ASHMOLEAN NOW

SOMA SUROVI JANNAT
CLIMATE CULTURE CARE

MALLICA KUMBERA LANDRUS

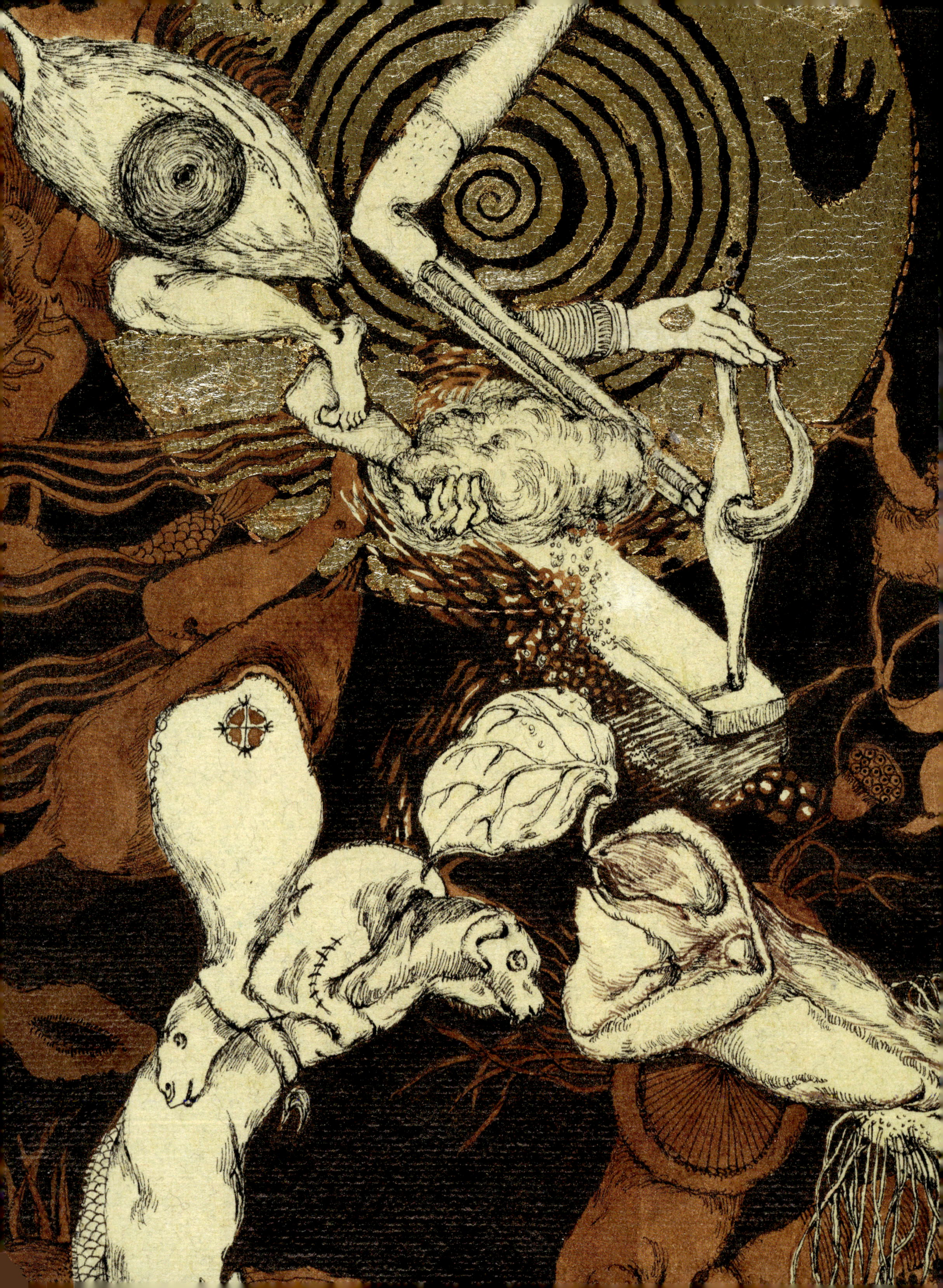

CONTENTS

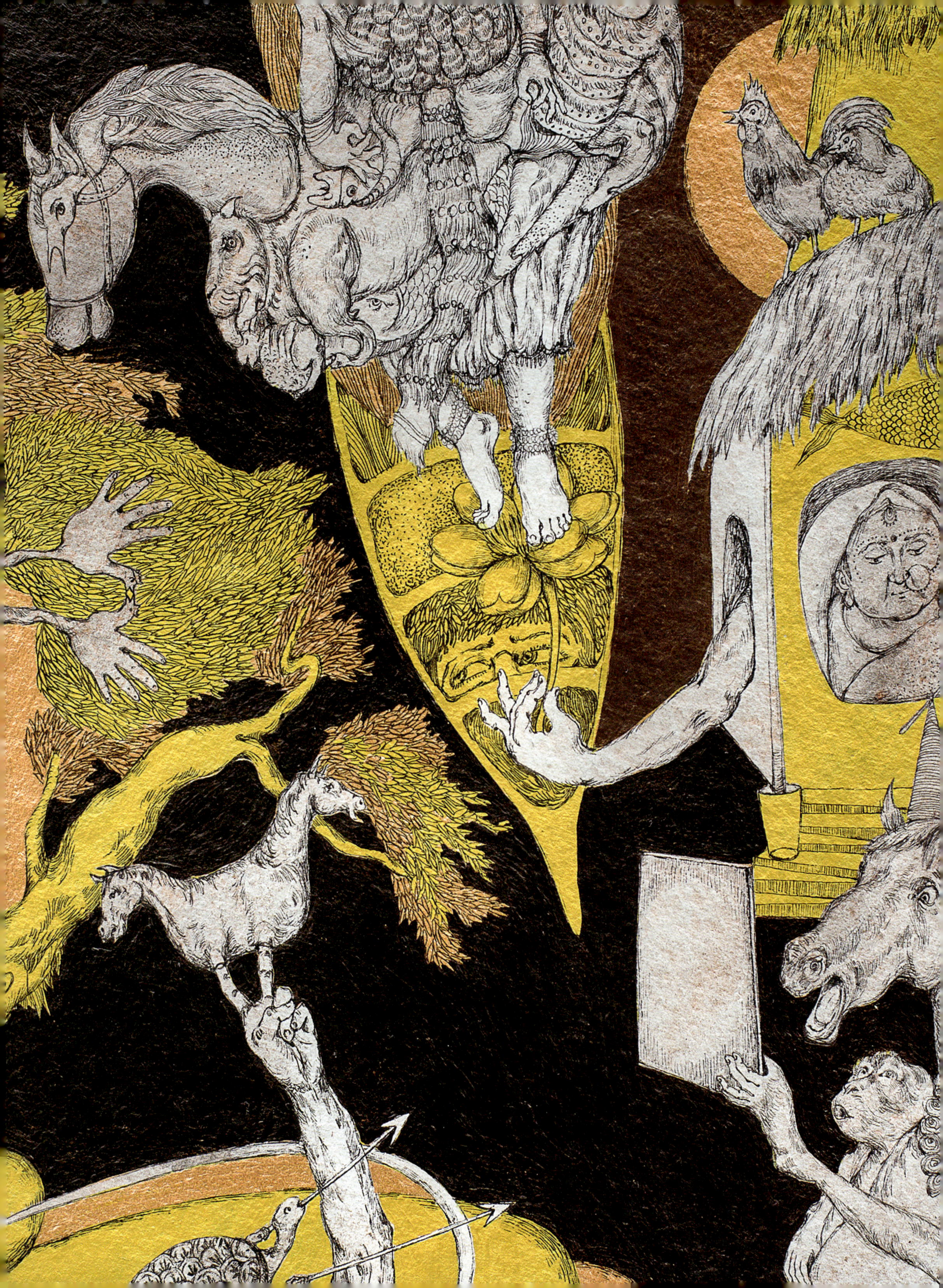

DIRECTOR'S FOREWORD

It is a great pleasure to present the work of Soma Surovi Jannat in the fifth exhibition of our series 'Ashmolean NOW', where we invite contemporary artists into the Museum to create new works which respond or relate to the historic works in our collections. In 2023 Surovi came to the Museum as the Ashmolean's first Frere Hall artist-in-residence, and this exhibition showcases the artist's works created since then. It marks the first solo exhibition dedicated to her in the UK, as well as the first solo presentation of any Bangladesh-based artist in a museum in this country. We hope and anticipate that this exhibition, unique in its scope and approach, will stimulate discussions around Bangladesh and its contemporary art, as we celebrate the country's 55th anniversary this year.

The creation of this exhibition derives from a collaborative and learning experience. The artist-in-residence programme provided both the artist and the exhibition's curator, Mallica Kumbera Landrus, the Ashmolean's Keeper of Eastern Art and curator of South Asian Art, with the time and space to engage in exploratory conversations around our collections. These discussions around South Asian art history, shared socio-political interests, historical narratives and connections to contemporary issues and concerns, allowed for and enabled rich and informed encounters with our collections. What emerges from this collaboration is a dialogue full of surprising visual similarities and differences that celebrates creativity, displays exceptional artistry and is informed by curatorial curiosity and expertise. This is an exhibition that is concerned with both the local and the global, and draws on historical traditions and narratives, while being focused on the present. As such, it has an entirely fitting home in the Ashmolean.

We are particularly grateful to Seher and Taimur Hassan, who generously support the Ashmolean's Frere Hall South Asia-based artist-in-residence programme and who also made this publication possible. I would also like to thank the British Council for their generous sponsorship as well as the Samdani Art Foundation. It is through their involvement that we were able to bring Surovi's works from Dhaka to Oxford. Further thanks are due to Sotheby's, Neha & Sumedh Jaiswal via Goldman Sachs Gives, Charles Wallace Bangladesh Trust and Gallery Espace, New Delhi, for their instrumental contribution to this project.

Last but by no means least, we would like to thank Surovi herself for her work and for her thoughtful and fruitful engagement with the Ashmolean and its collections.

Xa Sturgis

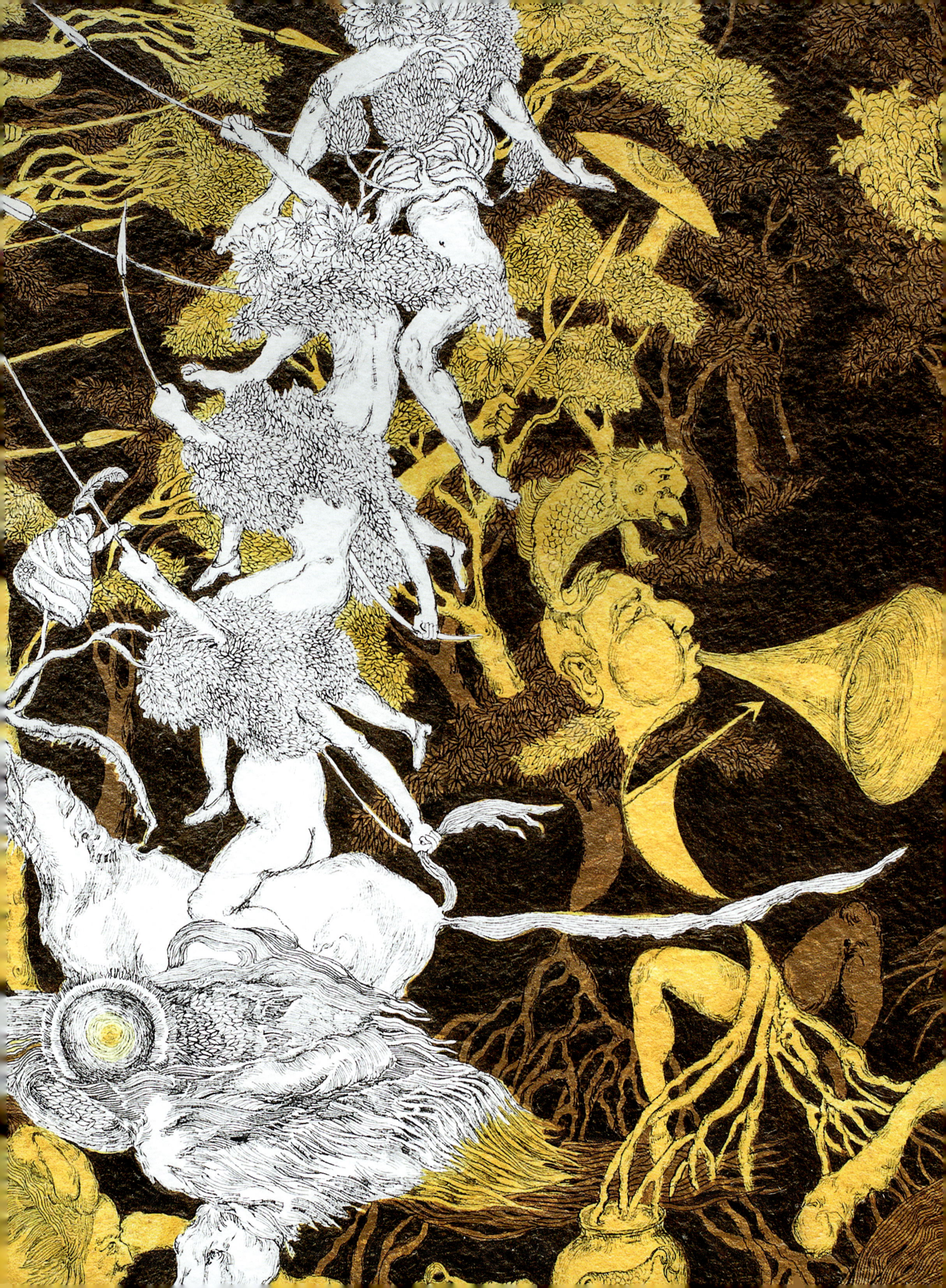

ACKNOWLEDGEMENTS

As the first university museum, and the first truly public museum globally, we are grateful to those who help us highlight and develop essential contributions to the history of art and visual culture at the Ashmolean Museum, University of Oxford. These contributions have improved our approach to addressing the gaps in our collection and programming of South Asian contemporary art.

We are honoured to showcase the exceptional works of Bangladesh-based artist Soma Surovi Jannat, whose exhibition stems from a collaborative effort between Taimur Hassan and the Ashmolean. Taimur's support of a South Asia-focused artist-in-residence programme at the Ashmolean has underscored the importance of backing the subcontinent. It is a programme that has, so far, allowed three South Asia-based artists in residence to benefit from their interactions with the Ashmolean collections. For understanding the value of giving for the region, for his selfless support, and friendship, I am deeply grateful.

The exhibition and accompanying publication are a joint effort with the artist. I would like to thank Soma Surovi Jannat for creating such insightful works for this exhibition, and for placing her trust in me to curate her pieces. Working with her has been a pleasure, and I greatly value her enthusiasm, generosity, time, and support throughout this project. She is an exceptional young woman, and I look forward to seeing how her practice develops in the coming years.

As is the case with any exhibition and publication of this magnitude, the contributions from donors were crucial. We are particularly thankful to The British Council Bangladesh for its generous assistance. Neha & Sumedh Jaiswal via Goldman Sachs Gives, Charles Wallace Trust Bangladesh, the Ashmolean Patrons, Sotheby's and Gallery Espace were all dedicated to ensuring the success of this endeavour, for which we are truly appreciative. I am especially thankful to Rajeeb and Nadia Samdani for their unwavering and generous support of Surovi. Without Rajeeb's meticulous attention towards various project-related details, this exhibition and publication would have faced significant challenges, especially considering the current political climate in Bangladesh.

Many colleagues from throughout the Ashmolean provided support to actualise this exhibition and publication, particularly Xa Sturgis, the Director, in his early backing of the project. The publications team, Declan McCarthy, Carrie Hickman and Lizzy Silverton, deserve applause for their insightful feedback and dedication to shaping this manuscript, and Ocky Murray for the design. I want to acknowledge Rohini Sampath, Development Executive, Agnes Valencak, Head of Exhibitions, and Catriona Pearson, Senior Exhibitions Project Manager for their essential help with various arrangements and plans for the show, as well as their consistent commitment to ensuring the exhibition materialised. I am grateful to Byung Kim for his collaborative efforts in designing the exhibition. My appreciation extends to Ally Greathead, Beth Twinn, Alex Baldwin, Nicky Lobaton, David Ronchka, Kevin Jacques, and Tim Crowley for their exceptional work in preparing the artworks for display in the exhibition. I am profoundly thankful to our Senior Graphic Designer, Krishna Balakrishna, Balwinder Meyrick in the Finance Office, Marie Sinclair, and our Registrar team Chrissie Gernon and Ilenia Scerra for their assistance. In Eastern Art, I extend my heartfelt thanks to my team, especially Alessandra Cereda, Ben Skarratt, and Yuliia Spolitak for their invaluable support to the artist. Special thanks to Marwa Ahmed for reading the draft and whose constructive feedback was very useful.

I am grateful to my friends and family for their encouragement, patience and kindness. To Matthew Landrus I express my immense gratitude for his unwavering support in all my pursuits these past three decades. His friendship, love, patience, and willingness to brainstorm is a constant source of inspiration and energy.

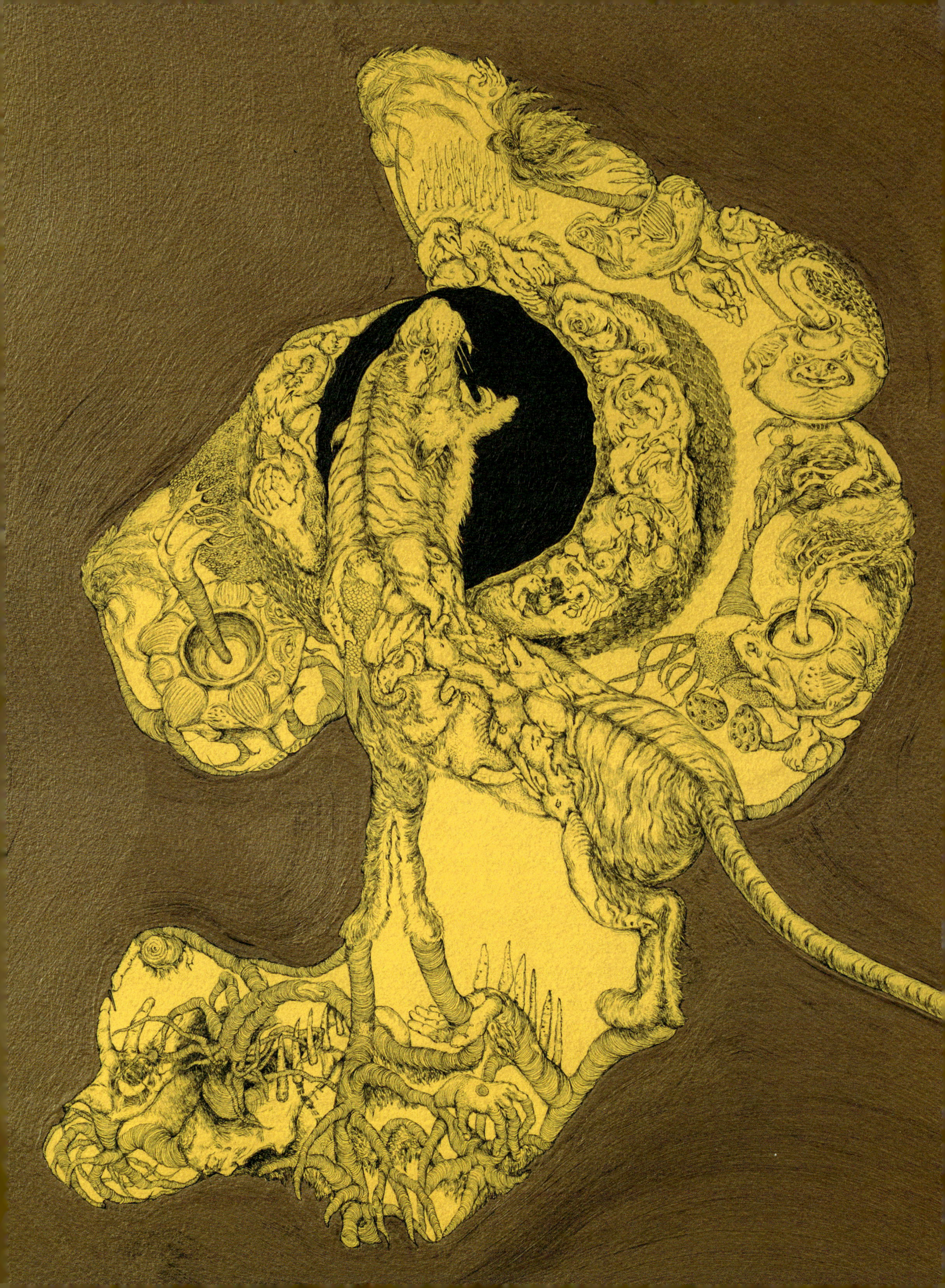

INTRODUCTION

Interposed between the sea and the plains of Bengal, lies an immense archipelago of islands ... They number in the thousands, these islands. Some are immense and some no larger than sandbars; some have lasted through recorded history while others were washed into being just a year or two ago ... There are no borders here to divide fresh water from salt, river from sea. The tides reach as far as two hundred miles inland and everyday thousands of acres of forest disappear underwater, only to reemerge hours later ... this archipelago is known as the Sundarban, which means the beautiful forest.

Amitav Ghosh, *The Hungry Tide* (Delhi, 2004)

This publication, and the exhibition it accompanies, features the work of Bangladesh-based artist Soma Surovi Jannat (b.1990), who has drawn inspiration from the Sundarbans and the Ashmolean Museum's collections to address the pressing climate crisis. All but one of her pieces were created following her Ashmolean residency in the summer of 2023. Inviting viewers to reflect on environmental issues and the interconnectedness of nature and humanity, Surovi (the artist's chosen name) examines environmental and social circumstances particularly in the Sundarbans, which is located south of Bangladesh. This extensive forest spans across the southern portion of Bangladesh and the southern part of the Indian state of West Bengal. Surovi asserts that central to her work is the importance of protecting the planet, future generations, and living beings.

A complex network of several hundred rivers weaves through Bangladesh. Included among these are the Brahmaputra-Jamuna, the Ganges (known as the Padma in Bangladesh), and the Meghna, all of which flow into the Bay of Bengal delta. The Sundarbans is part of this delta, the largest prograding delta on the planet. These river systems serve not only to transport water but also to carry silt across the country, which is essential for much of its agriculture. They play a significant role in Bangladesh's status as one of the countries most severely impacted by climate change. Due to climate change, it is anticipated that flooding in Bangladesh will increase because of cyclonic storm surges and rising sea levels. Much of the nation is at risk, as 80% of Bangladesh is composed of floodplains, with most of the land situated at a metre or less above sea level. While the rise in sea levels is considered a global emergency, Bangladesh remains one of the nations most affected.

A sprawling region of approximately 10,000 square kilometres shared between India and Bangladesh, the Sundarbans is home to the world's largest mangrove forest and an array of wildlife, as well as the endangered

Royal Bengal tiger. This biodiverse area is threatened by the effects of climate change, as rising sea levels diminish habitat, erode coastlines, and increase salinity in the water, endangering the essential Sundari trees (*Heritiera fomes*) that sustain the ecosystem. Around thirteen million people reside in this vulnerable region, facing significant challenges including flooding and the impact of natural disasters. People remain in the Sundarbans because of strong cultural and economic ties: the forest offers sustenance as well as providing a sense of identity. The inhabitants of the Sundarbans find themselves caught between a deteriorating environment and the absence of practical alternatives for relocation, confronting difficulties resulting from climate change, such as the increasing sea levels and land salinisation, that undermine their livelihoods and homes.

With a world population exceeding seven billion, the increasing consumption of resources, particularly from forests, has led to serious environmental consequences. Deforestation, urban development, river damming, and mining activities have contributed to a rise in carbon dioxide levels, resulting in global warming, shifting temperatures, and rising sea levels, which, in turn, threaten various plant and animal species. While some argue that the Earth has always gone through natural changes, what sets the current situation apart is that human action is the driving force behind these changes. Surovi's work highlights the relationship between natural disasters and social inequalities, serving as a powerful reminder and critique of the vulnerability faced by certain communities, particularly in the Global South. As climate-related disasters increase in frequency, it becomes essential to address the underlying causes that render marginalised communities more susceptible.

Surovi's work addresses the beauty and fragility of the Sundarbans, urging us to consider our responsibility toward the environment. Her pieces reflect the reality of flooding and its devastating effects on marginalised communities, illustrating the struggles faced by individuals and families as they navigate the hardships brought on by climate change. Through powerful imagery – such as contrasting landscapes before and after flooding – Surovi highlights the disparate ways in which various groups experience these disasters.

Amidst the chaos of natural and man-made calamities, her art also explores themes of grief and loss, utilising poignant symbols to convey the sorrow linked to environmental destruction. While some works portray serene landscapes, others depict the desperate search for safety, showcasing the resilience of communities affected by challenges and displacement. By engaging with her art, viewers are encouraged to reflect on their own relationship with nature and consider their role in safeguarding the planet for future generations. Through this exploration, the artist calls for collective action against the climate crisis, emphasising the interconnectedness of global ecological issues and the necessity of a sustainable, more equitable future, and urges viewers to confront these pressing issues directly.

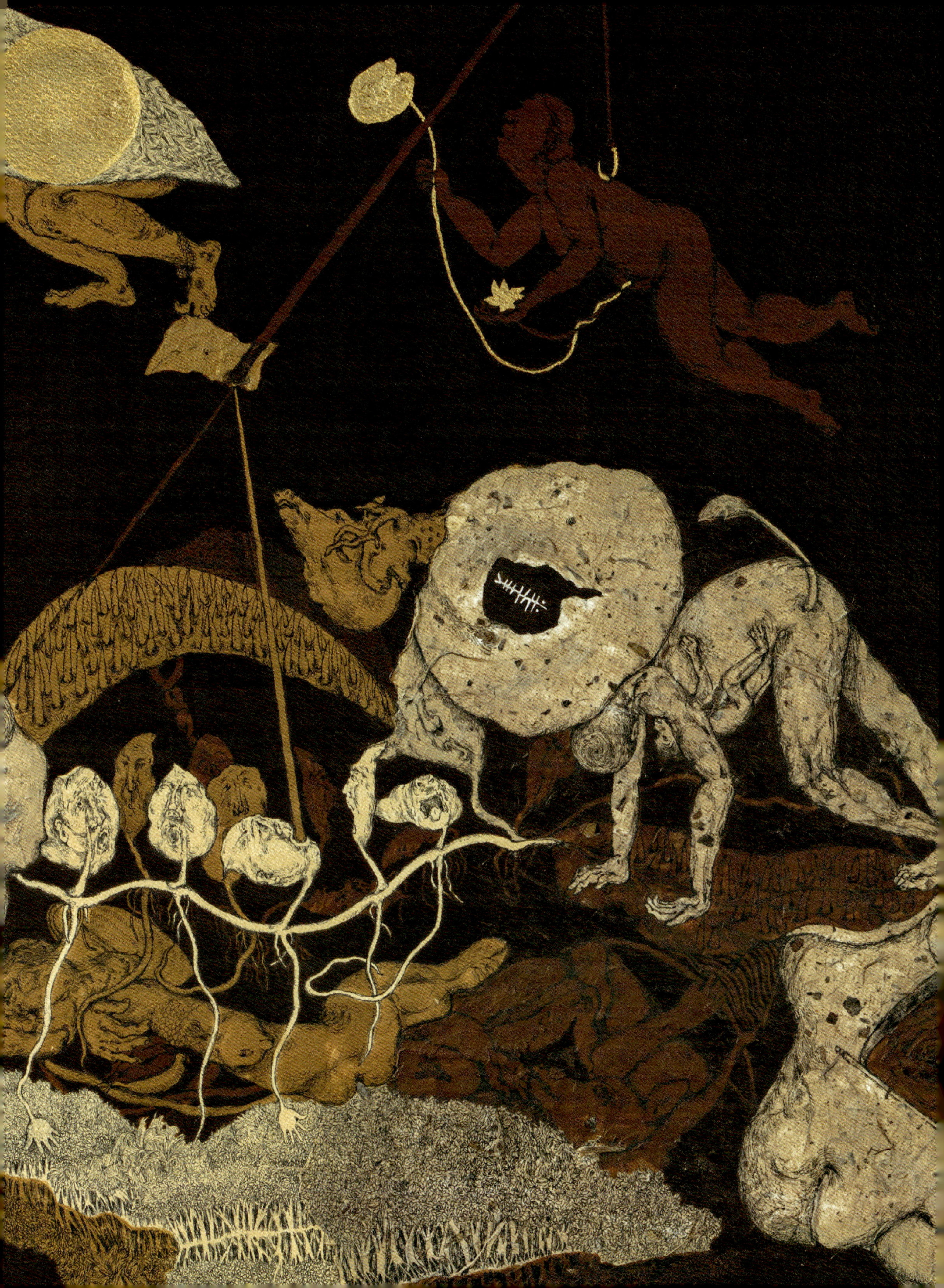

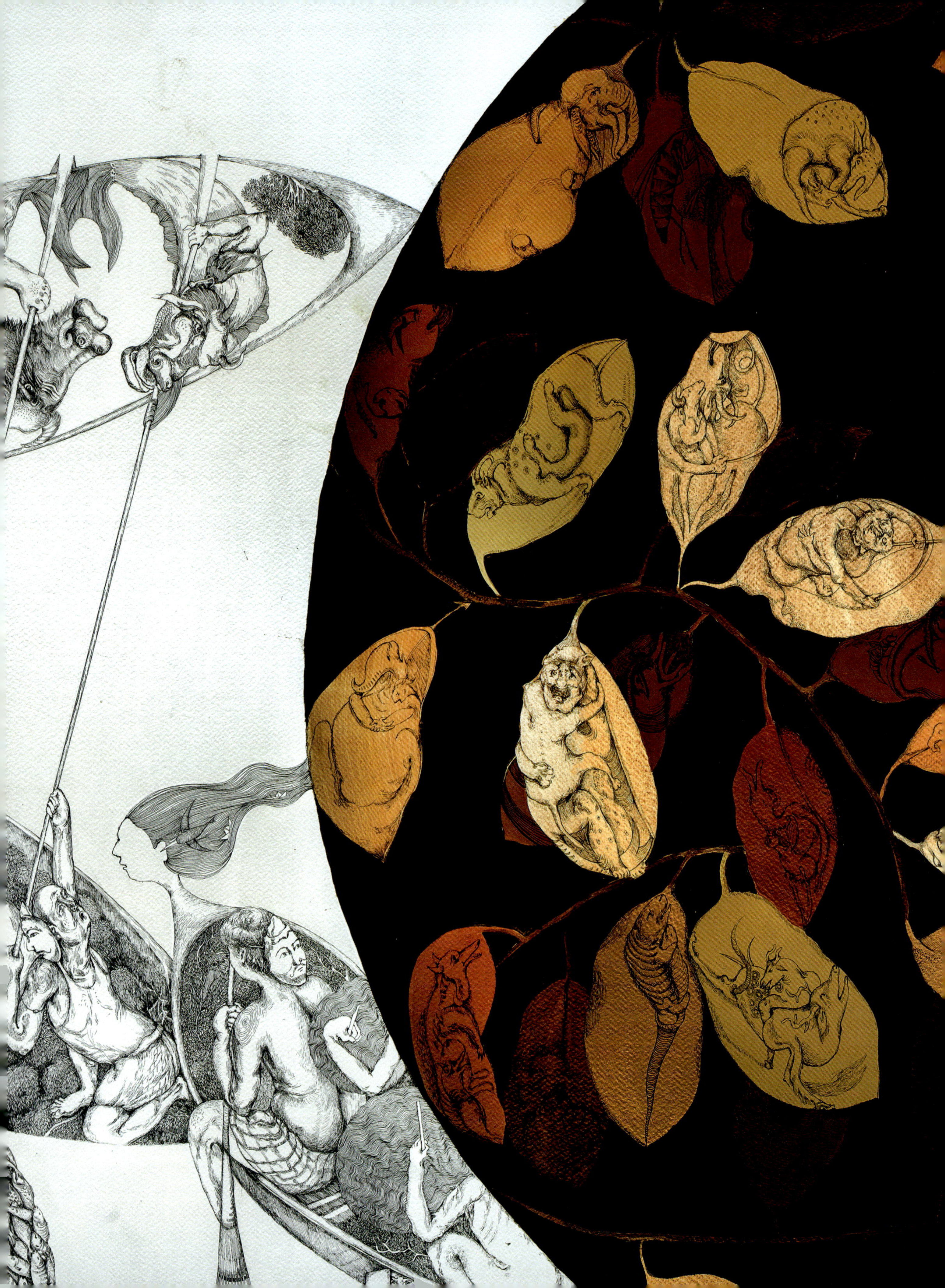

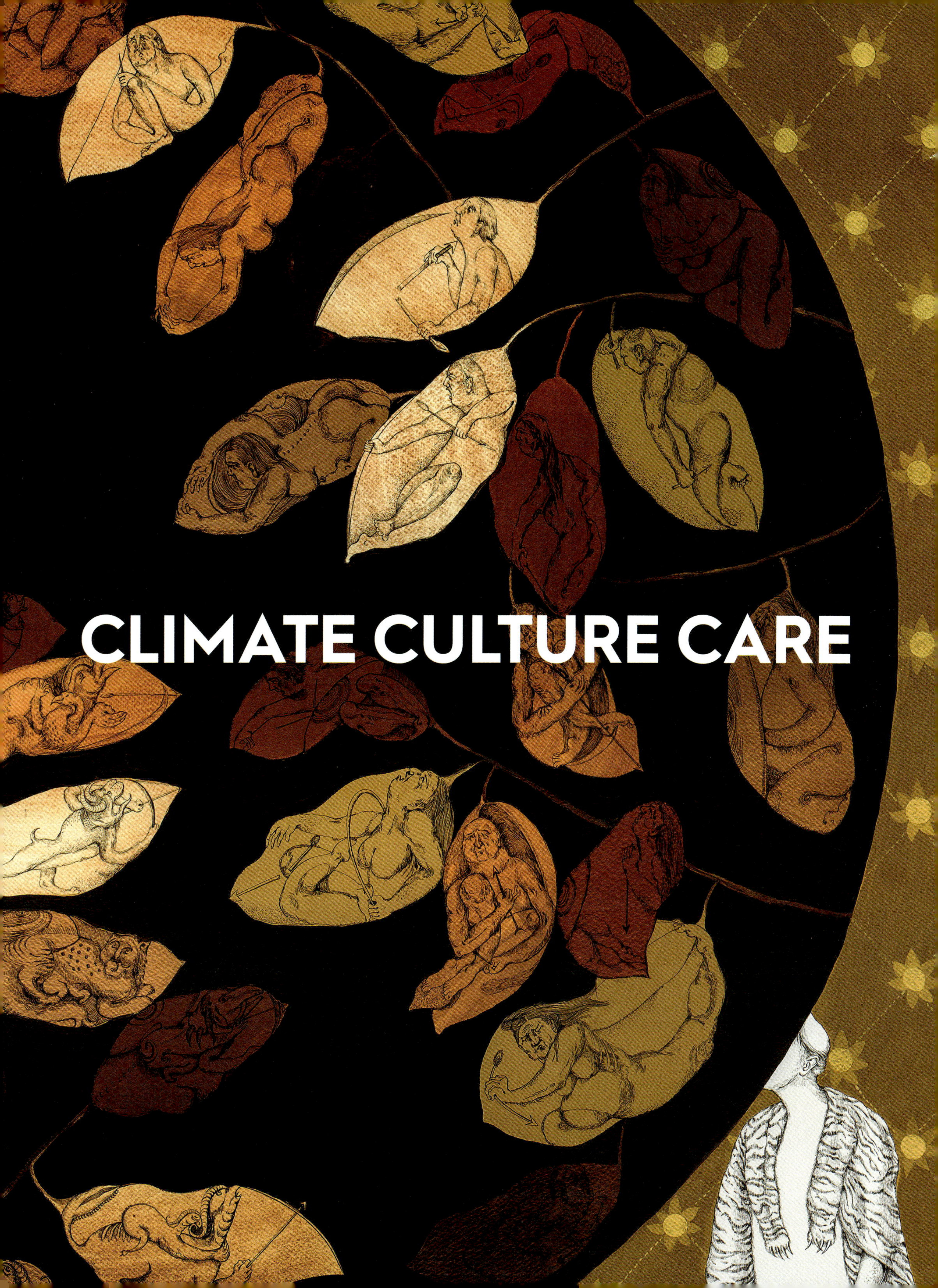
CLIMATE CULTURE CARE

CLIMATE CULTURE CARE

Soma Surovi Jannat is the inaugural artist from Bangladesh to be invited as an artist-in-residence (2023) at the Ashmolean Museum, University of Oxford. This exhibition marks her first solo show in the UK, and it is also the first solo show for any Bangladesh-based artist in a museum in this country. The works displayed were all created between 2023 and 2025, including the concept for her site-specific drawing, planned for 2026. All but one of the works featured in this publication were made for Surovi's exhibition at the Ashmolean.

Surovi is known for her captivating and surprising imagery, which she creates through a combination of free association and symbolism. Her work challenges traditional artistic practices by blending elements of disasters, whimsy, and clever new perspectives. Although she has classical academic training, the artist has opted to move away from realistic depictions in favour of embracing spontaneous expressions in distorted and exaggerated figures. She combines narratives with an analysis of policies, addressing those in power while emphasising the humour and optimism present in life. Her aim is to represent marginalised groups not as liabilities, but as individuals deserving of respect and dignity.

Her art often features striking dismembered figures set against surreal and dreamlike backgrounds, which can sometimes appear unsettling. Her intricately detailed figures exist within illusionistic spaces, creating a rich tapestry of visuals. Despite the abundance of detail and the array of figures, many of her works convey a profound sense of loneliness and silence, often situated in eerie, ominous settings. This intriguing combination of creativity and introspection encourages viewers to engage in and explore their own interpretations.

In a Timeless Sweet Land (fig.1)

Months prior to her arrival in Oxford, Surovi was inspired by her family's winter holidays in Lalmonirhat (northern Bangladesh), leading her to create a painting titled *In a Timeless Sweet Land* (2023). Contrasting significantly with the works she created after her time in Oxford, this piece depicts the artist (bottom-right corner) with her mother and cousins, in an idyllic scene, eating together. It is an image that captures the warmth of family life. The central figures, and the smaller images around them, symbolise the cherished and nostalgic memories of home and a carefree childhood. Around the time that this work was made, the artist began to think about climate migrants and the fundamental human right of every child to experience a childhood free from trauma, as well as the responsibility of all communities to enable refugee children to reclaim their sense of childhood.

(fig.1) ***In a Timeless Sweet Land*, 2023, archival ink pen on canvas with acrylic colour, 152 × 122 cm.** Collection of the artist. © Soma Surovi Jannat

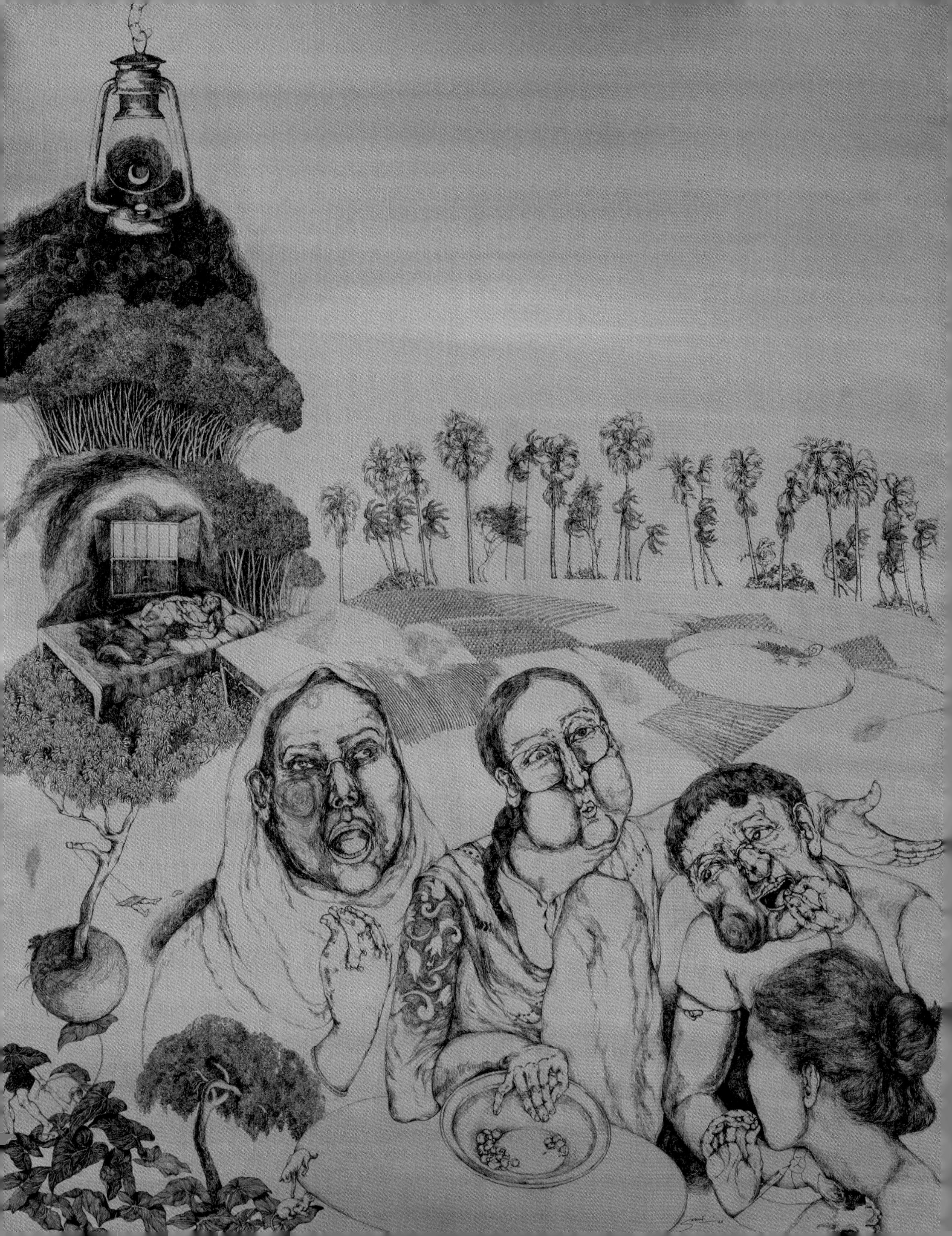

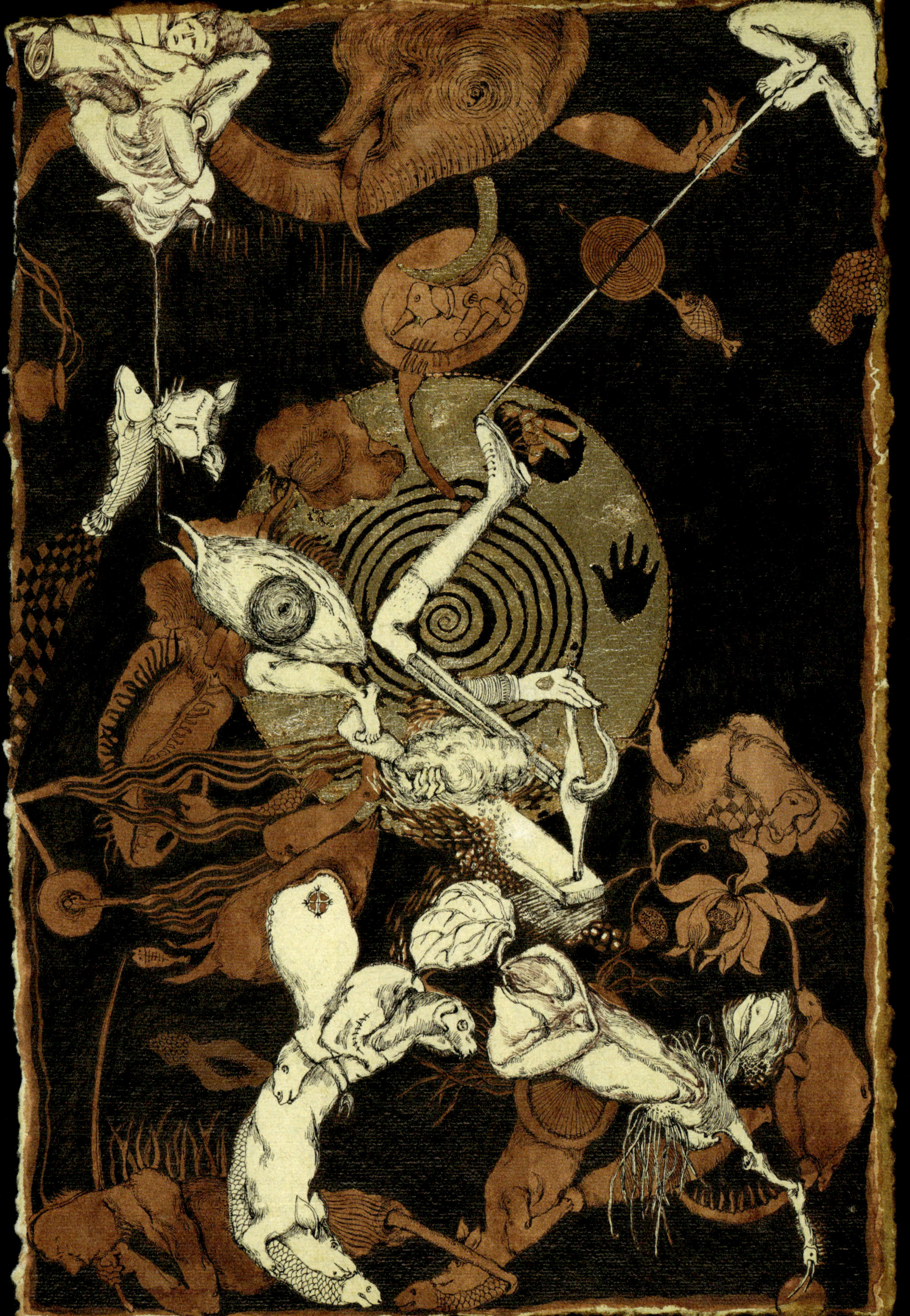

(fig.3) ***Bengali Vaisnava with drum*****, late 1800s, painted clay, metal armature, and fabric, 21.5 cm (height).** Ashmolean Museum, University of Oxford, EAX.7064

(fig.4) ***Grasscutter with bundle on head*****, late 1800s, painted clay, metal armature, and fabric, 27.4 cm (height).** Ashmolean Museum, University of Oxford, EAX.2451.a

(fig.5) ***Potter turning a pot on a wheel*****, late 1800s, painted clay, metal armature, and fabric, 14 cm (height).** Ashmolean Museum, University of Oxford, EAX.2455

(fig.6) ***Shoemaker*****, late 1800s, painted clay, metal armature, and fabric, 11 cm (height).** Ashmolean Museum, University of Oxford, EAX.2456

3

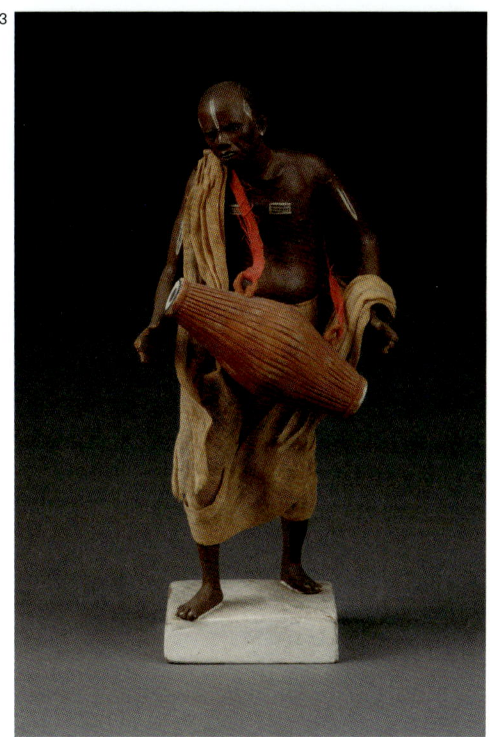

4

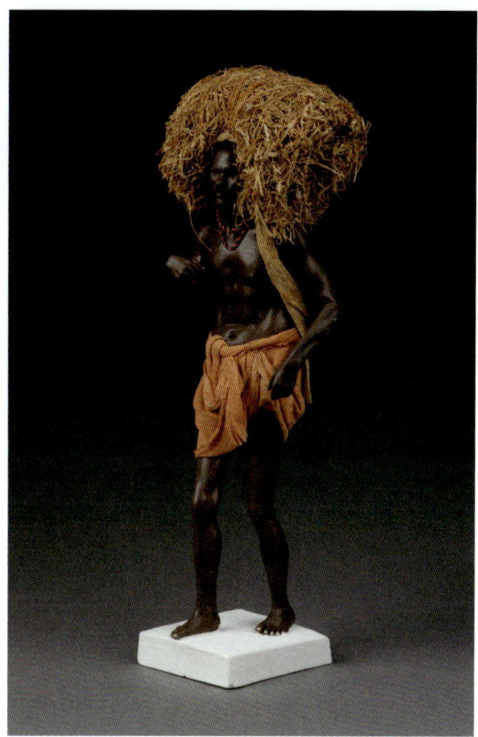

5

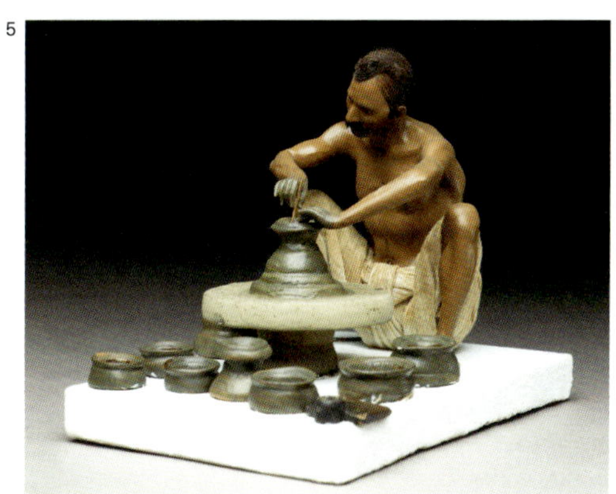

6

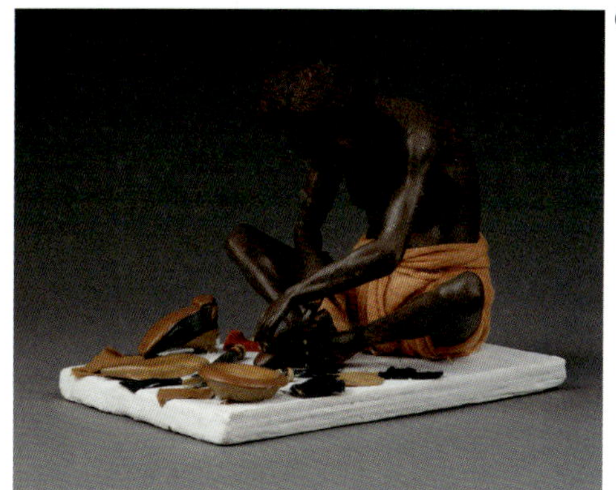

Resensitizing the Brown Narrative (fig.2)

Resensitizing the Brown Narrative (2023) reflects Surovi's creative journey during her residency in Oxford, where she lived in Jesus College and gathered materials from a local art shop. Influenced by her surroundings and the people she encountered, she explored symbolic aspects of the Ashmolean collection. Conversations about shades of brown, and her observations of clay figures portraying Indian castes (figs 3–6), enriched her artistic perspective. One of her key inspirations was Prabhakar Barwe's *The Blank Canvas* (translated edition, 2014), which emphasised the importance of patience in the creative process. During her time at the Ashmolean Museum, Surovi felt a sense of calm that allowed her to embrace new ideas amidst her discursive examination of the collection. She delighted in closely examining several hundred miniatures and other paintings, as well as sculptures and ceramics. Her resulting work encapsulates this transformative period, inviting viewers to explore all its elements.

(fig.2) ***Resensitizing the Brown Narrative*****, 2023, archival ink pen on paper with acrylic colour and gold leaf, 30 × 21 cm.** Collection of the artist. © Soma Surovi Jannat

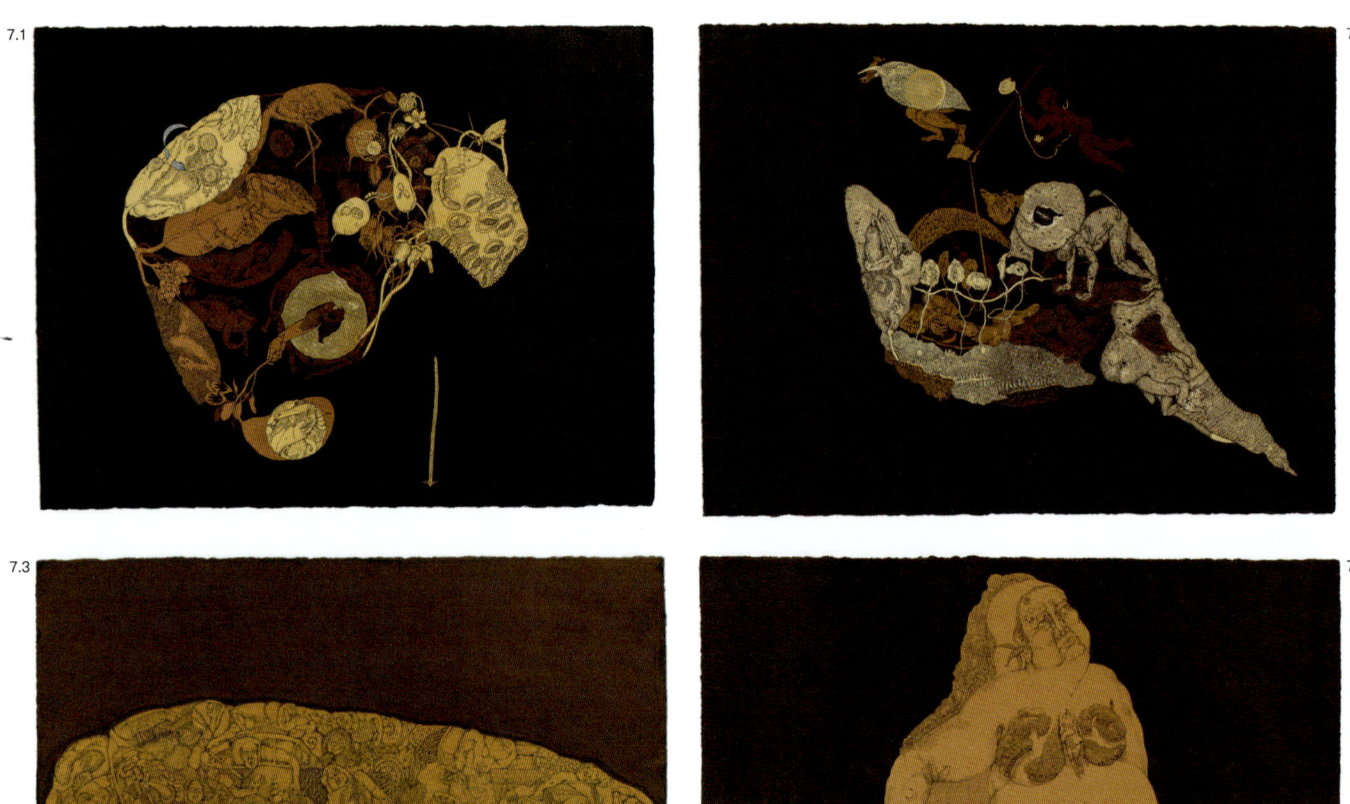

(fig.7.1–7.8) ***Where Every Leaf Holds a Tale*** **(*Chandeshar; Kalir Char; Ha Ja Ba Ra La; Dimer Char; Banishanta; Dhoenchabaria Char; Shyamnagar; and Tiger leg*), 2023–24, archival ink pen on paper with acrylic colour, gold and silver leaf, 76 × 57 cm (each).**
Ashmolean Museum, University of Oxford, EA2025.26.1–8. © Soma Surovi Jannat. Figs 7.1, 7.5, 7.6, 7.8 presented by the artist

7.5

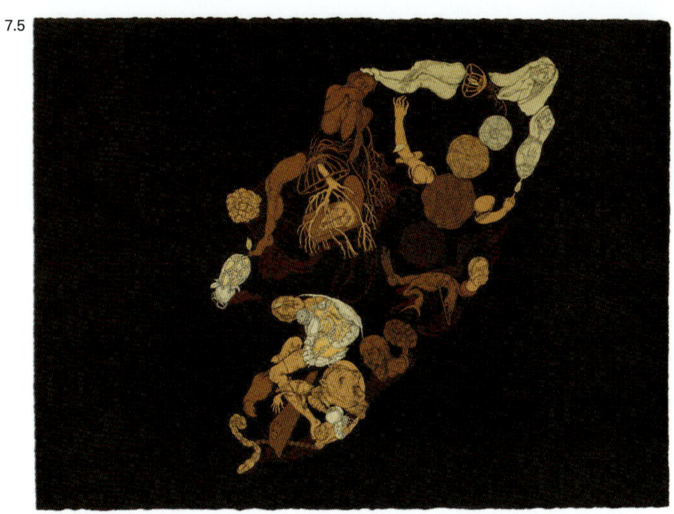

7.6

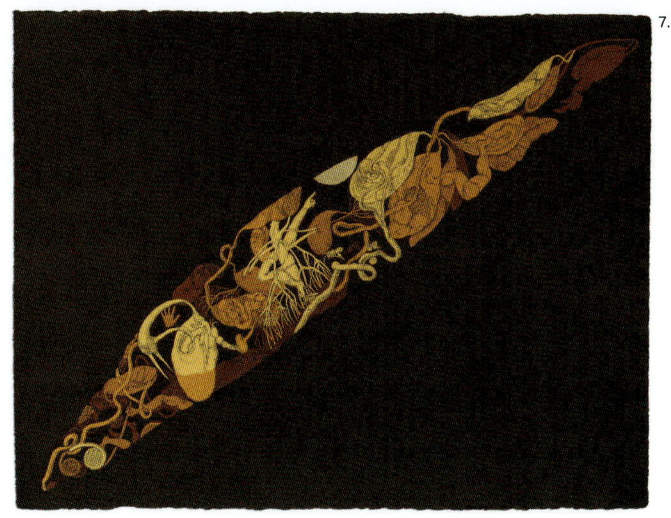

7.7

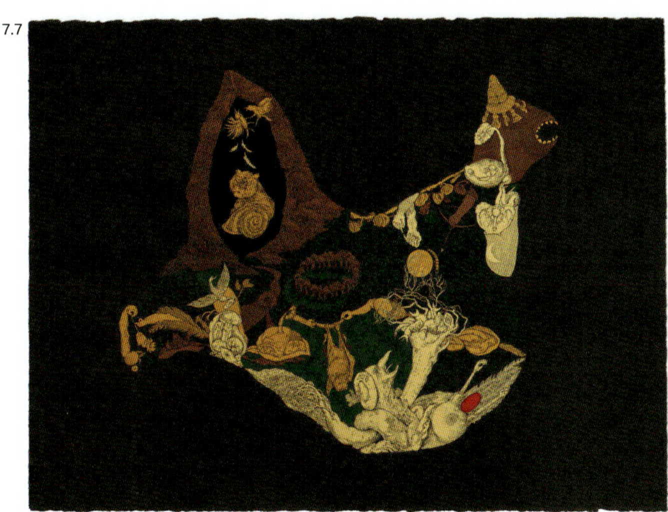

7.8

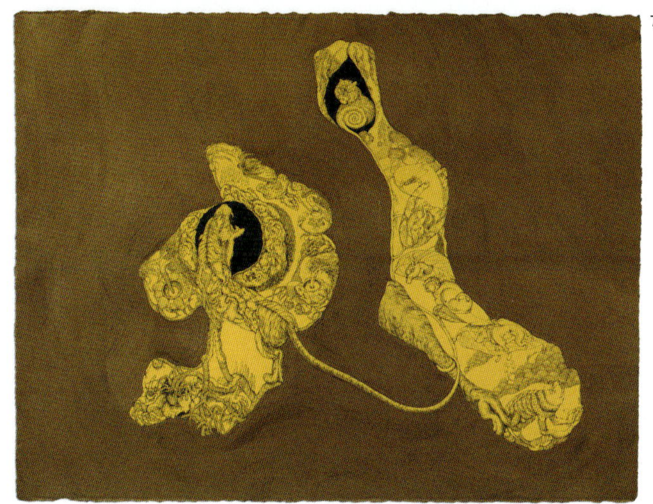

Where Every Leaf Holds a Tale (fig.7)

Surovi is deeply influenced by the natural world, particularly the mangrove forests of the Sundarbans and the ecosystems associated with them. In her 2023–24 series of eight works, *Where Every Leaf Holds a Tale*, she highlights the importance of mangrove forests, which thrive along tropical and subtropical coastlines. These trees, with their intertwined roots, serve as a natural barrier against storms and play a significant role in reducing the impact of climate change, capturing carbon more effectively than other tropical trees. Yet, despite their ecological significance, mangrove forests have faced severe decline. Mangroves are a vital ecosystem, providing breeding grounds for various marine species and supporting local fishing industries, which in turn contribute to food security and economic stability in many communities. They also attract ecotourism, bringing further economic benefits through recreational activities such as birdwatching and kayaking. Importantly, mangrove roots trap sediment, preventing coastal erosion and protecting coral reefs and seagrass meadows. As the threat of climate change leads to increased severe weather events, the preservation of mangroves becomes essential, proving more cost effective than constructing artificial barriers.

In the waters of Bangladesh, the alarming rise in salt levels and pollution has made survival difficult for fish populations, which many communities depend upon. Overfishing has led to the endangerment of numerous species within the Sundarbans, while shrimp farming – despite being a significant economic activity – often disregards regulatory standards, exacerbating water pollution.

During her exploration of the region, Surovi observed the contrast between the dense, dark appearance of the forest from the outside and the much less dense areas found deeper within, due to illicit logging. She became mindful of the impressive sensory abilities of plants, paralleling her own artistic process of exploring and expressing similar sensory interests through her work. By drawing leaves that symbolise these incredible sensory abilities, Surovi seeks to deepen the connection between her art and the narrative of the mangrove forests, their struggles, and their potential for recovery.

Before visiting the Sundarbans, Surovi prepared by exploring the area through Google Maps. As she navigated the maps, she noted significant loss of greenery over time and the diminishing size of the Sundarbans. She was struck by the shrinking islands and the alarming pollution, with waters in some areas appearing dark brown, almost black, instead of clear. The islands diminish in size primarily due to rising sea levels and the erosion of their coastlines. Storms and hurricanes can worsen this erosion, leading to the loss of land, while the increased salinisation of fresh water from encroaching salt water can render islands uninhabitable and threaten their food supplies. If an island's landmass is unable to keep up with the rate of sea-level rise and the effects of storms, it decreases in size, eventually disappearing beneath the ocean.

Meanwhile, the waters in the Sundarbans look dark as a result of pollution from multiple sources, such as black carbon (soot) due to incomplete burning, heavy metals and chemicals released by industries, fertilisers, sewage, microplastics, and untreated wastewater from urban and industrial regions. These contaminants build up in both the water and sediment, leading to discolouration and a decline in overall water quality. In her works, Surovi uses a dark brown to represent these murky waters, while also celebrating the beauty of the mangrove trees and their intricate, twisted roots. The outlines of her pieces echo the shapes of the islands, named in their subtitles, encouraging viewers to engage more closely. Rich with details reminiscent of the miniature painting tradition of the Indian subcontinent, which flourished under the Mughal Empire from the sixteenth century, Surovi cites such works as inspiring her approach. Indian miniatures, renowned for their intricate details and vibrant colours, blended influences from Persian and Indian cultures (figs 8–12). The art form evolved through various regional schools, each developing unique styles and themes, including religious narratives, scenes from royal courts, and portraits.

(fig.8) ***Composite figure of an elephant ridden by a lady*****, 1800s, watercolour on board, 26.6 × 35.3 cm.** Ashmolean Museum, University of Oxford, EA1959.46

(fig.9) ***Grotesque animals*** **India, mid-eighteenth century Gouache on paper, 27.9 × 40.6 cm.** Ashmolean Museum, University of Oxford EA1958.30

8

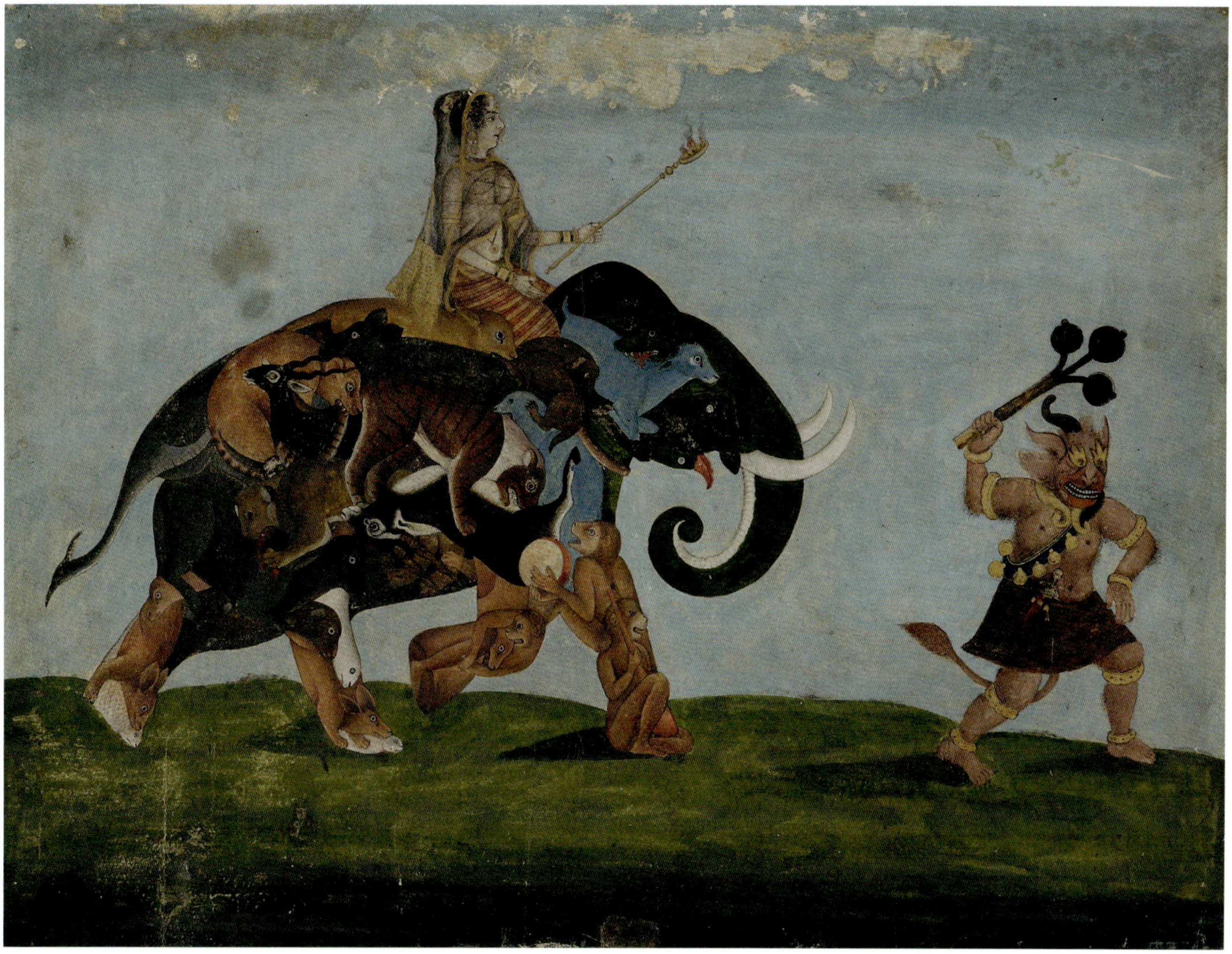

9

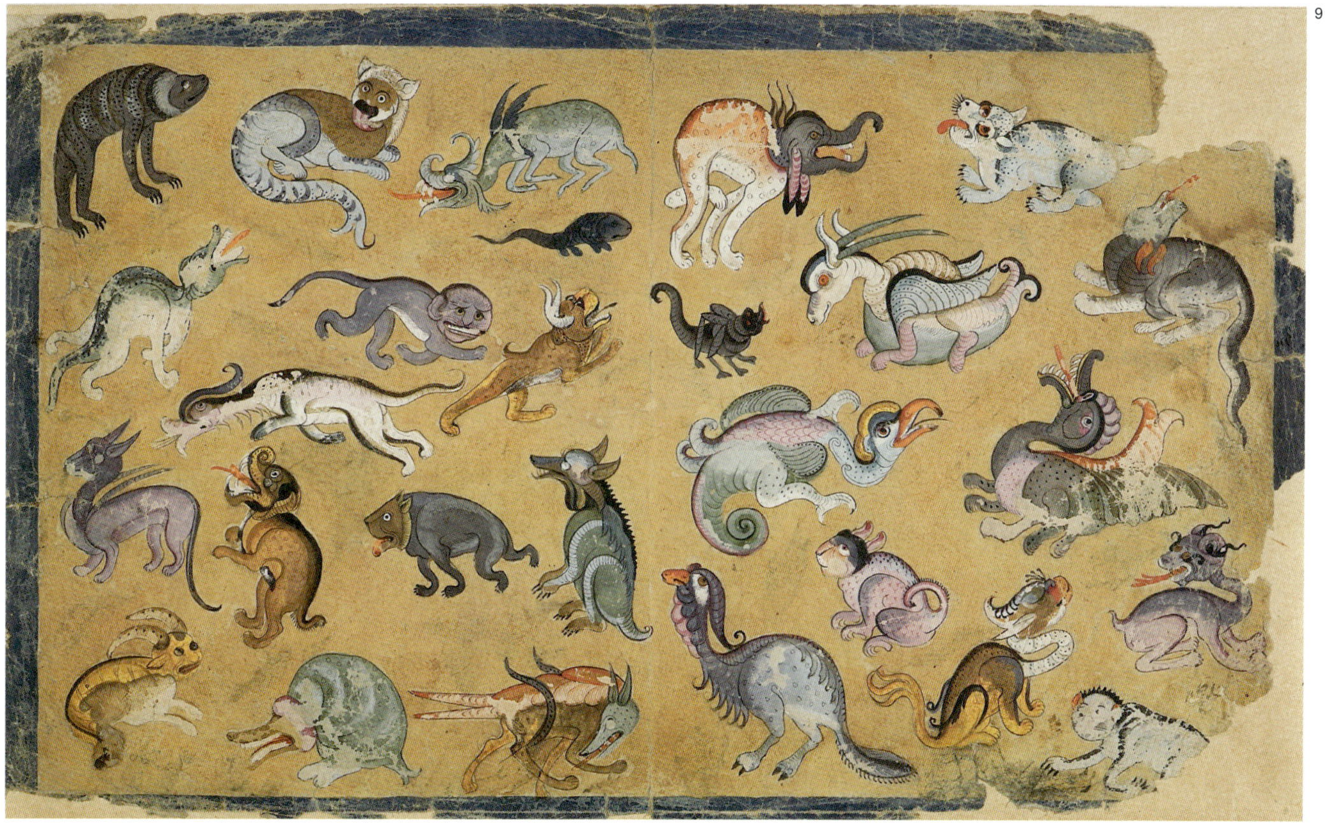

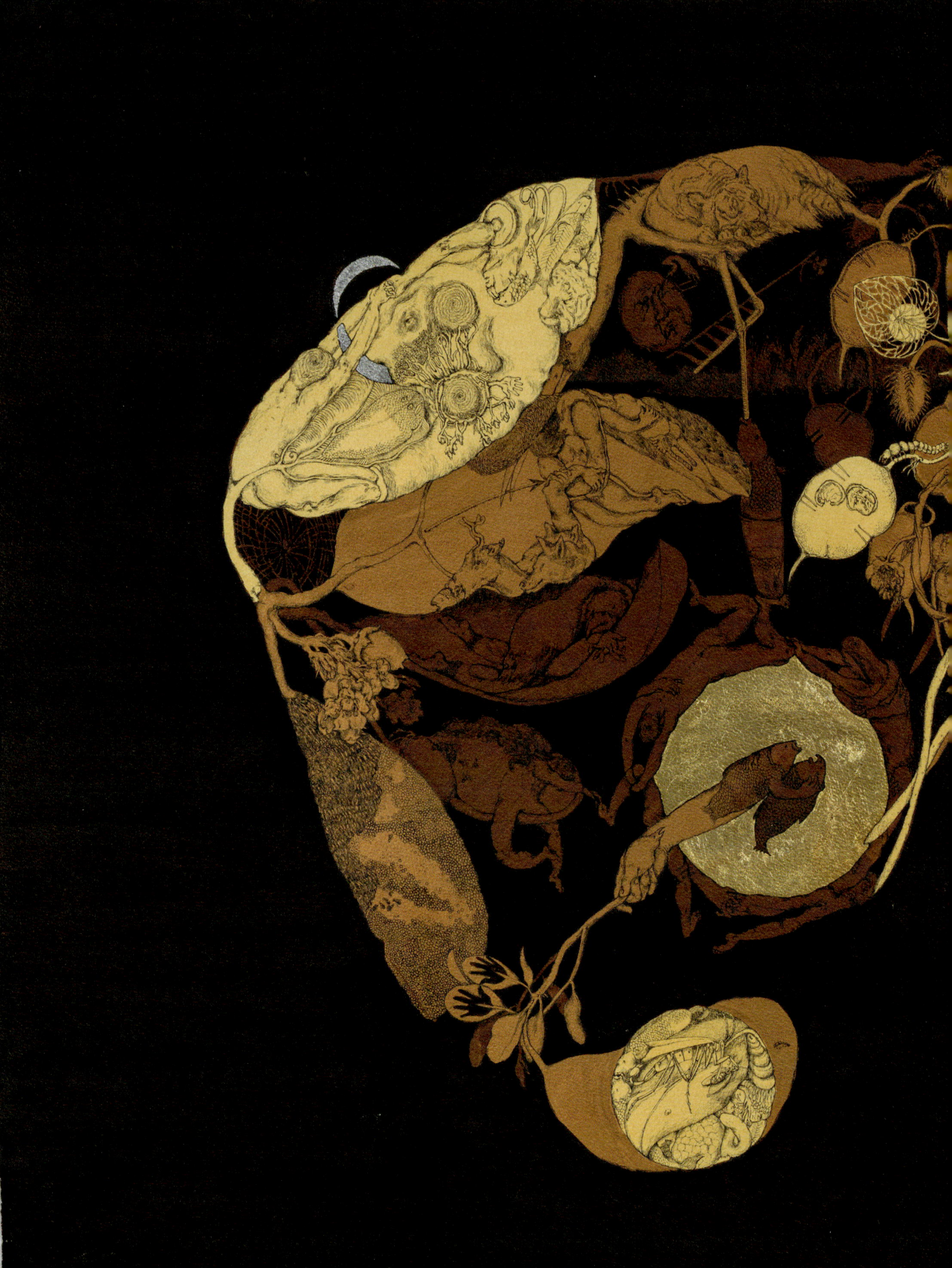

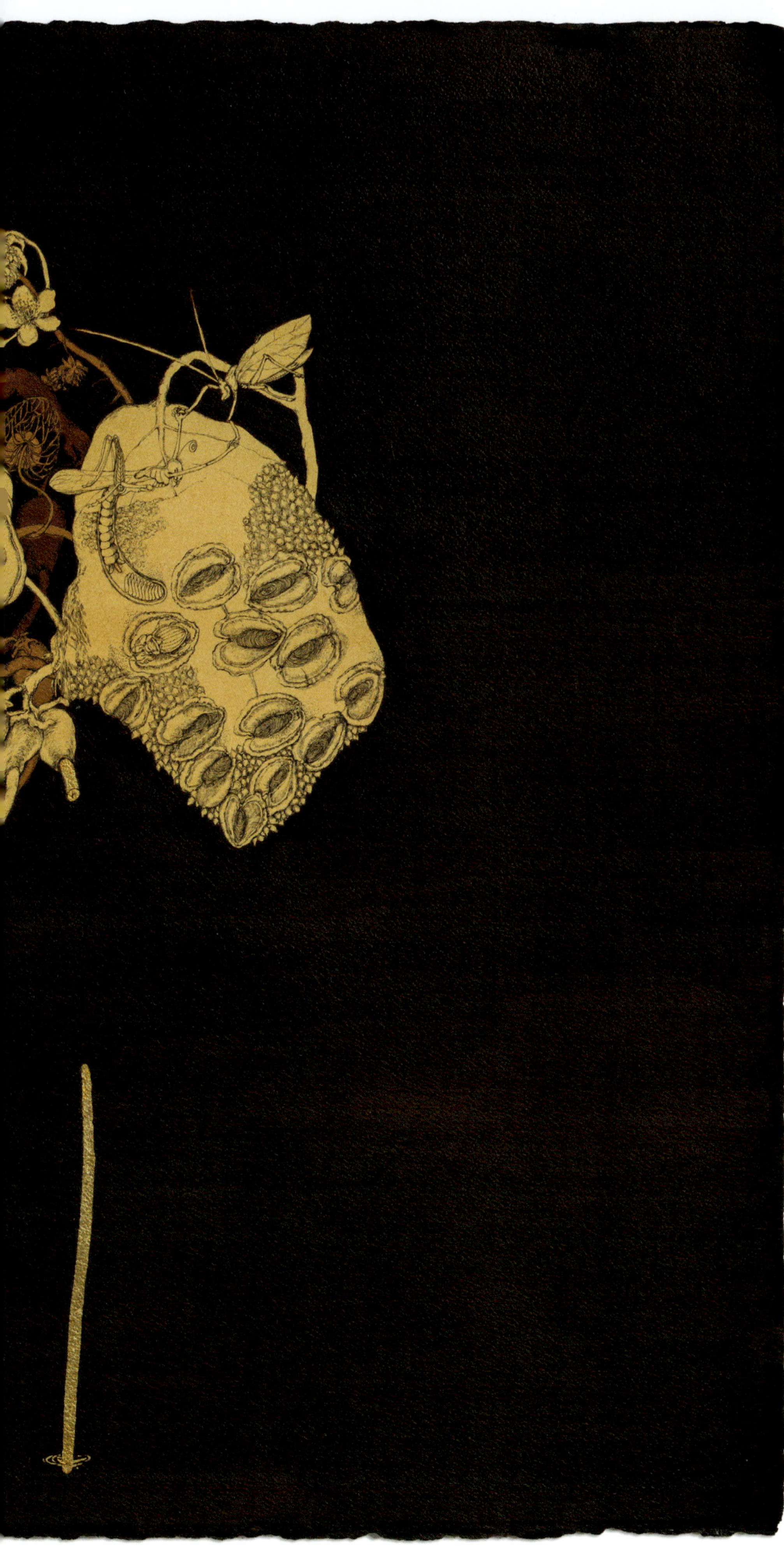

(fig.7.1) *Where Every Leaf Holds a Tale* (*Chandeshar*), 2023, archival ink pen on paper with acrylic colour, gold and silver leaf, 76 × 57 cm. Ashmolean Museum, University of Oxford, EA2025.26.1. © Soma Surovi Jannat. Presented by the artist

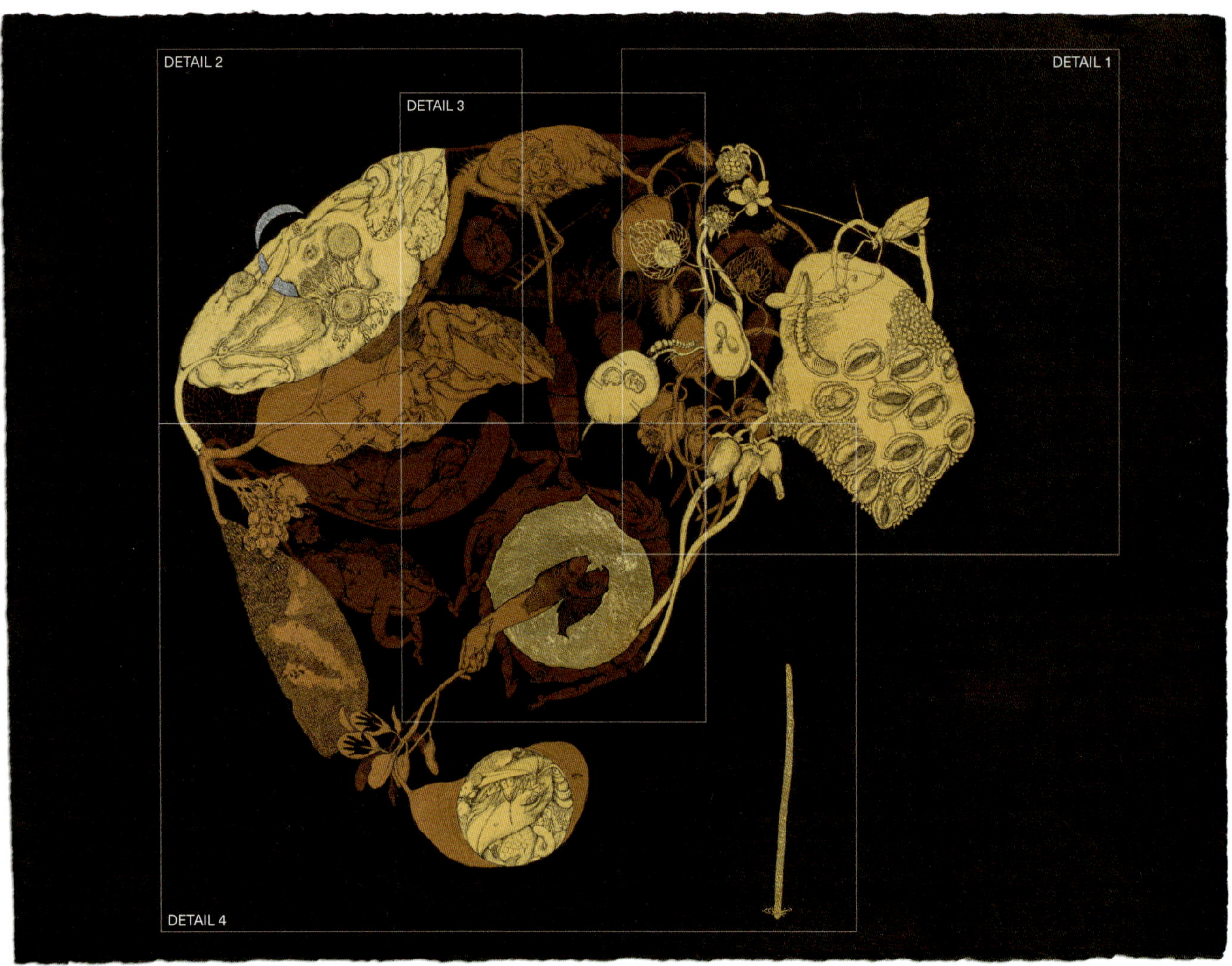

Where Every Leaf Holds a Tale (Chandeshar) (fig.7.1)
Chandeshar (Moon God) is one of the first islands depicted by Surovi in this series. It is characterised by a half-moon shape in the top-left corner. The moon is essential for making Earth habitable and enabling life to thrive by stabilising the climate, generating tides that are important for numerous marine organisms, and offering night-time light that affects the behaviour of nocturnal animals. The work symbolises life and support, particularly evident in the depiction of two grasshoppers grasping hands, the female laying eggs (detail 1). One egg is adorned with gold leaf; Surovi highlights this element, signifying the value of new life. Like many of her pieces, the visual narrative can be interpreted in multiple directions, with each detail representing a unique story.

Below the half-moon, an elephant is positioned between a man and woman, its crescent tusk reaching upward (detail 2). Surovi incorporates various narratives into her works. Here she weaves in a famous children's tale from the subcontinent about a tiger with a bone lodged in its throat. A heron assists the tiger by pulling the bone out, stressing a dynamic of interdependence between different animals and, by extension, communities. At the top centre, a tiger reclines on a bird, while the same bird's leg is ensnared in the mouth of a fish, and the fish struggles inside a half-filled glass of water, further illustrating the complicated relationships within the ecosystem (detail 3).

On the left is a group of Goran trees (*Ceriops decandra*) with the falling fruit painted gold to highlight nature's bounty. This tree naturally propagates in the Sundarbans and reproduces through vivipary, where the seeds of the fruit germinate and grow before detaching from the tree, falling into tidal waters, floating with currents, and settling in muddy areas to root and grow, supporting the ecosystem's regeneration (detail 4). The piece encompasses a rich diversity of life, including fish, elephants, insects, and humans, symbolising the intricate web of existence. At the bottom, a grasshopper gazes at a dead bee, underscoring the link between life and death. Overall, inspired by various composite and other works (figs 8–12), the artwork paints a vivid tapestry of life, reflecting the cycle of existence in nature.

10

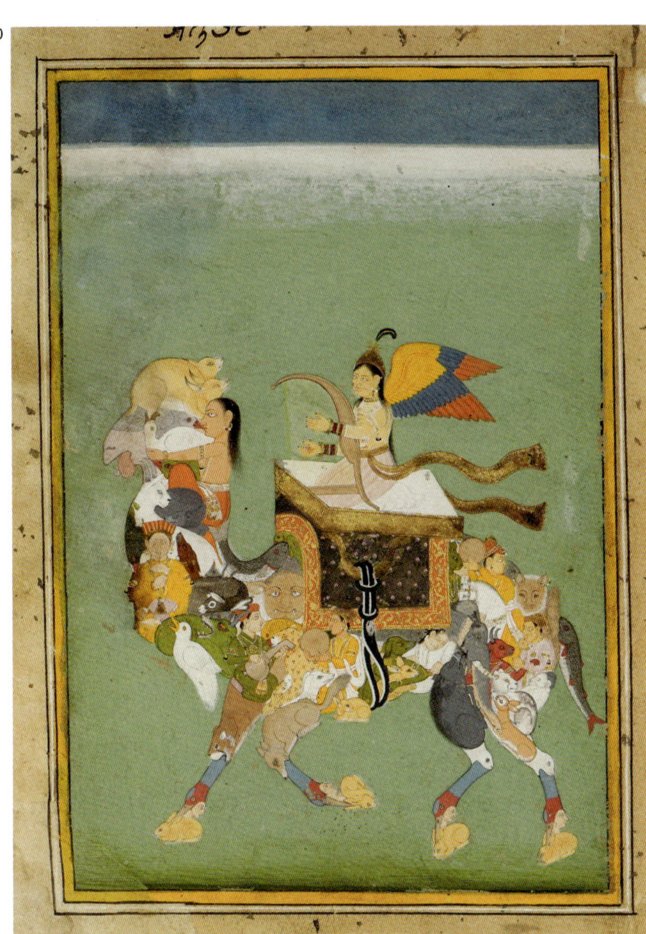

11

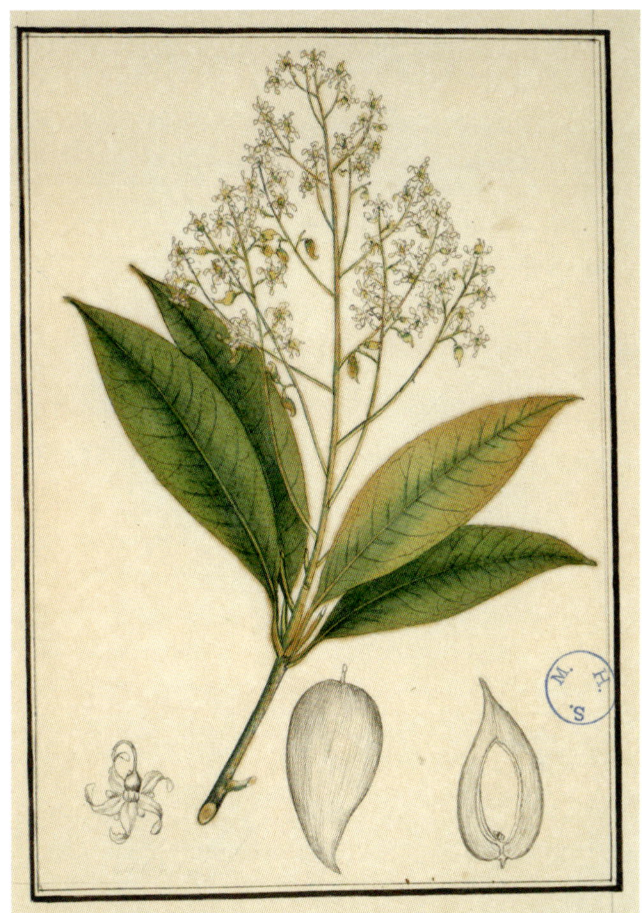

12

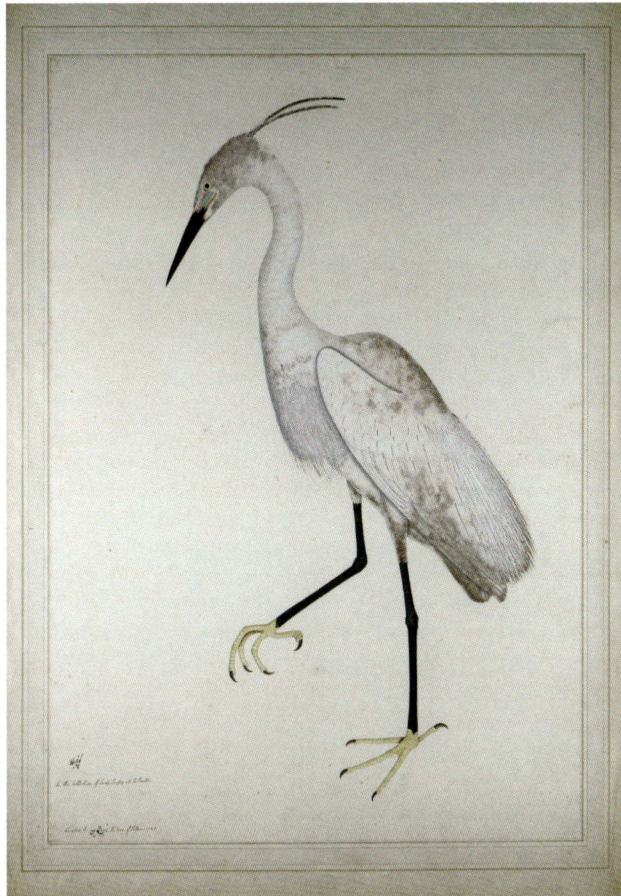

(fig.10) ***A peri, or fairy, riding a magic camel*, c.1680, gouache with gold on paper, 27 × 19.5 cm.** Ashmolean Museum, University of Oxford, EA2003.1

(fig.11) ***A study of Mangifera sylvatica, or wild Himalayan mango*, late eighteenth century, pen, ink, and watercolour on paper, 23.5 × 16.7 cm.** Ashmolean Museum, University of Oxford, EA2022.151

(fig.12) ***Little egret in breeding plumage* (*Egretta garzetta*), 1781, gouache on paper, 90.2 × 61.9 cm.** Bodleian Libraries, University of Oxford, LI901.15

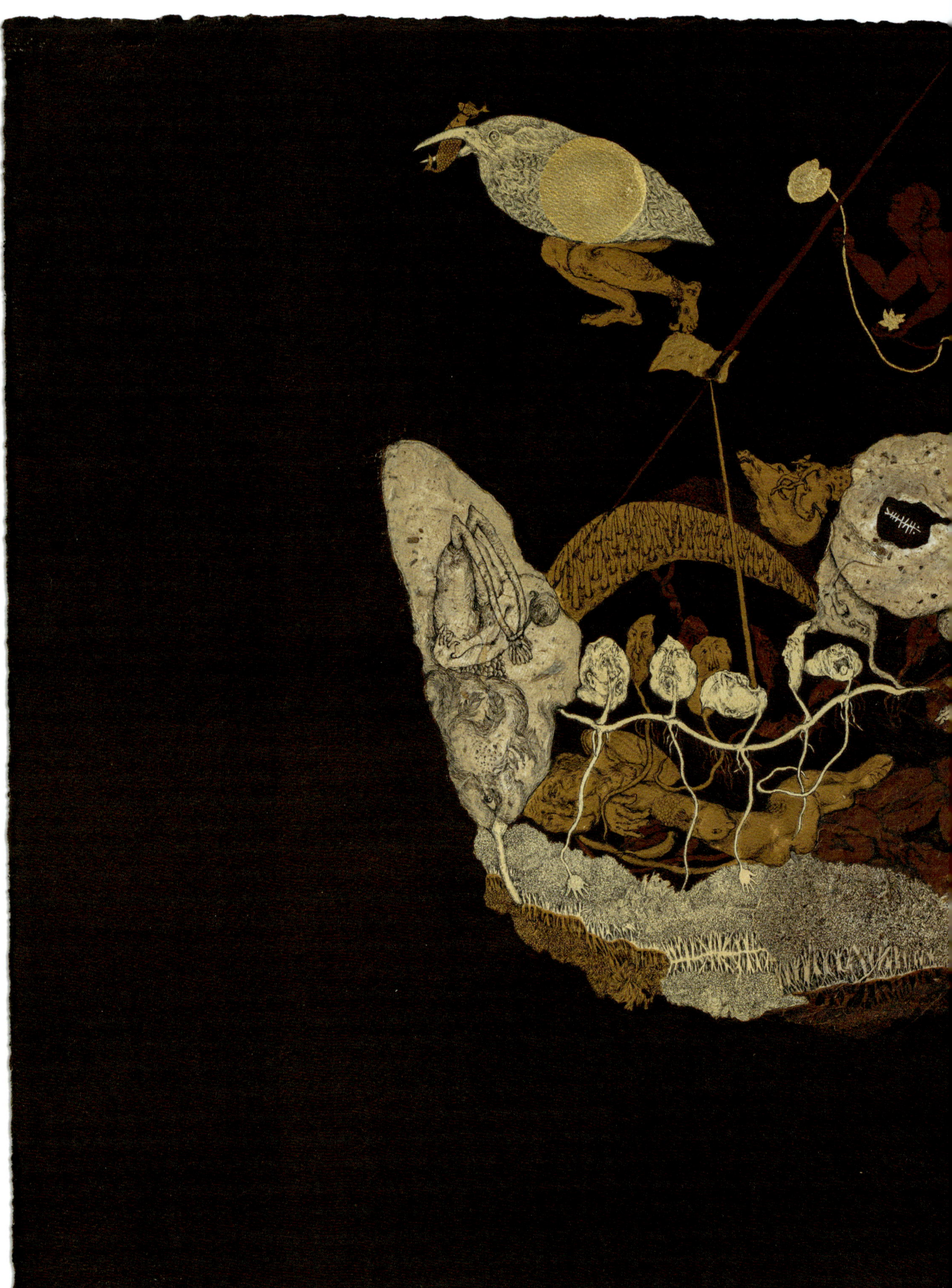

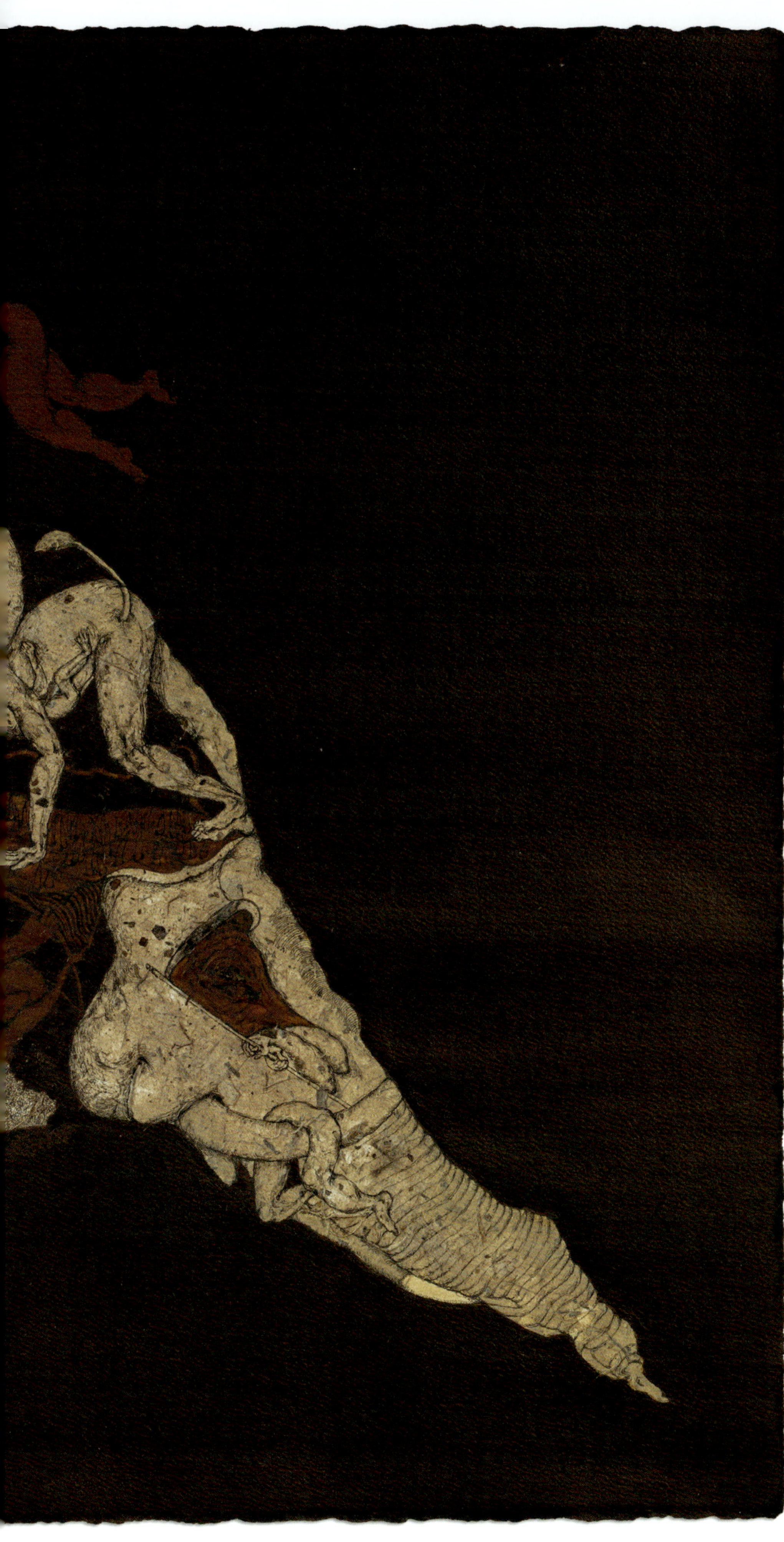

(fig.7.2) ***Where Every Leaf Holds a Tale*** **(*Kalir Char*), 2023, archival ink pen on paper with acrylic colour, gold leaf, 76 × 57 cm.** Ashmolean Museum, University of Oxford, EA2025.26.2. © Soma Surovi Jannat.

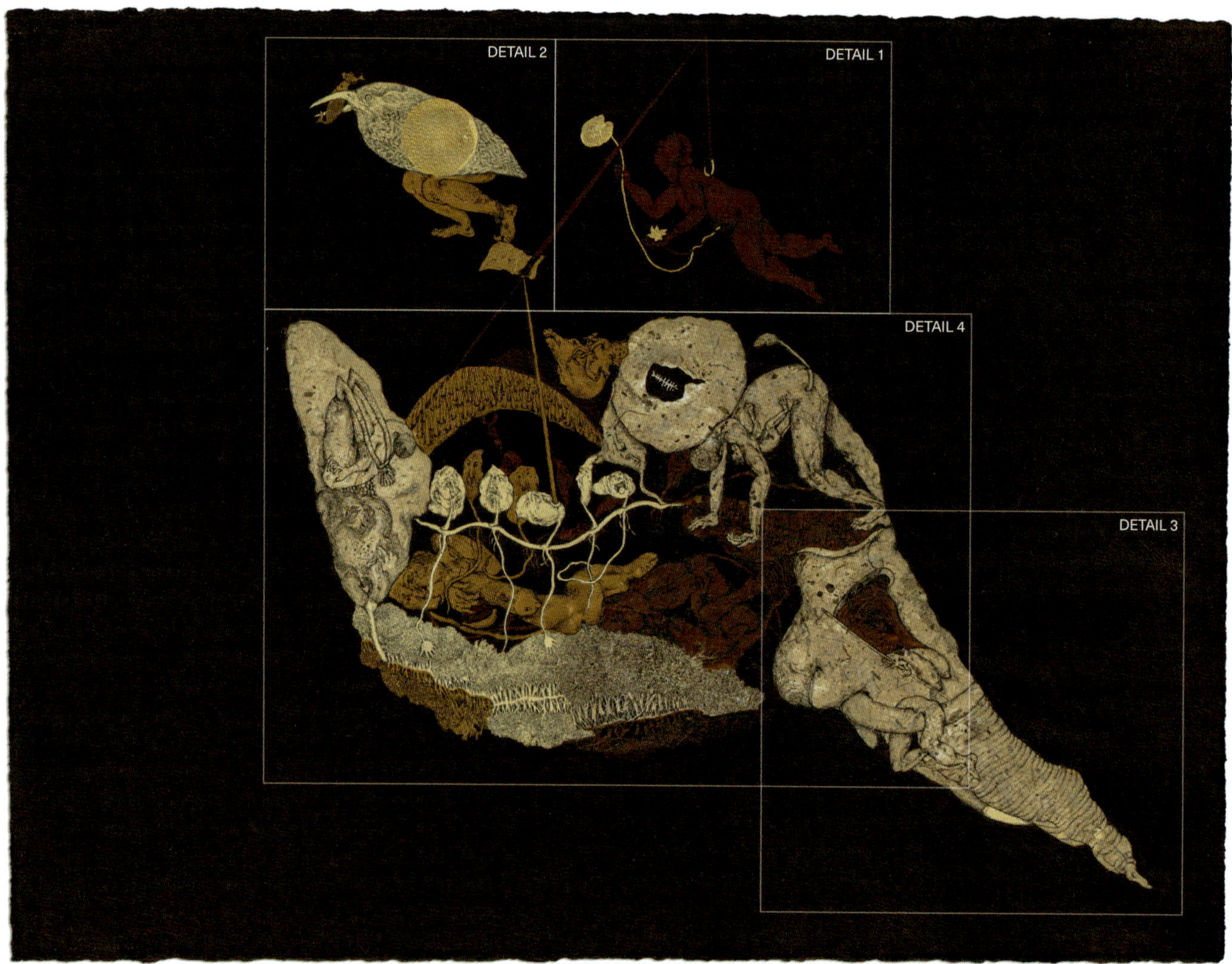

Where Every Leaf Holds a Tale (Kalir Char) (fig.7.2)
On Kalir Char (Kali's Island), Surovi encountered a striking artwork featuring a woman suspended on a hook (detail 1), evoking the traditional rituals depicted in mica paintings at the Ashmolean (fig.13). This imagery reflects the sacrifices women endure, particularly the pain of childbirth, and symbolises the deep bond represented by the umbilical cord. Drawing from the strength embodied by Hindu deities, such as Kali and Durga, she explores themes of motherhood through various symbols.

Influenced by another painting on mica in the Ashmolean, Surovi integrates a bird motif and the concept of wearing masks, which represents the burdens of humanity and the need for balance (detail 2 and fig.14). The inclusion of a fishbone, which can get stuck in the throat (fish on the subcontinent is often cooked with the bone), metaphorically highlights the discomfort and challenges faced by humans and animals. In the lower-right corner of the artwork, an elephant's face emerges, accompanied by a man perched on its trunk (detail 3), showing their interdependence. Two deer interact (inspired by figs 15 and 16), with one biting the other's neck, while surrounding faces convey visible struggle and tension, including a monkey clinging to a man (detail 4).

(fig.13) ***Street and ritual performers*****, c.1790, gouache on mica, 10.2 × 14 cm.** Ashmolean Museum, University of Oxford, EAX.447.o

(fig.14) ***Street and ritual performers,*** **c.1790, gouache on mica, 10.2 × 14 cm.** Ashmolean Museum, University of Oxford, EA1968.41.v

13

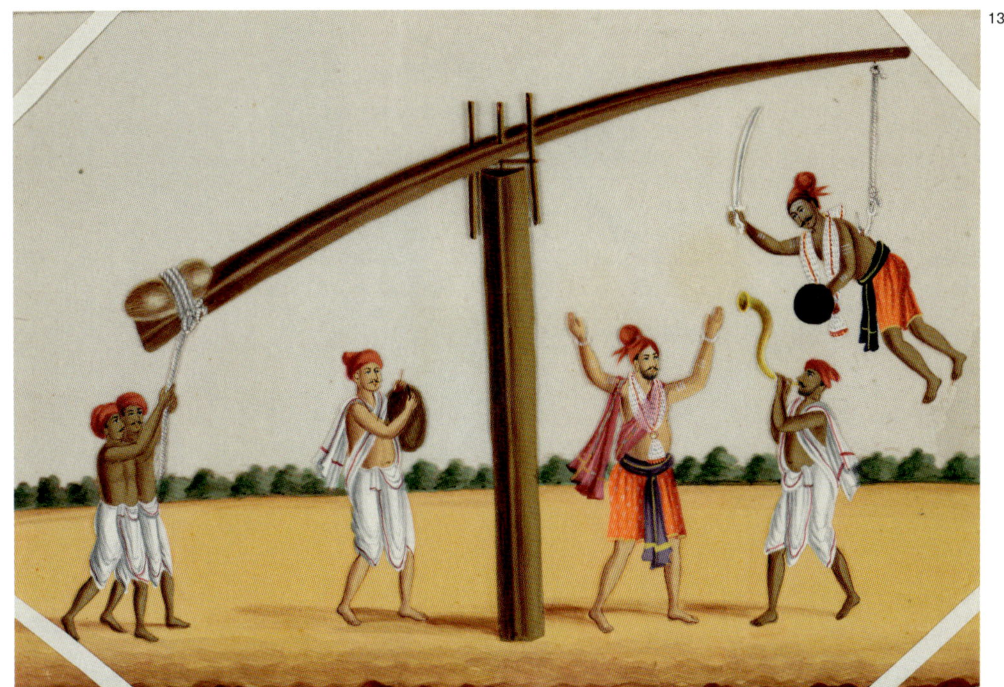

14

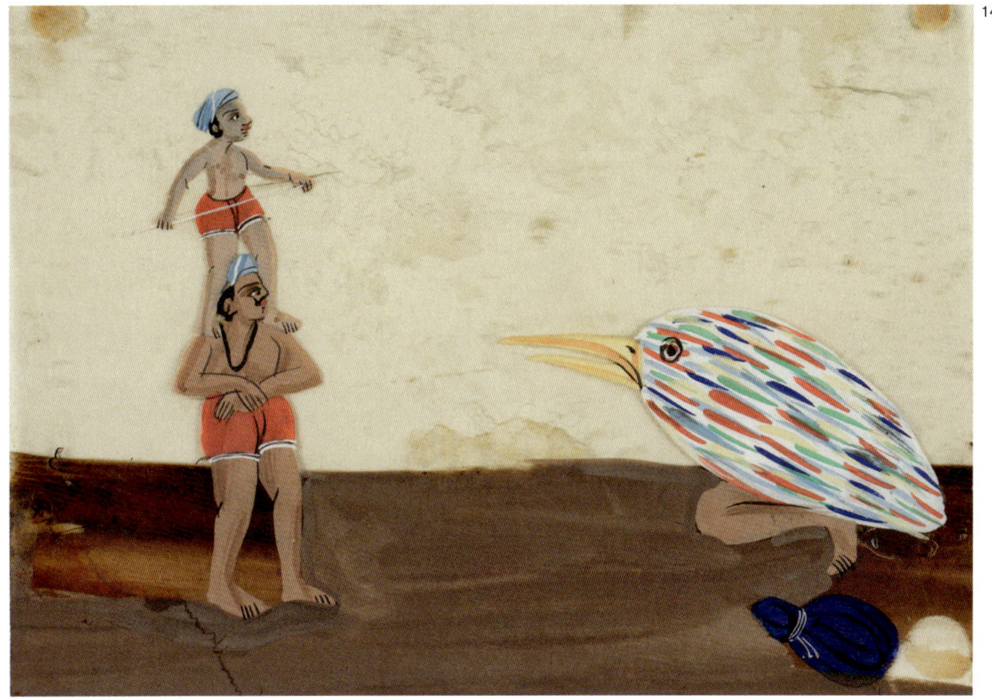

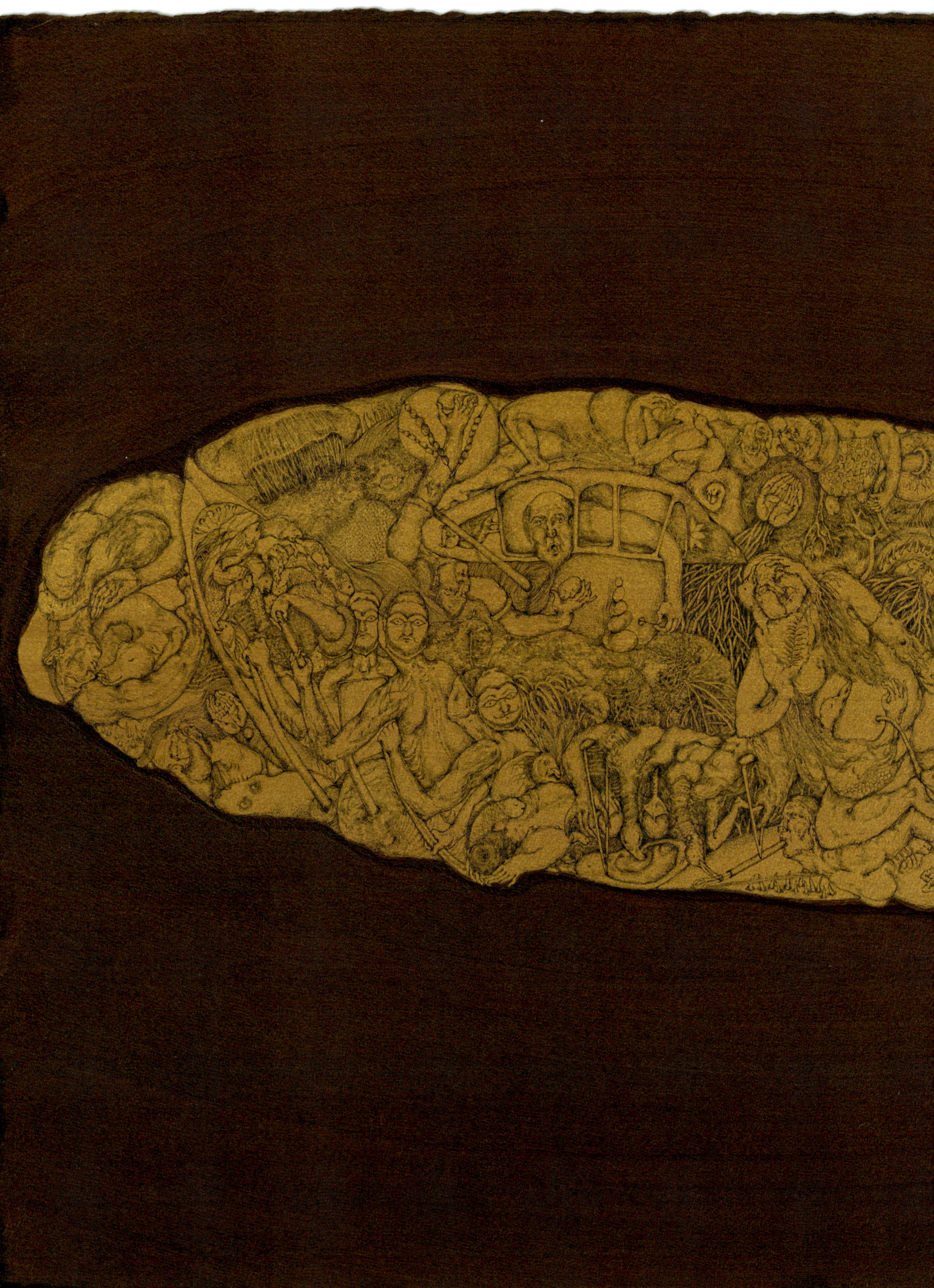

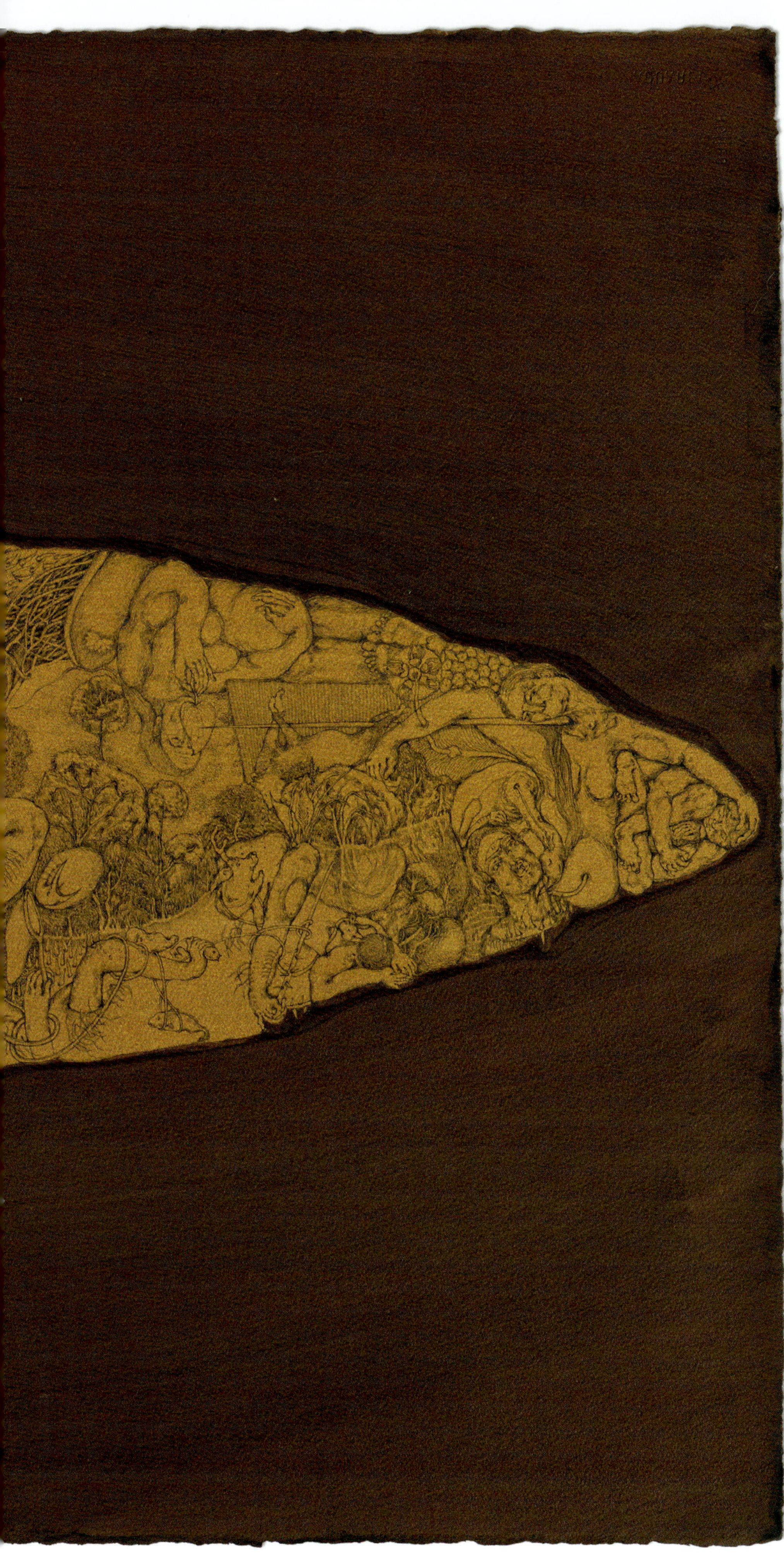

(fig.7.3) ***Where Every Leaf Holds a Tale*** **(*Ha Ja Ba Ra La*), 2023–24, archival ink pen on paper with acrylic colour, 76 × 57 cm.**
Ashmolean Museum, University of Oxford, EA2025.26.3.

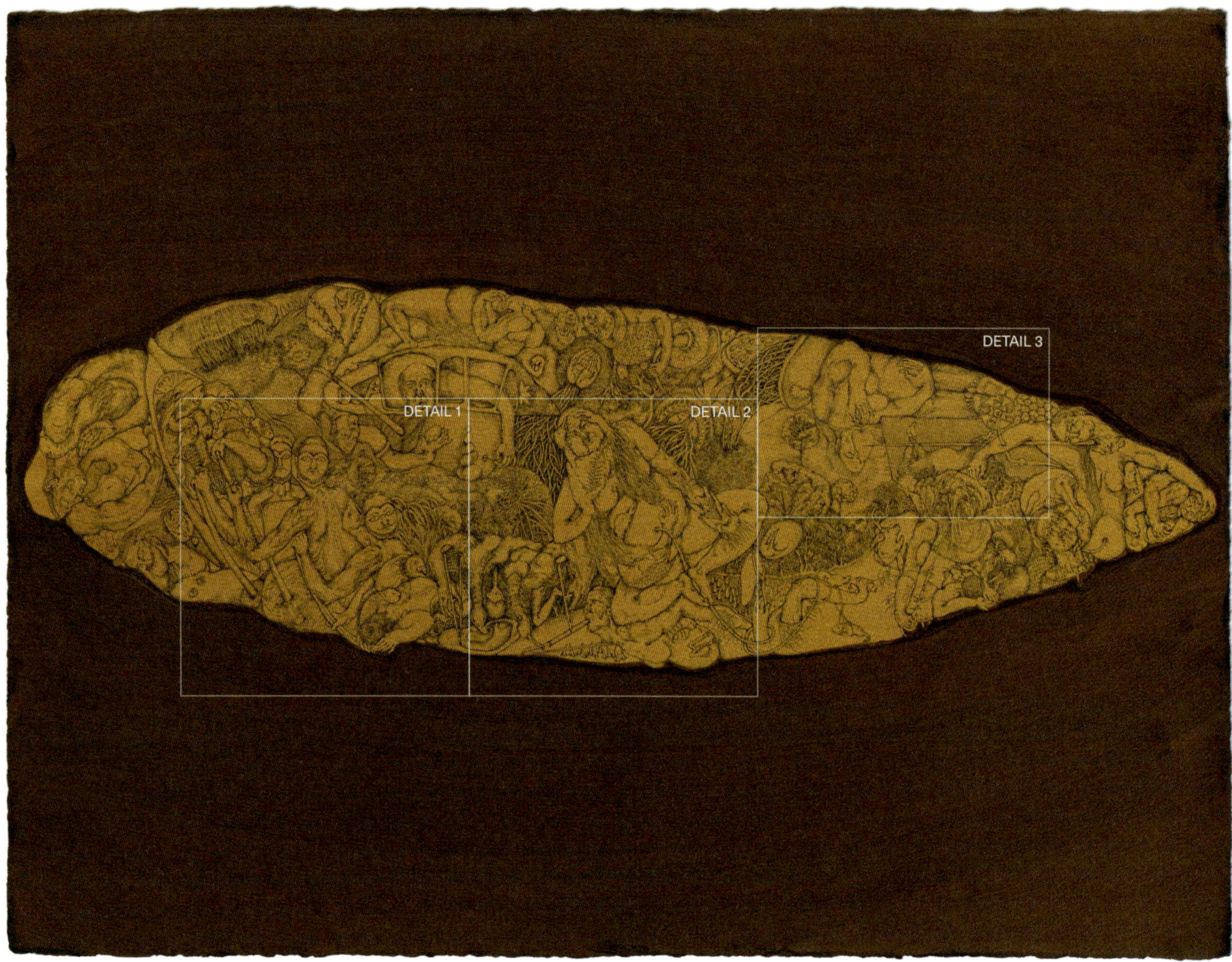

Where Every Leaf Holds a Tale (Ha Ja Ba Ra La) (fig.7.3)
In this work, Surovi delves into the concept of chaos through her exploration of an island named Ha Ja Ba Ra La, a term derived from Bengali that embodies a sense of clutter. The painting captures this notion; every inch of the island is filled with intricate details, creating a sense of almost chaotic complexity. Surovi drew inspiration from a 2023 article by Annu Jalais titled 'The Tiger Charmers of the Sundarbans', which highlighted the close relationship between local communities and wildlife. Among its narratives was a story from 1999, detailing an innovative, yet controversial, tactic employed by forest officers to deter tiger attacks: providing villagers with masks to wear on the back of their heads (detail 1), based on the belief that tigers typically strike from behind. While intended to protect, the masks were met with scepticism, as many villagers preferred to rely on the protection of Bonobibi, the deity of the forest, rather than adopt a strange mask strategy they felt was imposed upon them. This dynamic reflects broader issues of power and belief, showcasing how marginalised communities often feel undervalued and treated as experiments, rather than as respected participants in their own safety.

Through her readings and conversations with Sundarbans' inhabitants, Surovi uncovered local narratives about the villagers' resilience and their spiritual connection to the land. Her composition presents a bird's-eye view of Ha Ja Ba Ra La, intertwining various experiences and challenges faced by the community, with Bonobibi as the central figure (detail 2). Surrounding her are depictions of villagers, including one woman cradling her belly, partially veiled with a ceremonial bridal leaf, and sat against a traditional *shilpatta*, a flat stone used for grinding spices (detail 3). For Surovi, the *shilpatta* is a metaphorical representation of the oppression of women through laborious tasks. She connects these elements through Bonobibi's umbilical cord, creating a visual narrative that celebrates life, culture, and environmental stewardship. While the imagery may appear unsettling, with dismembered limbs intertwined with animals, it suggests a deeper connection and serves as a reminder of the greater whole beyond the visible parts. The painting invites viewers into an infinite space where only fragments of a larger story are presented, allowing for personal interpretations of what lies beyond.

(fig.15) Figure of a reclining stag, *c*.1670, porcelain and polychrome overglaze enamels, 17.2 × 21 × 11.5 cm. Ashmolean Museum, University of Oxford, EA2001.5.a

(fig.16) Figure of a reclining hind, *c*.1670, porcelain and polychrome overglaze enamels, 15 × 20 × 12 cm. Ashmolean Museum, University of Oxford, EA2001.5.b

15

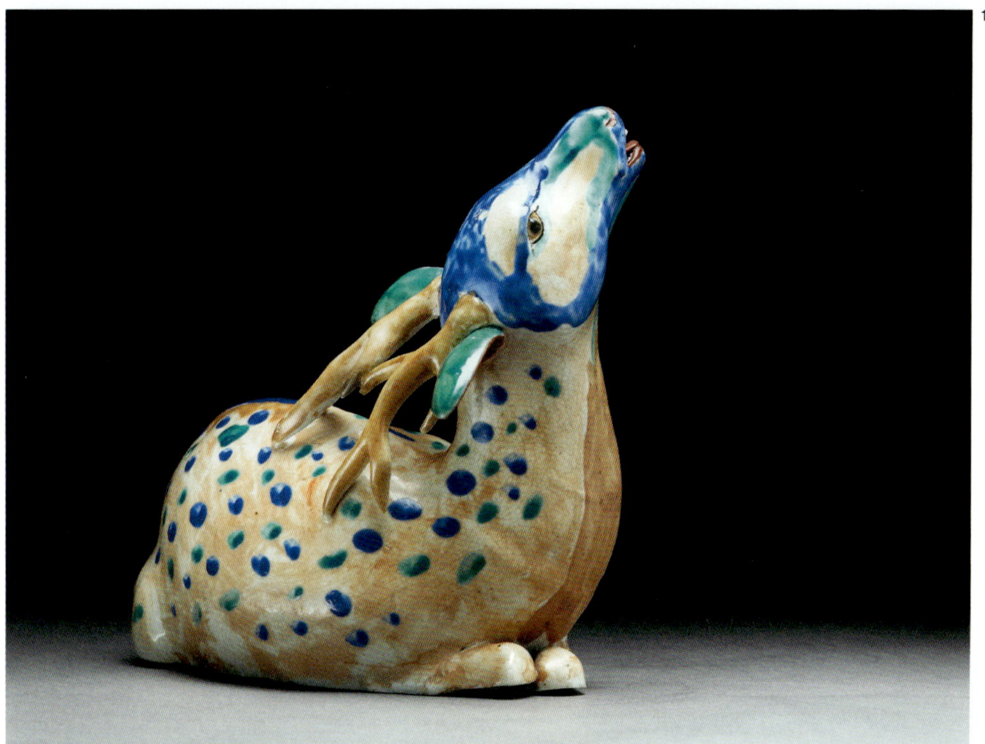

16

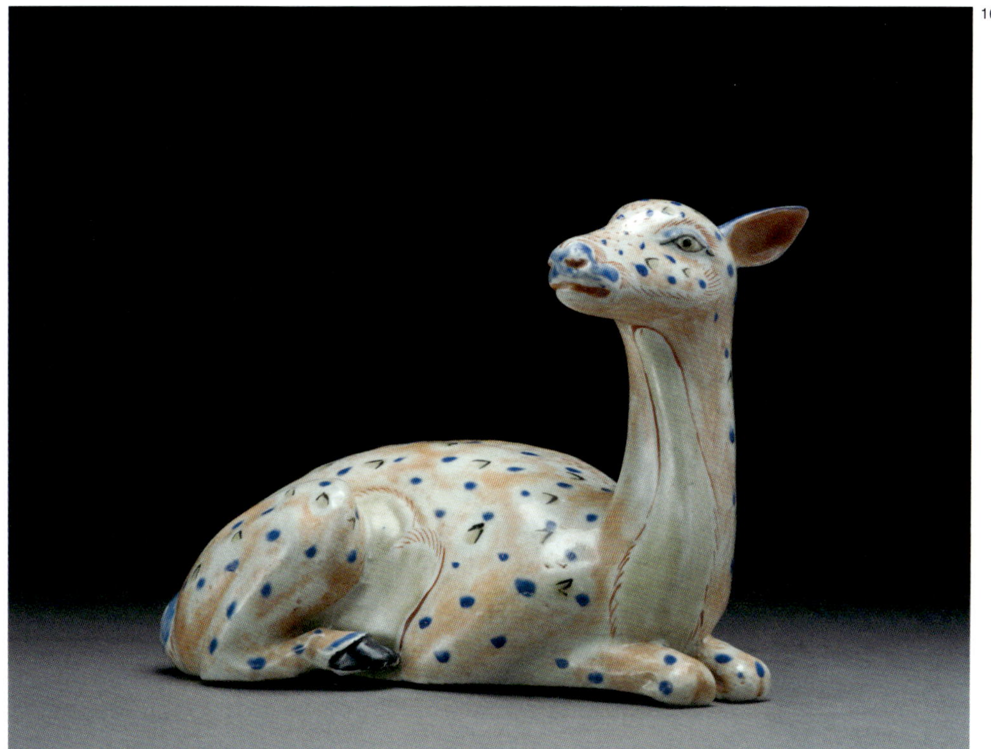

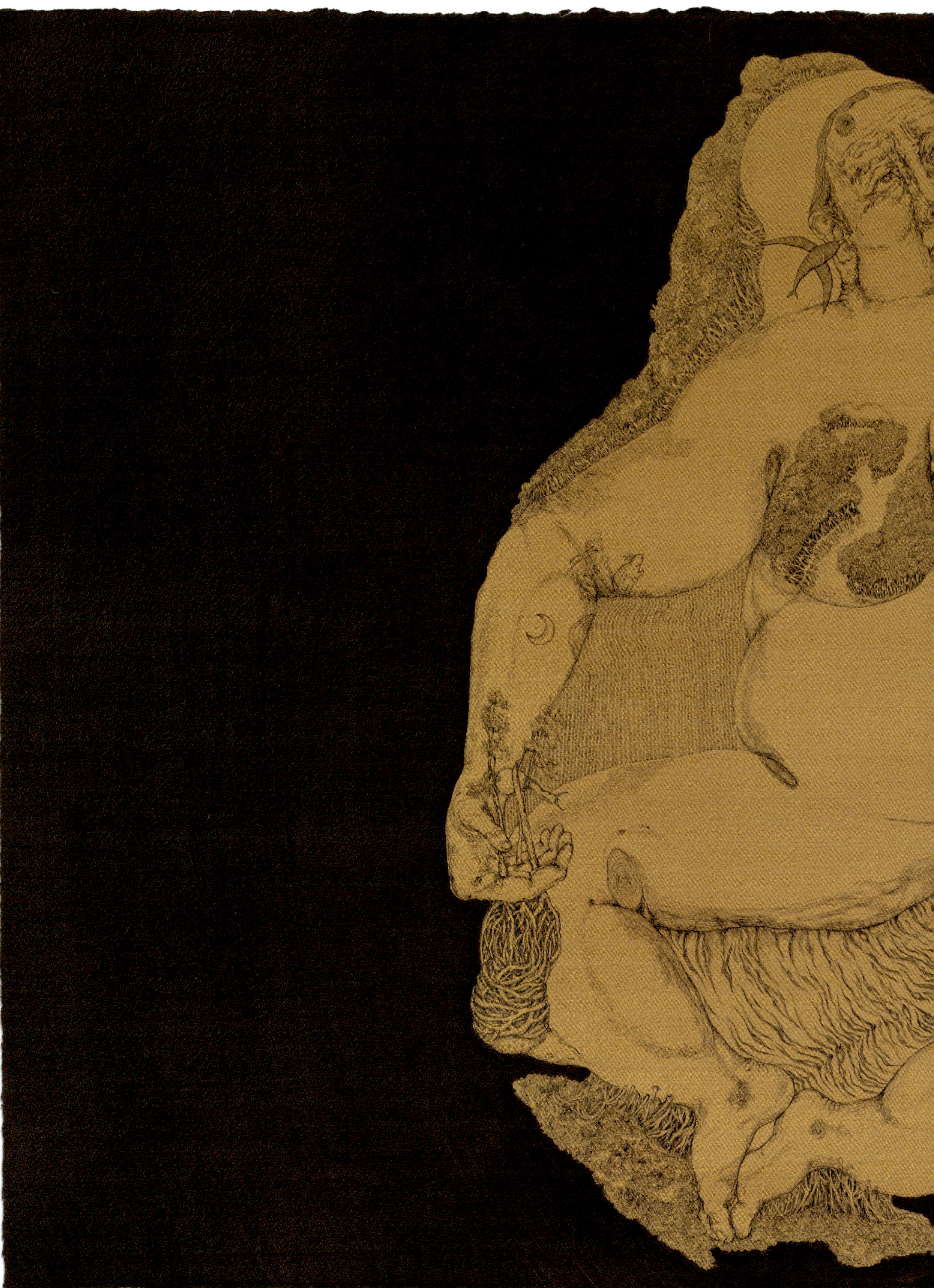

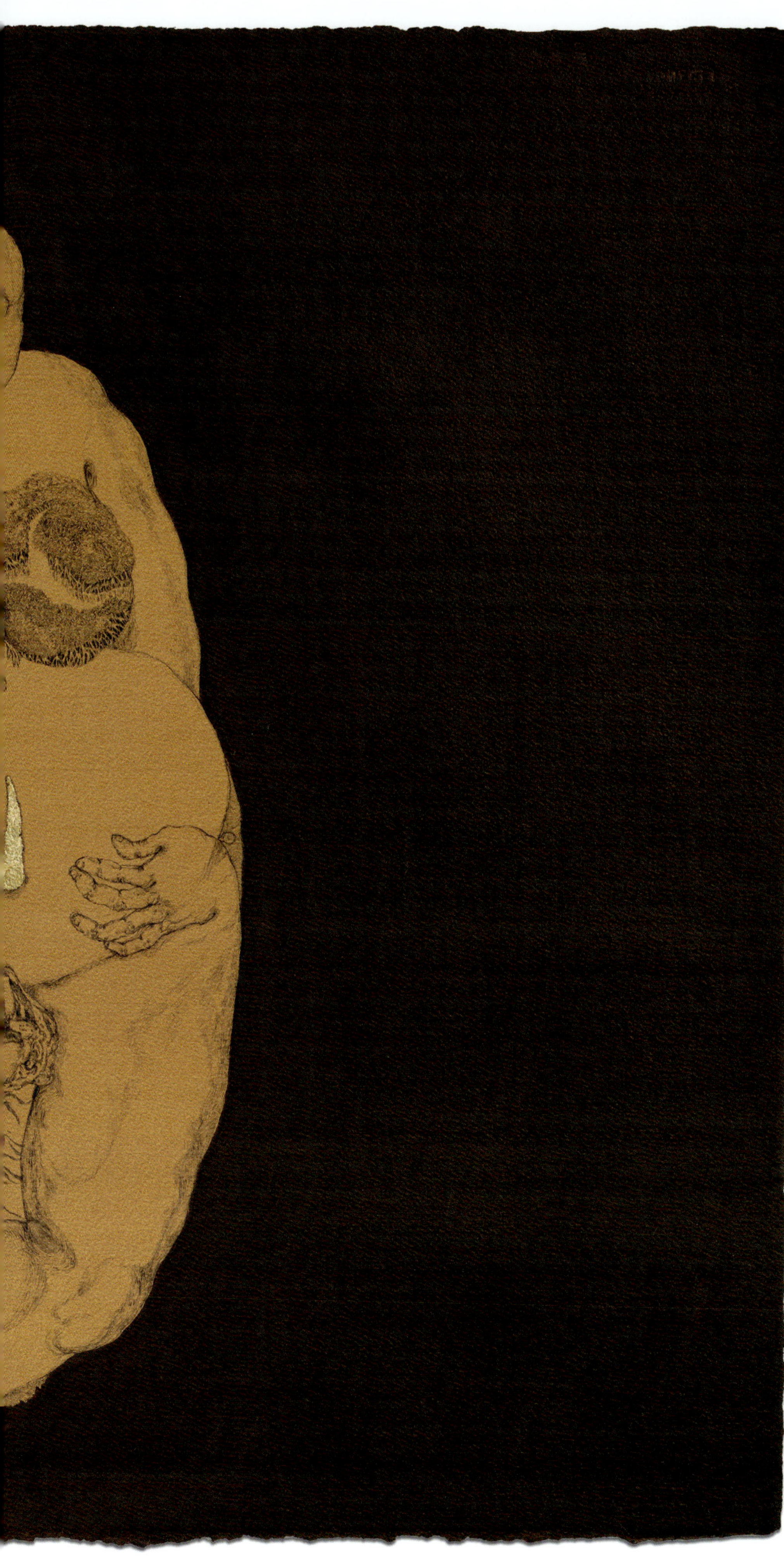

(fig.7.4) *Where Every Leaf Holds a Tale* (*Dimer Char*), 2024, archival ink pen on paper with acrylic colour, gold leaf, 76 × 57 cm.
Ashmolean Museum, University of Oxford, EA2025.26.4.
© Soma Surovi Jannat.

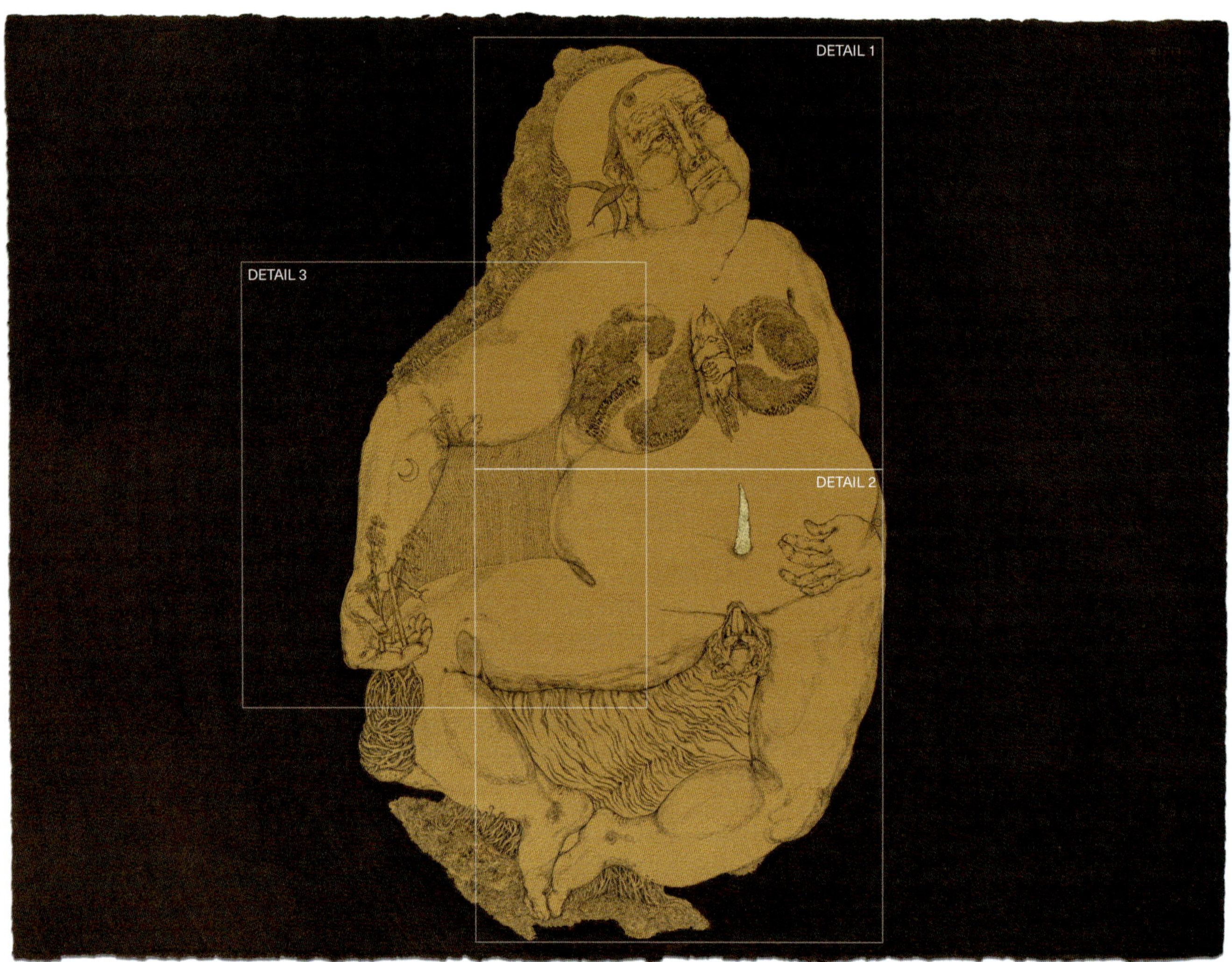

Where Every Leaf Holds a Tale (Dimer Char) (fig.7.4)
Dimer Char (Egg Island) derives its name from its distinctive egg-like shape. Surovi draws inspiration from figures such as the terracotta Yakshi (nature spirit) in the Ashmolean (fig.17), which symbolises nature, femininity, and Surovi's own identity. Central to the artwork is a representation of a mother figure, portrayed as a powerful force of nature. In South Asia, a kala tikka, or black dot, is placed on a child's face to protect them from the evil eye – a malevolent glare driven by envy or ill will. Surovi suggests that even Mother Nature warrants such protection, adorning her forehead with a *kala tikka* (detail 1). Mother Nature's head is covered, reminiscent of older women in Bangladesh. One bird speaks into her ear while she cradles a second lifeless bird on her mangrove-covered breasts. A mangrove root emerges from her navel, while a tiger, representing nature's ferocity, roars between her legs (detail 2). The figure's expression is one of concern as she holds her pregnant belly, signifying both creation and the weight of loss. Her right arm is teeming with vibrant details of forest life, including a playful squirrel, reflecting the rich environment that sustains her (detail 3). This piece captures themes of pain, grief, loss, and also hope and resilience, portraying a complex narrative where even a broken woman like Mother Nature embodies strength and power despite her sorrow.

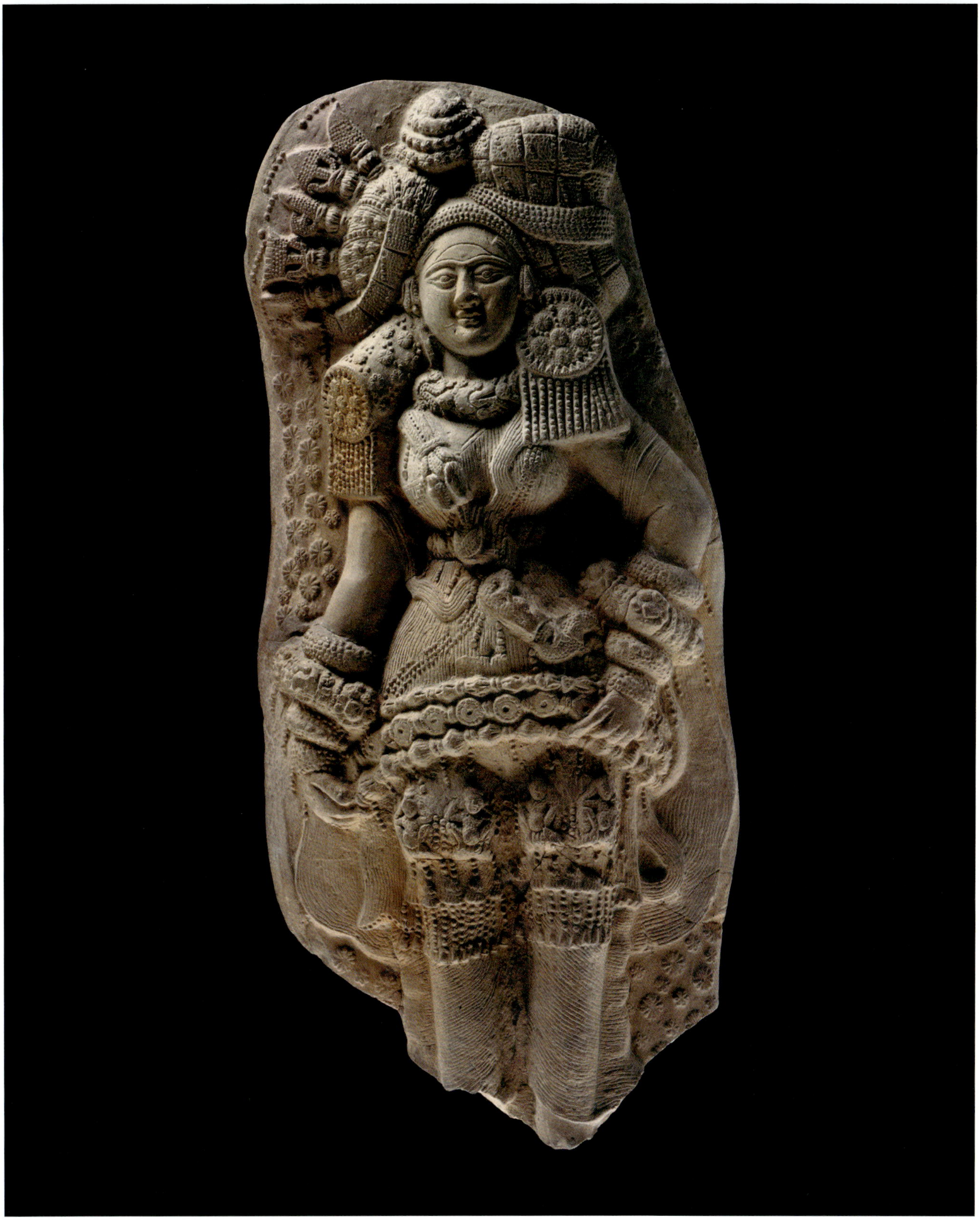

(fig.17) *Plaque with Yakshi (nature spirit) or mother goddess*, second century BCE, terracotta, 21.7 cm (height). Ashmolean Museum, University of Oxford, EAX.201

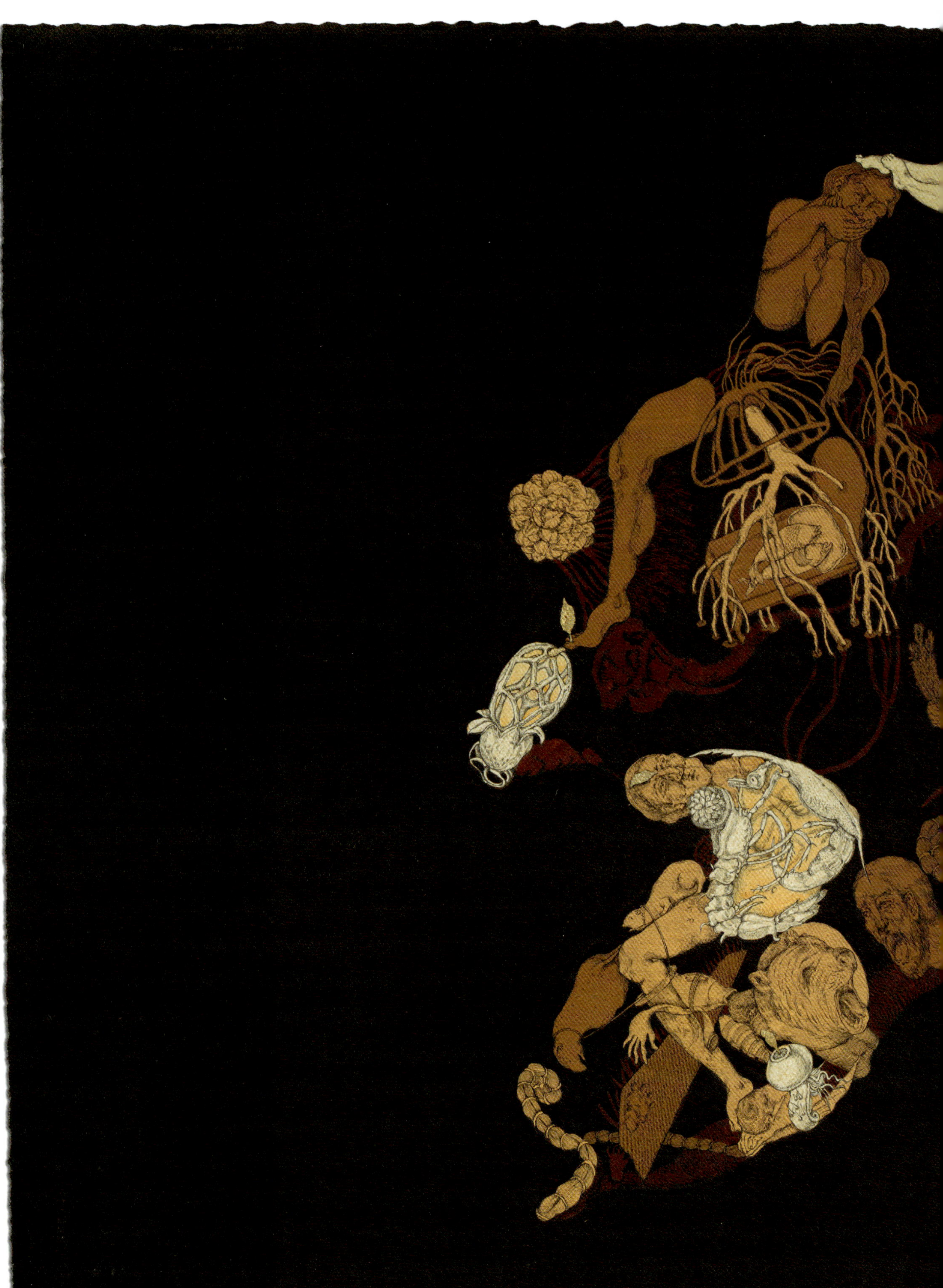

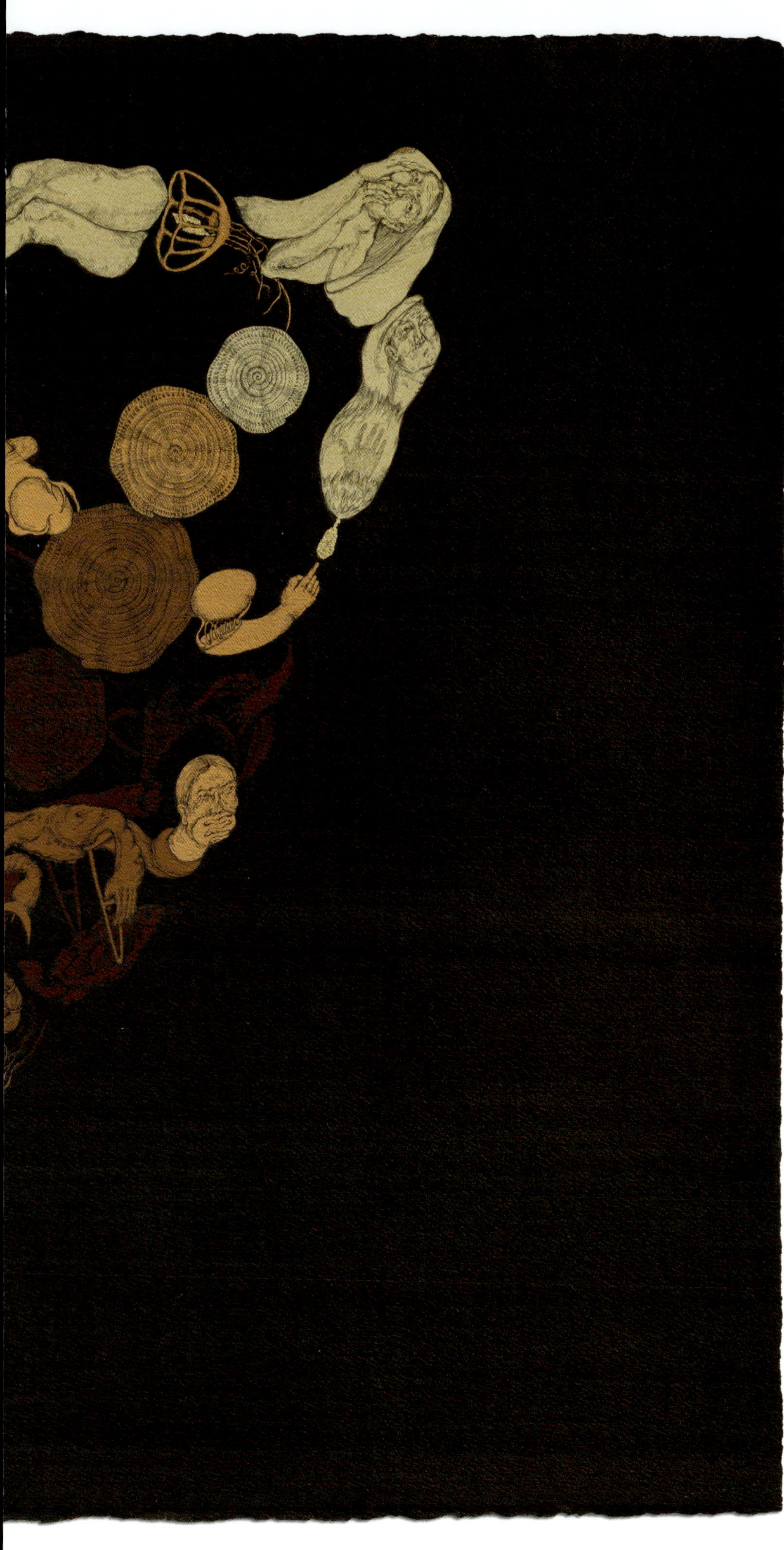

(fig.7.5) *Where Every Leaf Holds a Tale* (*Banishanta*), 2024, archival ink pen on paper with acrylic colour, gold leaf, 76 × 57 cm.
Ashmolean Museum, University of Oxford, EA2025.26.5. Presented by the artist.

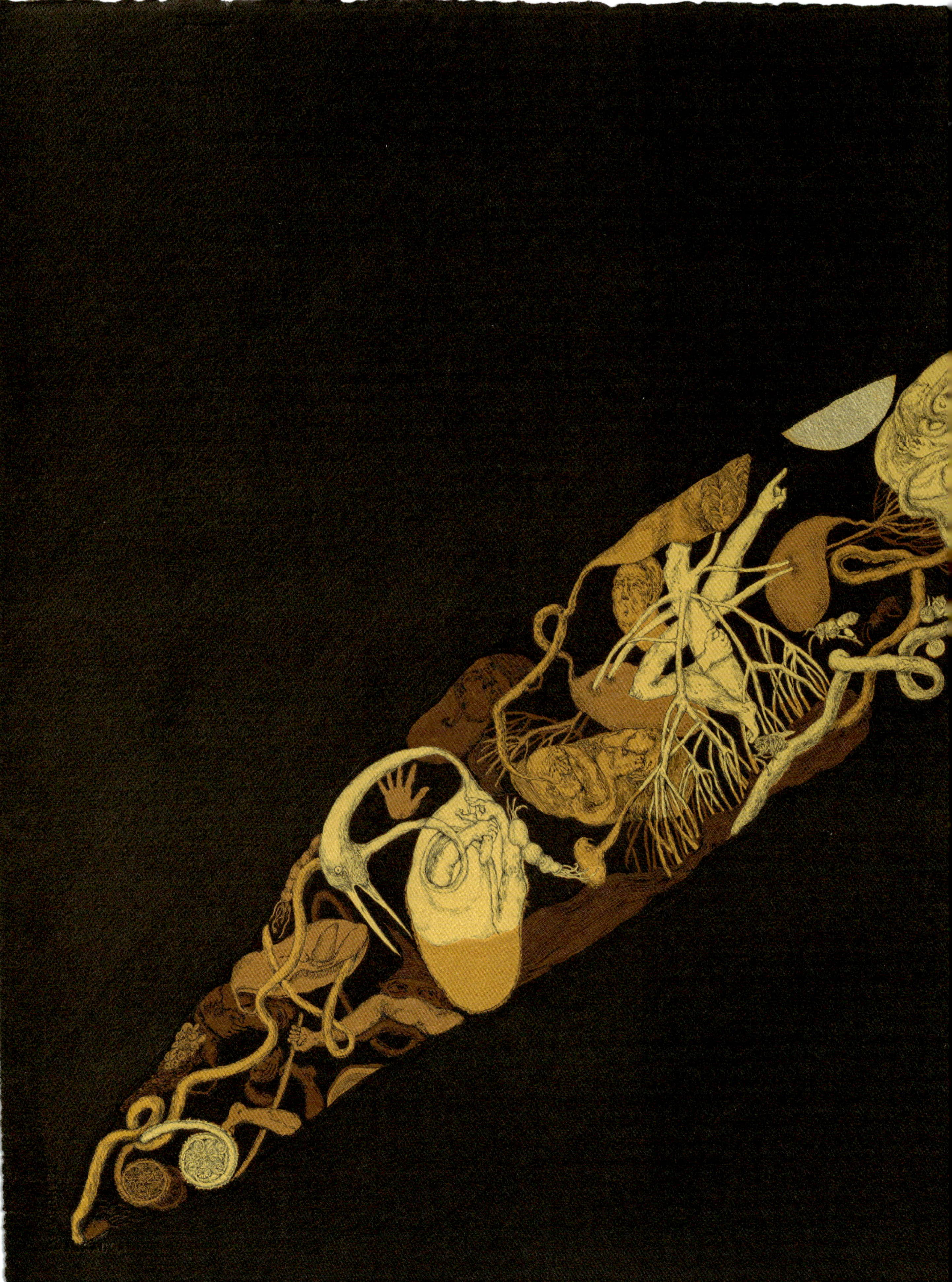

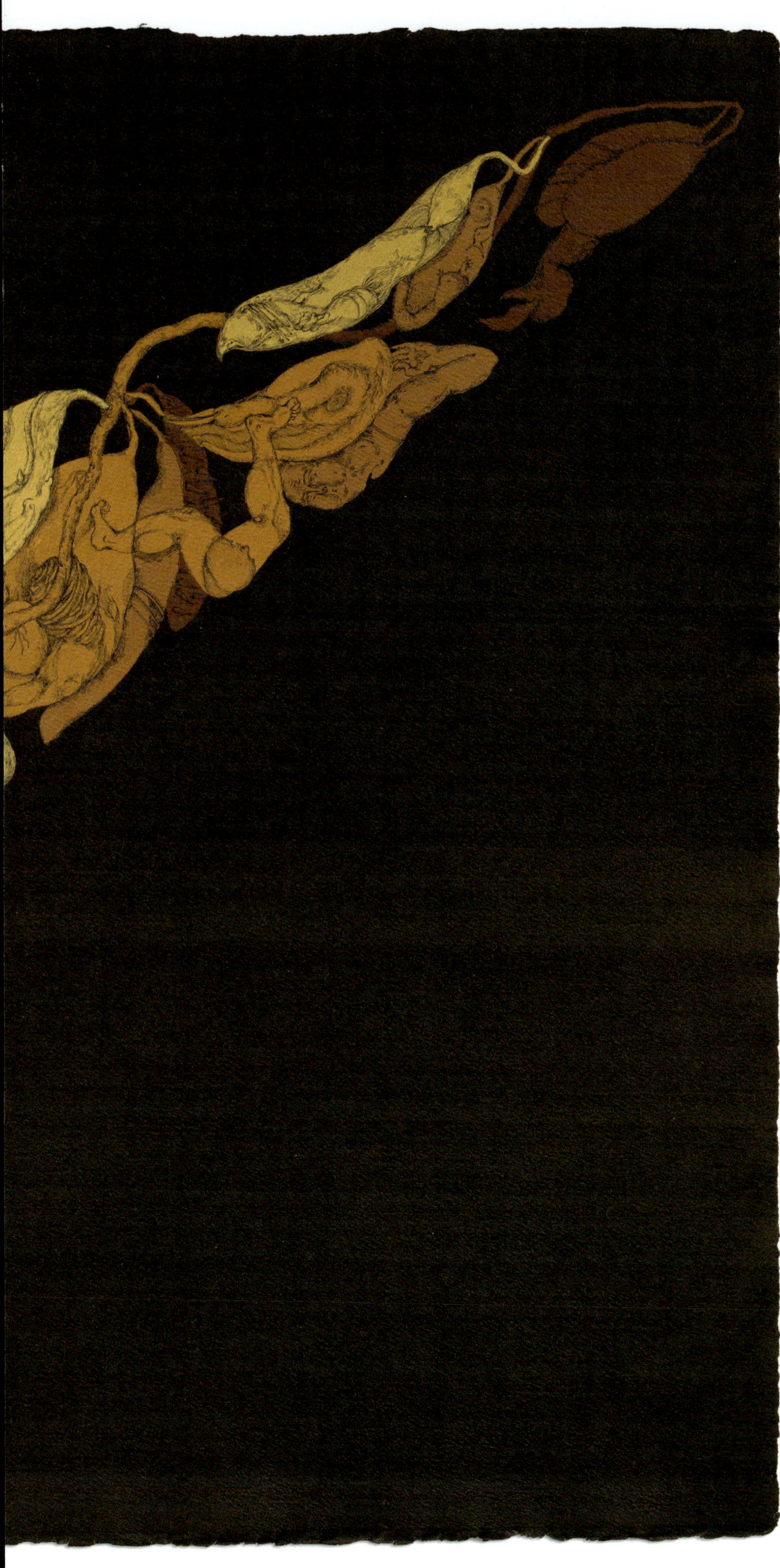

(fig.7.6) *Where Every Leaf Holds a Tale* (*Dhoenchabaria Char*), 2024, archival ink pen on paper with acrylic colour, gold leaf, 76 × 57 cm. Ashmolean Museum, University of Oxford, EA2025.26.6. © Soma Surovi Jannat. Presented by the artist

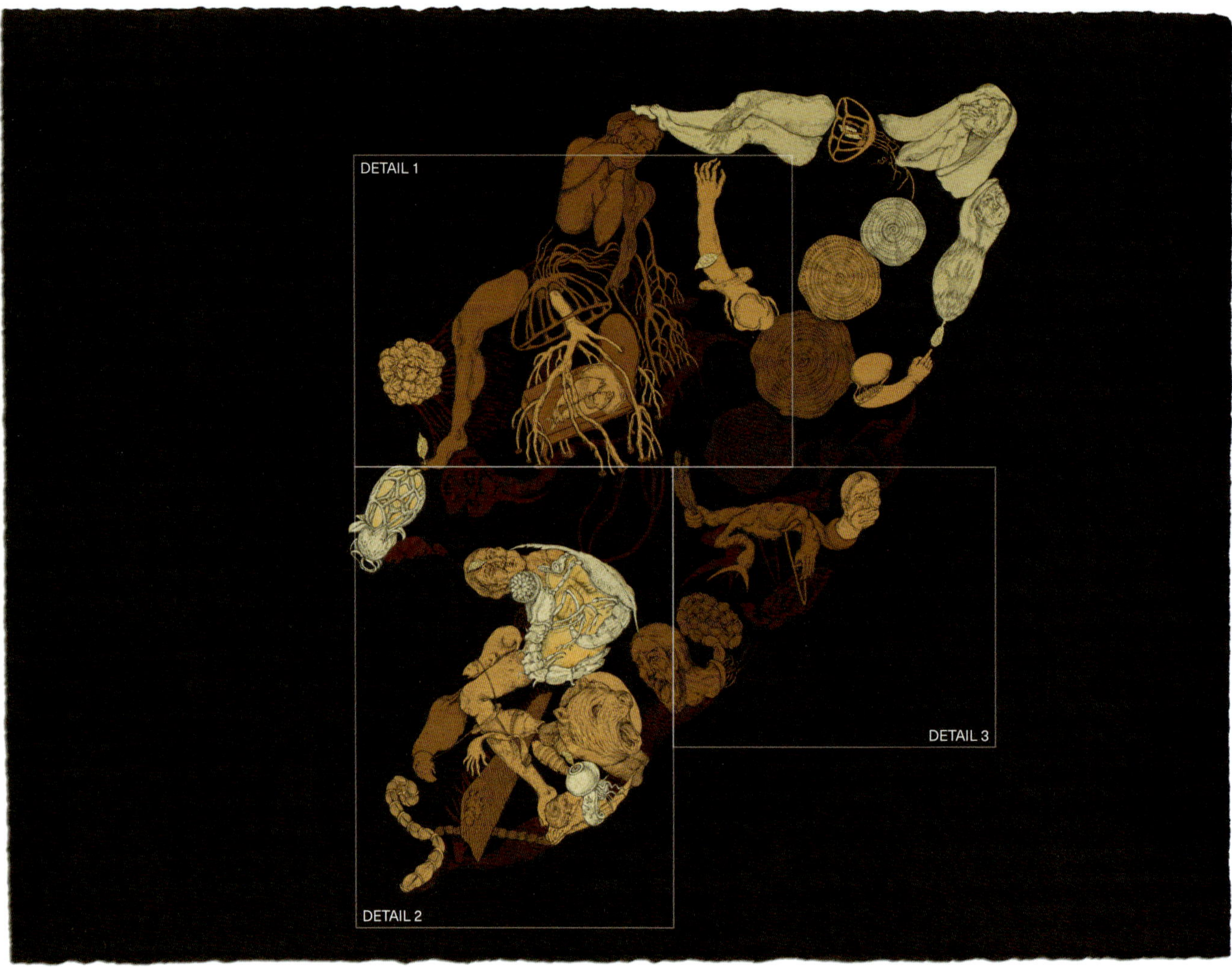

Where Every Leaf Holds a Tale (Banishanta) (fig.7.5)
The term 'bania' denotes a mercantile caste in the Indian subcontinent, and the island of Banishanta exemplifies this with its combination of trade, tourism, and shrimp farming. However, beneath the surface of this vibrant locale lies a growing eco-anxiety among the populace, stemming from the loss of natural greenery and land. The landscape of the Sundarbans, marked by a complex network of tidal rivers and mangrove forests, relies on a delicate balance between river flow, sediment, and salt-tolerant vegetation for its health. During a visit to Banishanta, Surovi was struck by the sight of withering and dead Sundari trees (detail 1). To her, nature seemed to convey an anguish reminiscent of women in distress, suffering in silence. Human activities, particularly the extensive practices of shrimp farming, have led to increased salinity in the waters, significantly impacting the local ecosystem. Shrimp farming in Bangladesh depends on utilising salt water to form saline ponds in coastal areas, but this method results in significant land and water salinity problems. The creation of these ponds leads to the permanent salinisation of soil, making it unfit for traditional rice cultivation or other crops.

This alteration of land and water resources due to rising salinity is a key factor in environmental degradation, loss of livelihoods, and social conflicts, affecting small-scale farmers as well as the broader community. While the government has planted new trees, the core issues remain unresolved. With the depletion of fish populations due to salt water intrusion, locals have begun training otters to assist in fishing (detail 2). This adaptation of otters serves as a means of attraction for tourists, even in the face of pressing environmental challenges.

Surovi portrays two fish (detail 1) rested among the mangrove roots, representing a fleeting peace amid the ecological turmoil. Scattered throughout the landscape are golden leaves, symbolising beauty and rarity amidst destruction. The work features a hand holding peacock feathers being sold in the market, accompanied by a

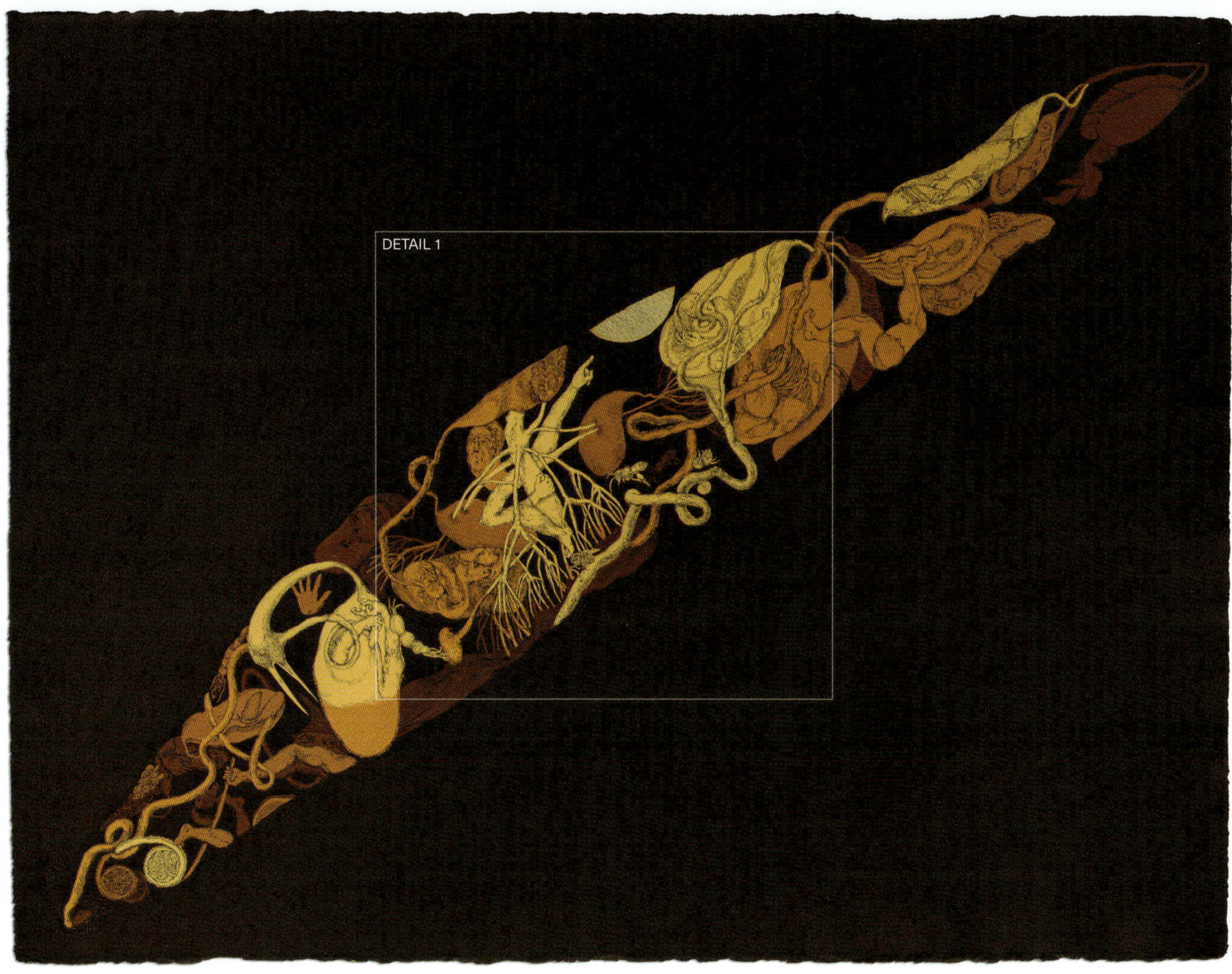

humorous portrayal of peacocks protesting the plucking of their tails (detail 3). Beneath the water, a turtle swims, symbolising age, wisdom, and an understanding of nature's rhythms. Surovi's depiction of a human figure shouting near the turtle evokes questions surrounding communication and awareness. Organic forms merge to create a shadow, resembling a human face, suggesting the intertwining of humanity and the natural world. Overall, the visit to Banishanta left Surovi with a profound sense of tranquillity mixed with concern for the environment, highlighting the urgent need for harmony between human activity and nature.

Where Every Leaf Holds a Tale (Dhoenchabaria Char) (fig.7.6)

The narrative in this work centres around the island Dhoenchabaria, whose shape inspired the composition of the piece. Though Surovi did not visit this island, she was intrigued by its contours.

On the various islands of the Sundarbans, collecting honey is a task undertaken by many men. One honey collector told Surovi that, on discovery of a honeycomb, they point and say, 'Allah Allah'. This signal emphasises a sense of divine purpose in their labour. At the centre of this work, an extended arm points toward a shimmering honeycomb (detail 1). The honeycomb's metallic hue symbolises its distinctive qualities, representing the complexity of nature's creations. This focal point invites viewers to appreciate the intricate patterns and unique structure of the honeycomb, encouraging them to think more deeply about its significance. Honeycombs are becoming increasingly scarce due to environmental destruction, particularly in areas like the Sundarbans, where they were once plentiful.

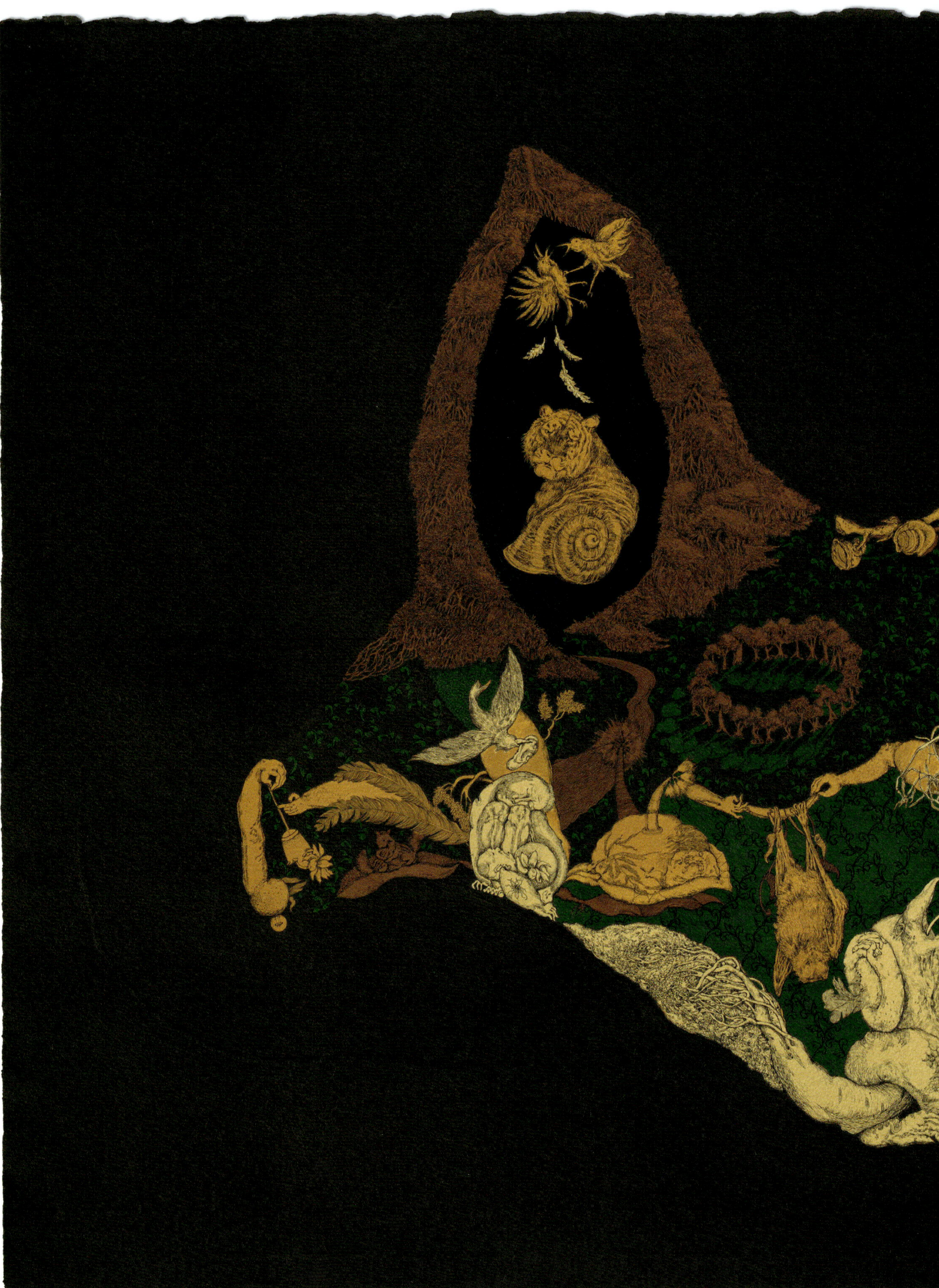

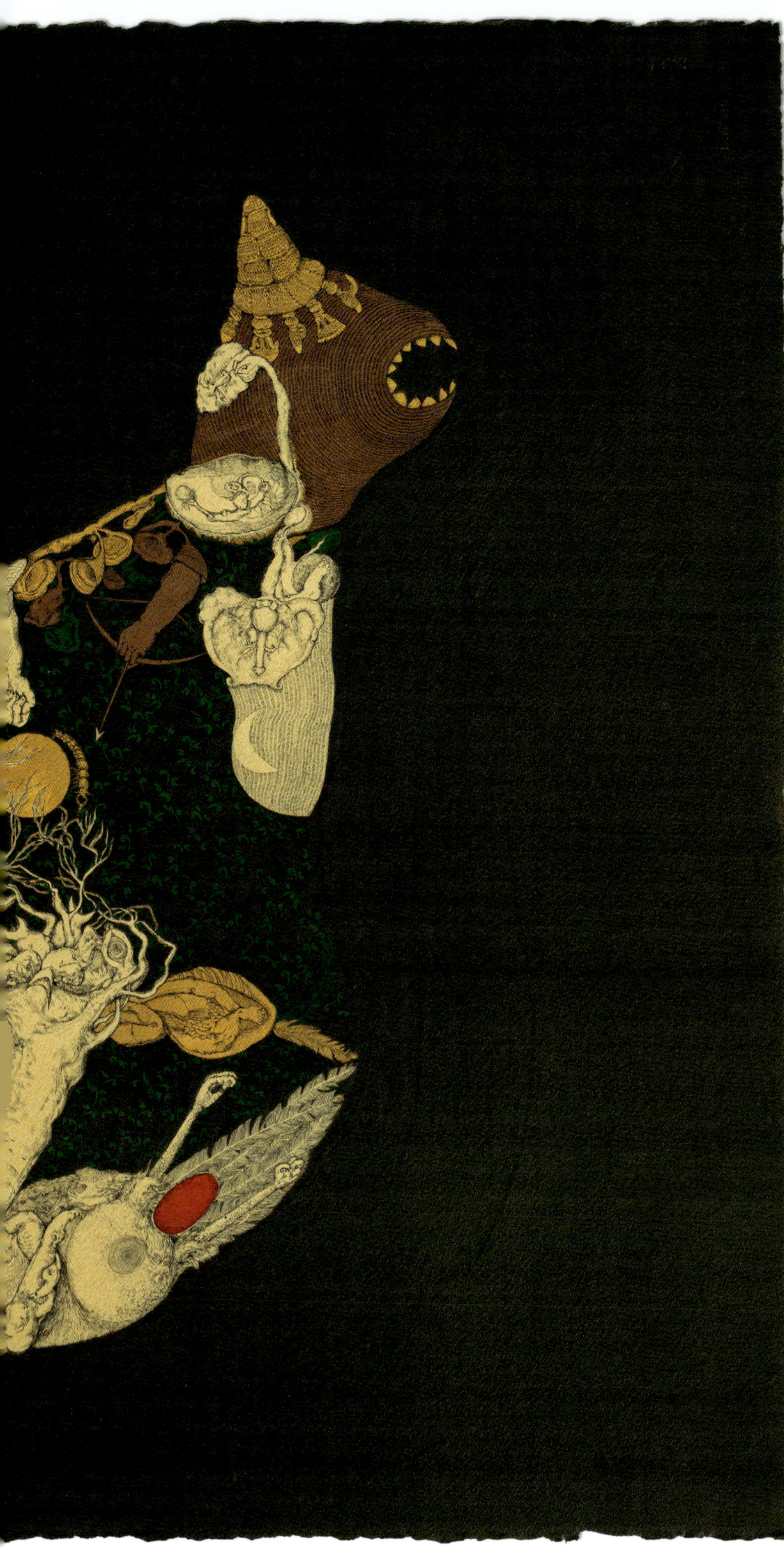

(fig.7.7) ***Where Every Leaf Holds a Tale*** **(*Shyamnagar*), 2024, archival ink pen on paper with acrylic colour, gold leaf, 76 × 57 cm.**
Ashmolean Museum, University of Oxford, EA2025.26.7. © Soma Surovi Jannat.

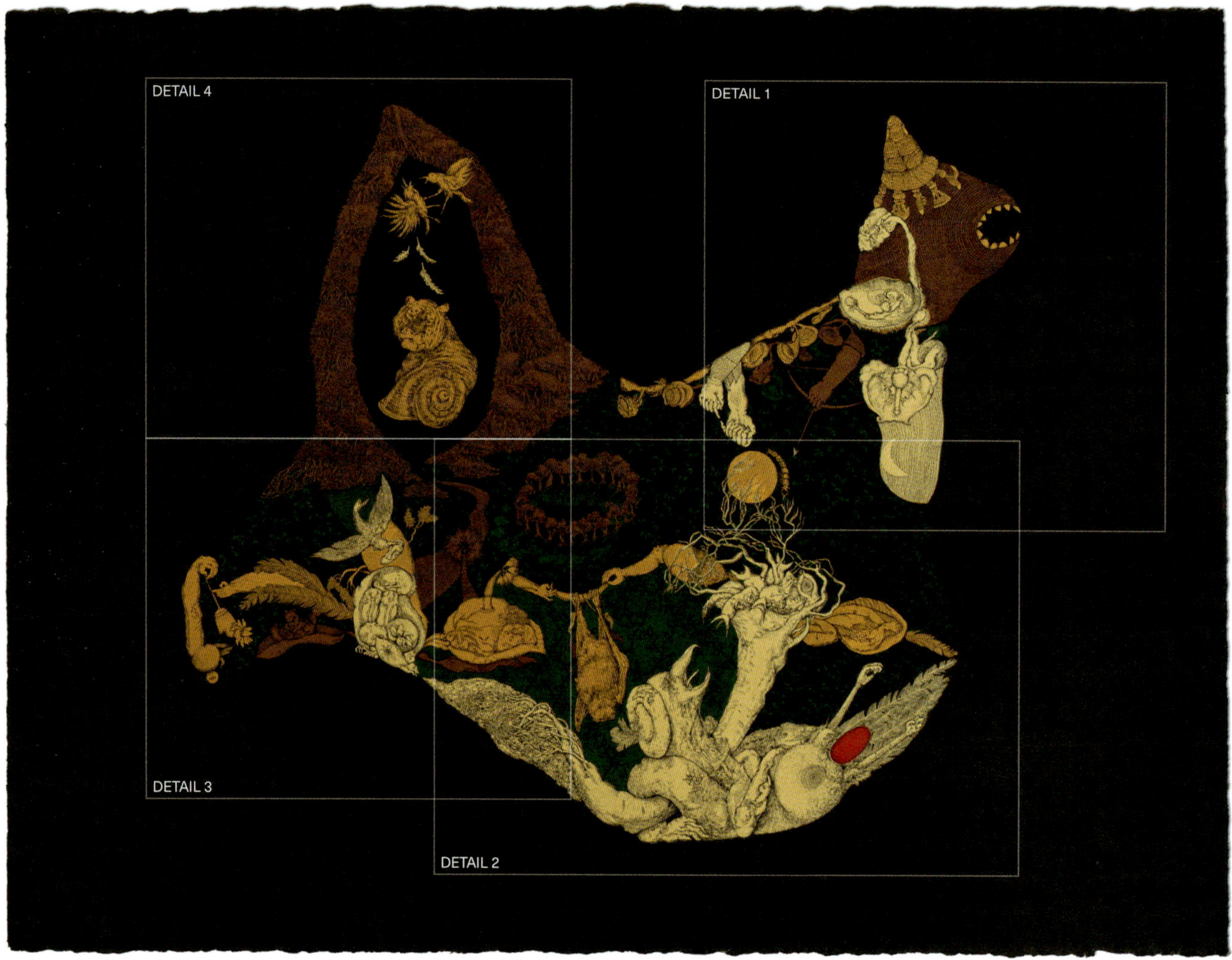

Where Every Leaf Holds a Tale (Shyamnagar) (fig.7.7)
The seventh work in this series is focused on the culturally significant island of Shyamnagar. The name 'Shyam' invokes images of the Hindu god Krishna, known for his dark complexion and romantic relationships with numerous partners. Among his notable devotees, figures like Meera and Radha exemplify deep admiration and love. Shyamnagar's bird-like shape adds a unique visual element to the artwork, which includes an imaginative twist: a mouth added to the 'bird' that doesn't exist in the shape of the island. Surovi once again drew inspiration from the Ashmolean's Yakshi (fig.17), particularly its distinctive headdress, which she reinterprets here by positioning it upside down on the bird's head (detail 1).

Exploring themes of parenthood, the viewer is presented with a distressed mother bird screaming for her young, who cry from their position within an exposed root system beneath a fallen tree (detail 2). A red dot on the mother bird's back points to the struggles and experiences of motherhood; the use of red in this context suggests blood, intensifying the emotional depth perhaps related to Surovi's own personal journey. The composition also features a man resting while a bird interacts with him (detail 3). This interaction subtly references the Bengali proverb, '*Chile kan niyece*', which literally means, 'A kite has stolen the ear'. The phrase refers to the spreading of unfounded rumours. Here, when the kite takes the man's ear, he does not run after the bird or chase the misinformation. Instead, he sits calmly, holding his child on his lap, embodying acceptance amid the surrounding chaos. The presence of two squirrels, a mother and her baby, alongside the man tenderly holding his child, represents the deep bond between parents and children, a recurring theme in Surovi's work during this period.

The painting depicts a contrast of destruction in nature with the fragile relationships between its elements. Inspired by two images in the Ashmolean (figs 18–19), Surovi's powerful tiger, depicted with sorrowful energy,

18

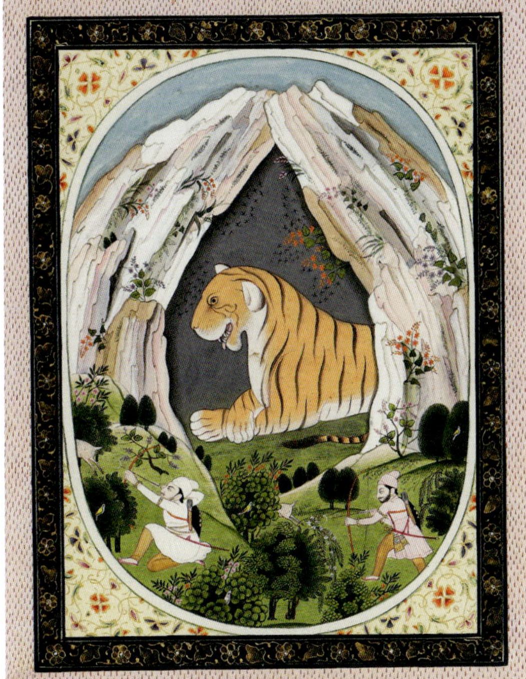

19

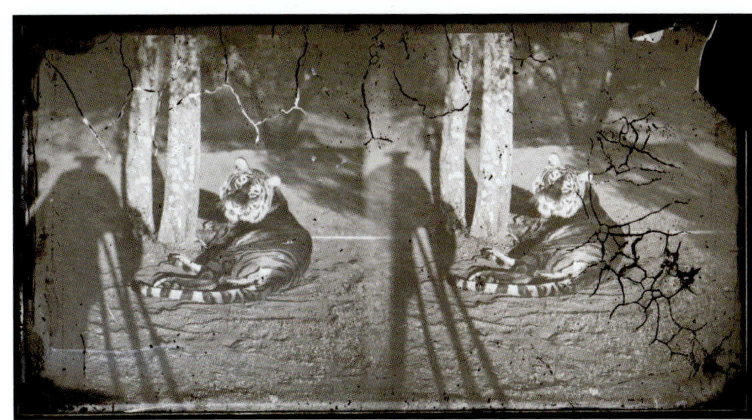

(fig.18) ***Tiger in a cave*, *c*.1800, gouache with gold on paper, 18.8 × 13.5 cm.** Ashmolean Museum, University of Oxford, EA2007.255

(fig.19) Eugene Clutterbuck Impey (1830–1904), *Untitled* (tiger with tripod/photographer's shadow), *c*.1851–78, digital positive from a stereoscopic glass negative. Ashmolean Museum, University of Oxford, GB/0000/ECI/1/1/247

serves as a symbol of hope and renewal alongside feelings of fear and loss (detail 4). Above the tiger, birds further illustrate this theme, with one appearing ready to fall while the other screeches in distress. The background, a vibrant green representing life, contrasts with elements of decay, illustrated through hints of brown. This combination highlights the urgent degradation of the environment. Additionally, bats in this artwork, which often evoke fear in the context of Bangladesh, enhance the sense of foreboding (detail 2).

Surovi incorporates her brother's *ek-tara* (a one-string musical instrument, (detail 3), symbolising personal and cultural connections amidst a narrative of destruction caused by human actions. This instrument has a single neck and a resonator, traditionally made from a dried gourd or coconut, covered with a stretched animal skin. The instrument is played by plucking the single string and is often used by holy men on the subcontinent to accompany their songs and prayers.

In 2024, during the political protests and unrest in Bangladesh, with widespread misinformation, it was difficult to reach and receive medical care on time in Dhaka. Surovi tragically lost her unborn child, Izhaan, before she completed this painting. This deeply personal loss resonates with the concerns in this series, particularly the last two works (figs 7.7–7.8). The colours employed reflect Surovi's feelings and the turbulent environment surrounding her, conveying a sense of fragility and isolation in challenging times. While she explored dark, murky colours effectively in this series to depict the tumultuous waters of Bangladesh, she has shared her deep emotional experience, allowing viewers to connect with her journey. The solitary tiger in a cave (upper left, detail 4) conveys profound sadness, encapsulating a time marked by mixed emotions of hope and heartache.

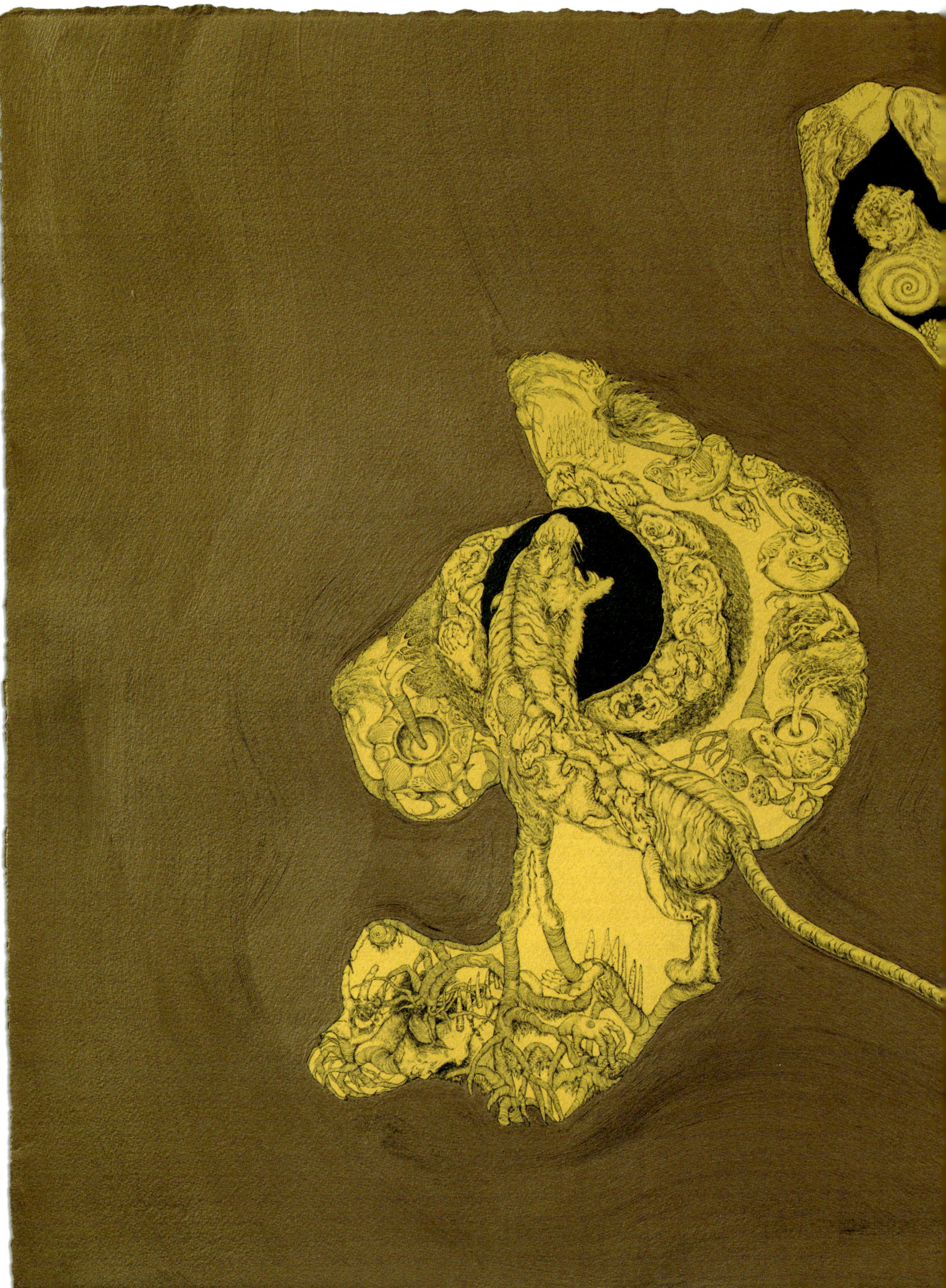

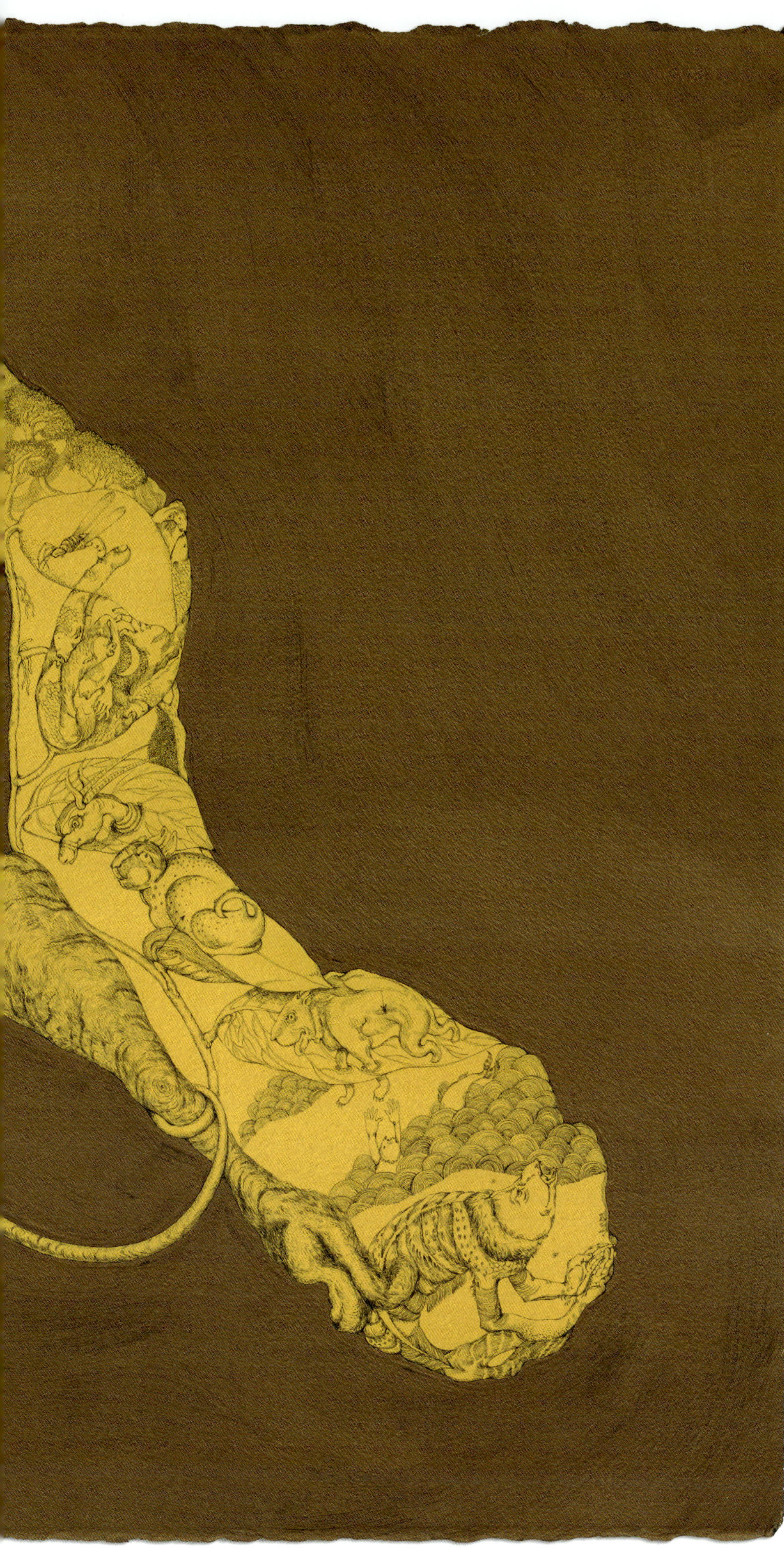

(fig.7.8) ***Where Every Leaf Holds a Tale*** **(*Tiger Leg – Bangladesh and India*), 2024, archival ink pen on paper with acrylic colour, 76 × 57 cm.** Ashmolean Museum, University of Oxford, EA2025.26.8. © Soma Surovi Jannat. Presented by the artist

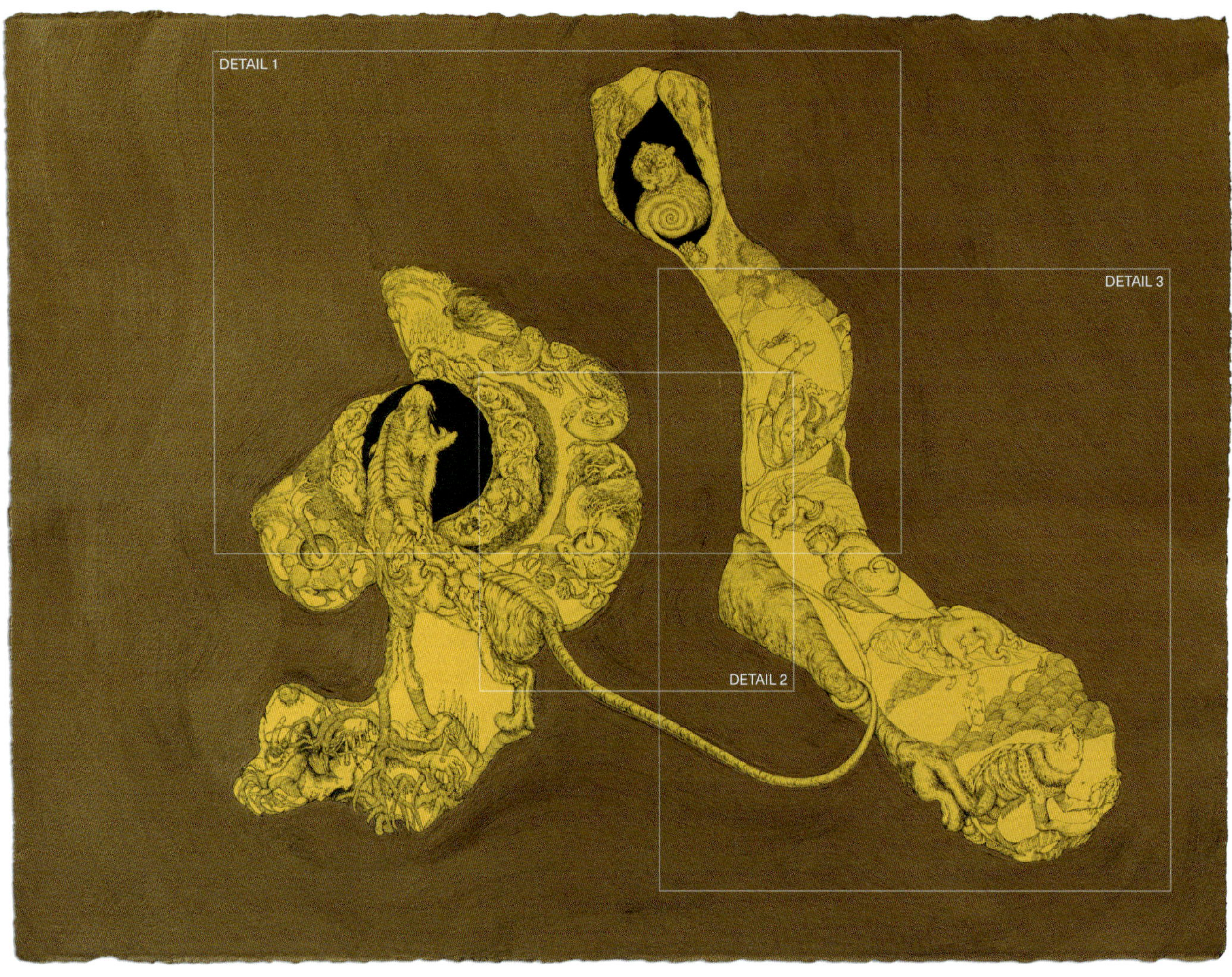

Where Every Leaf Holds a Tale
(Tiger Leg – Bangladesh and India) (fig.7.8)
Tiger Leg Island, located at the border between Bangladesh and India, serves as a poignant backdrop for an exploration of climate, culture, and care on the subcontinent. A river bisects the island, highlighting the geographical boundary that exists, yet Surovi muses that the tigers residing in this region are blissfully unaware of such divisions. The imagery features a poignant drawing of a tiger separated from its cub, invoking a sense of loss as the once-vibrant greenery of the island now appears dry and parched. The desolation starkly contrasts with the rich browns and greens that once dominated the landscape.

On the Indian side of the artwork, the tiger roars towards her distant cub (detail 1 and figs 18–20), symbolising the separation of land. She represents the Indian tiger with three legs on its side, with one leg stretching toward Bangladesh. The tiger's tail curves across the border to connect with the tail of the cub (signifying Bangladesh) on the other side. This is a visual metaphor for a mother and her offspring reaching across boundaries. The graceful tail connects the two tigers and two pieces of land suggesting an innate desire for communication, unity, and continuity despite physical divisions.

The work incorporates other animals, including a frog (detail 2), which resonated deeply with Surovi

20

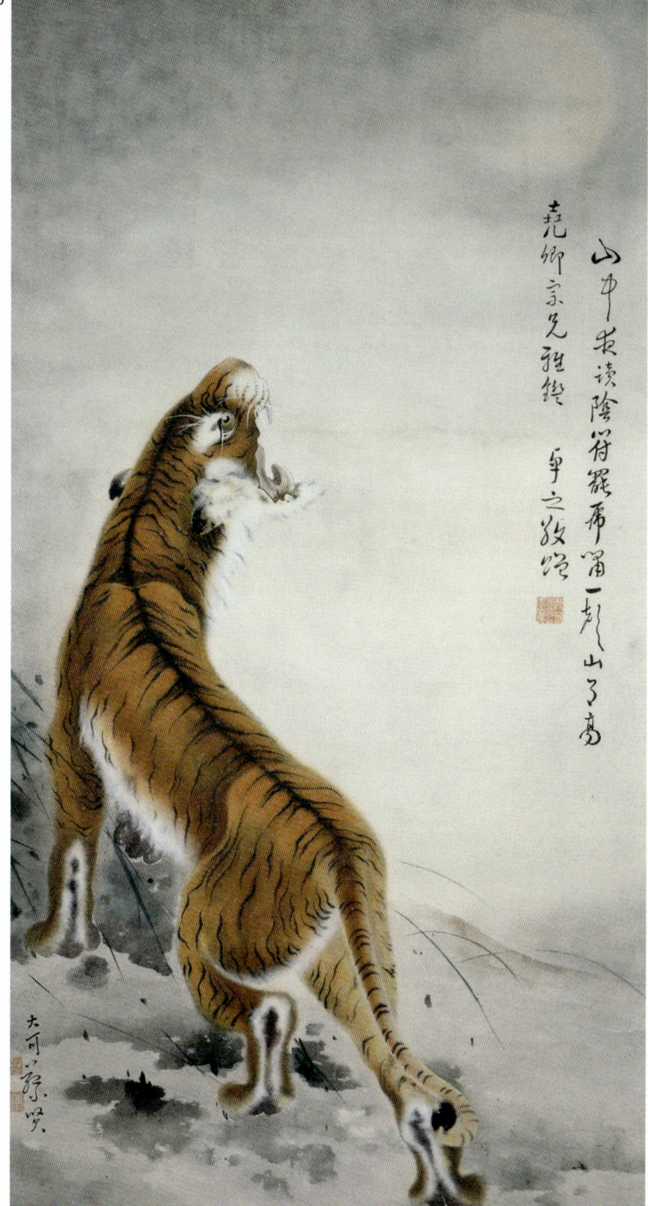

21

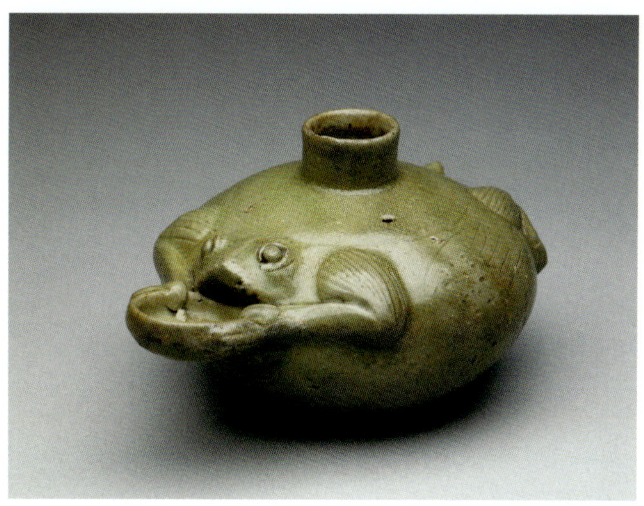

(fig.21) *Greenware water pot in the form of a frog*, 4th century CE, ceramic, 8 × 14.5 × 11.3 cm.
Ashmolean Museum, University of Oxford, EA1956.950

(fig.20) After Gao Qifeng (1889–1933), *Tiger*, 1889, ink and colour on paper, 164 × 88 cm.
Ashmolean Museum, University of Oxford, EA1995.249

after encountering a greenware water pot in the form of a frog in the Ashmolean collection (fig. 21). During the rainy season in Bangladesh, the lively sound of frogs permeates the nights, serving as inspiration for her reflections on their ecological significance. From programmes at Dhaka University, Surovi learned about various initiatives aimed at raising awareness about frogs, recognising their crucial role in the ecosystem, despite their underappreciation by many.

Surovi emphasises the alarming reality of species decline by drawing the water in a brown hue, deliberately shifting away from the dark shades of previous works, to draw attention to the tigers and the themes they embody. Her engagement with stories about the Sundarbans further enriches her understanding of communities and nature, underscoring the urgent need to restore and protect the natural world for future generations. Through her art, she expresses a deep concern for the environment and the vital relationships that persist despite borders and the encroaching threat of environmental destruction. She aims to convey the depth of these experiences by highlighting how leaves (detail 3) carry the memories and stories of the land, merging narratives that reflect both the environment and the lives of the people.

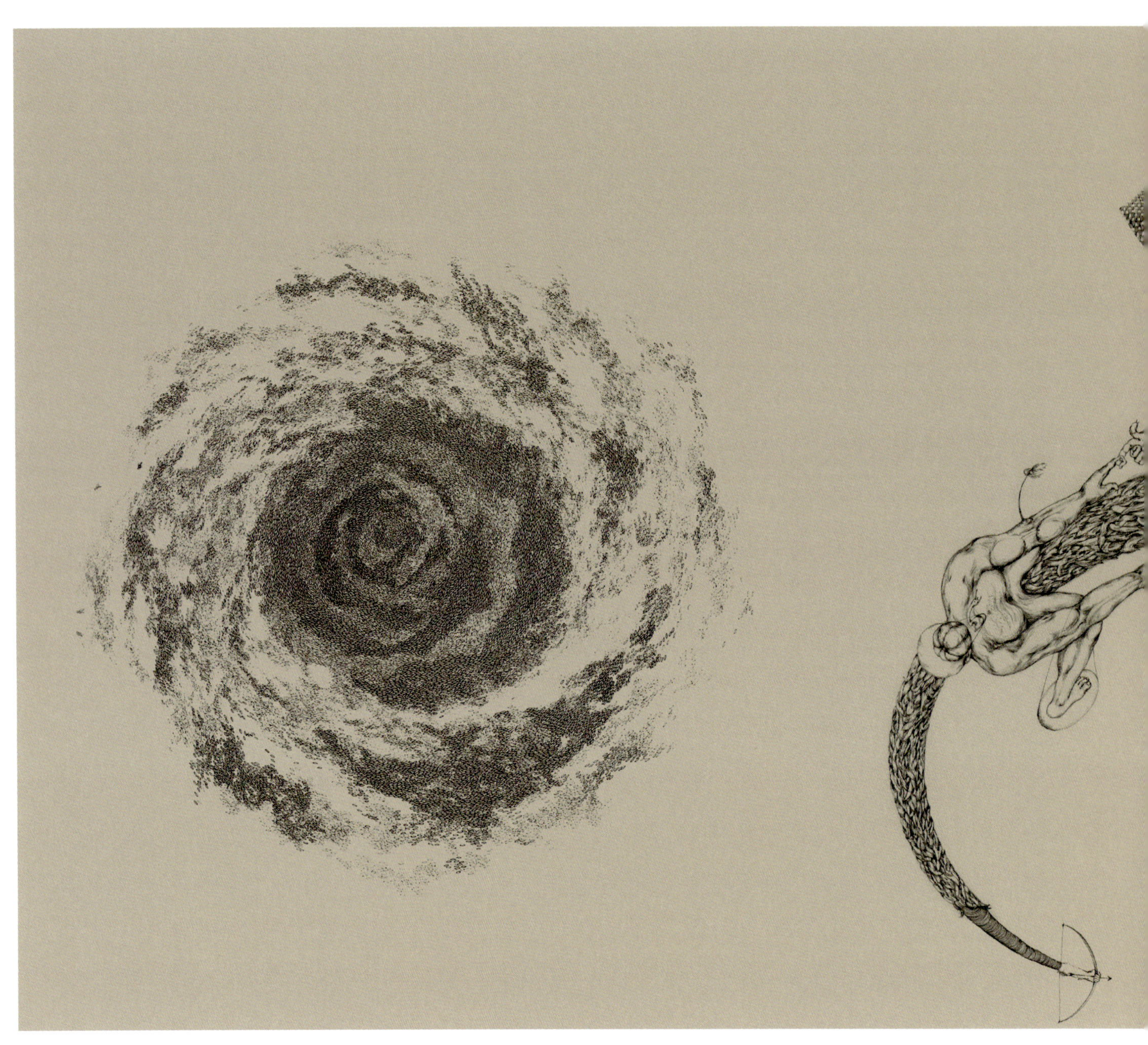

(fig.22) Digital rendition of *She Carries the River in Her Skin* (detail).
Ashmolean Museum, University of Oxford. © Soma Surovi Jannat

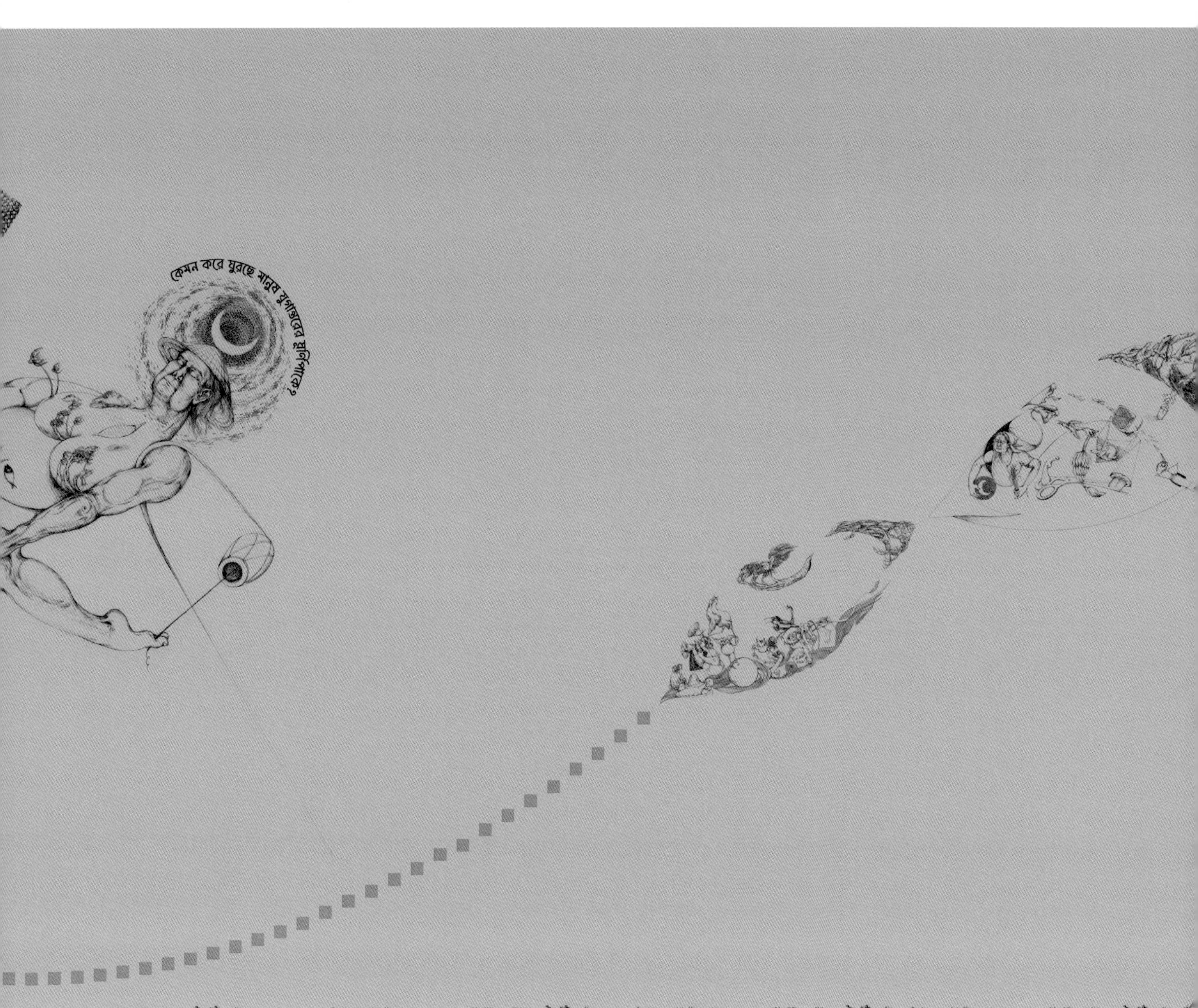
কেমন করে ঘুরছে মানুষ যুগান্তরের ঘূর্ণিপাকে?

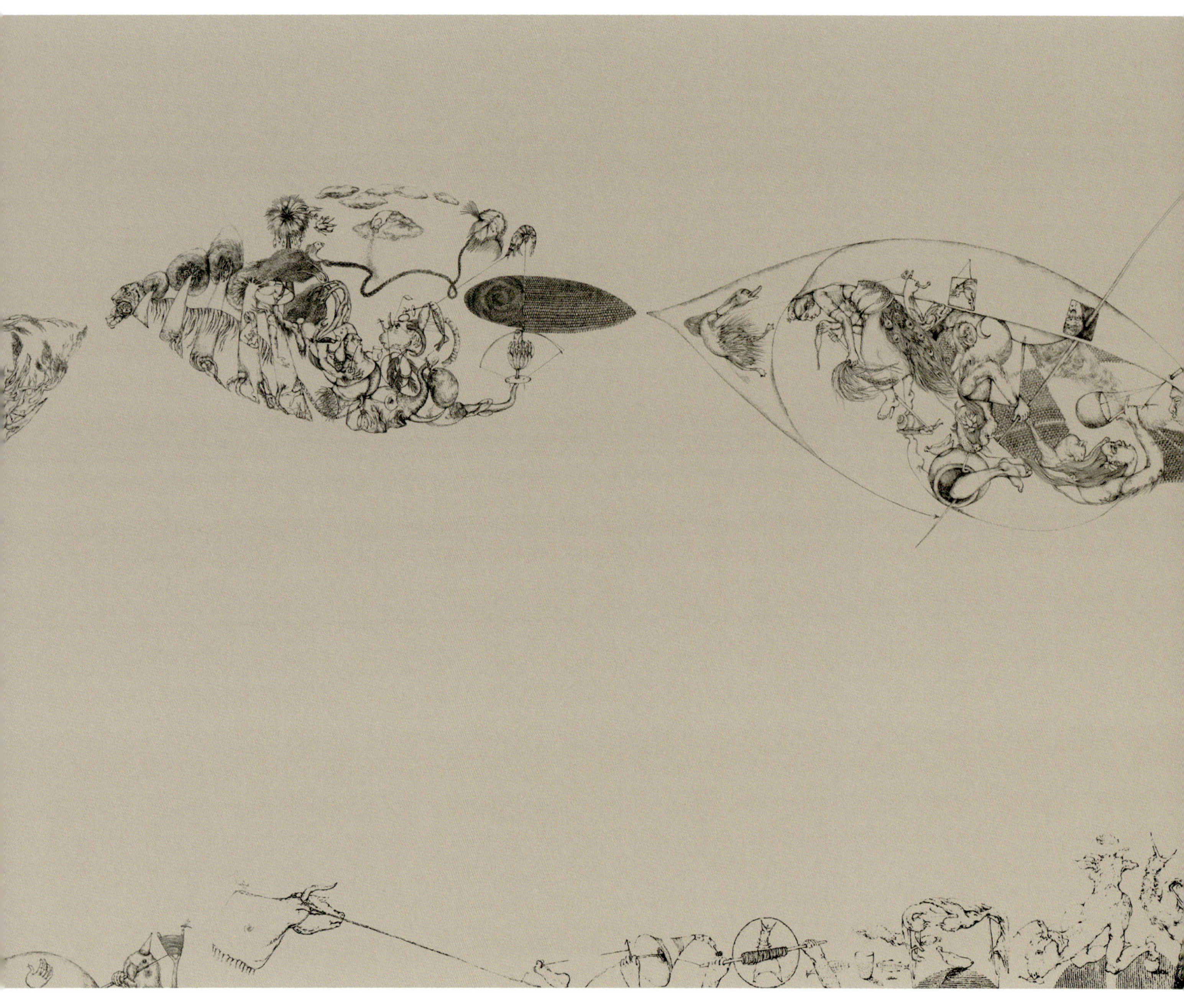

(fig.22) Digital rendition of *She Carries the River in Her Skin* (detail).
Ashmolean Museum, University of Oxford. © Soma Surovi Jannat

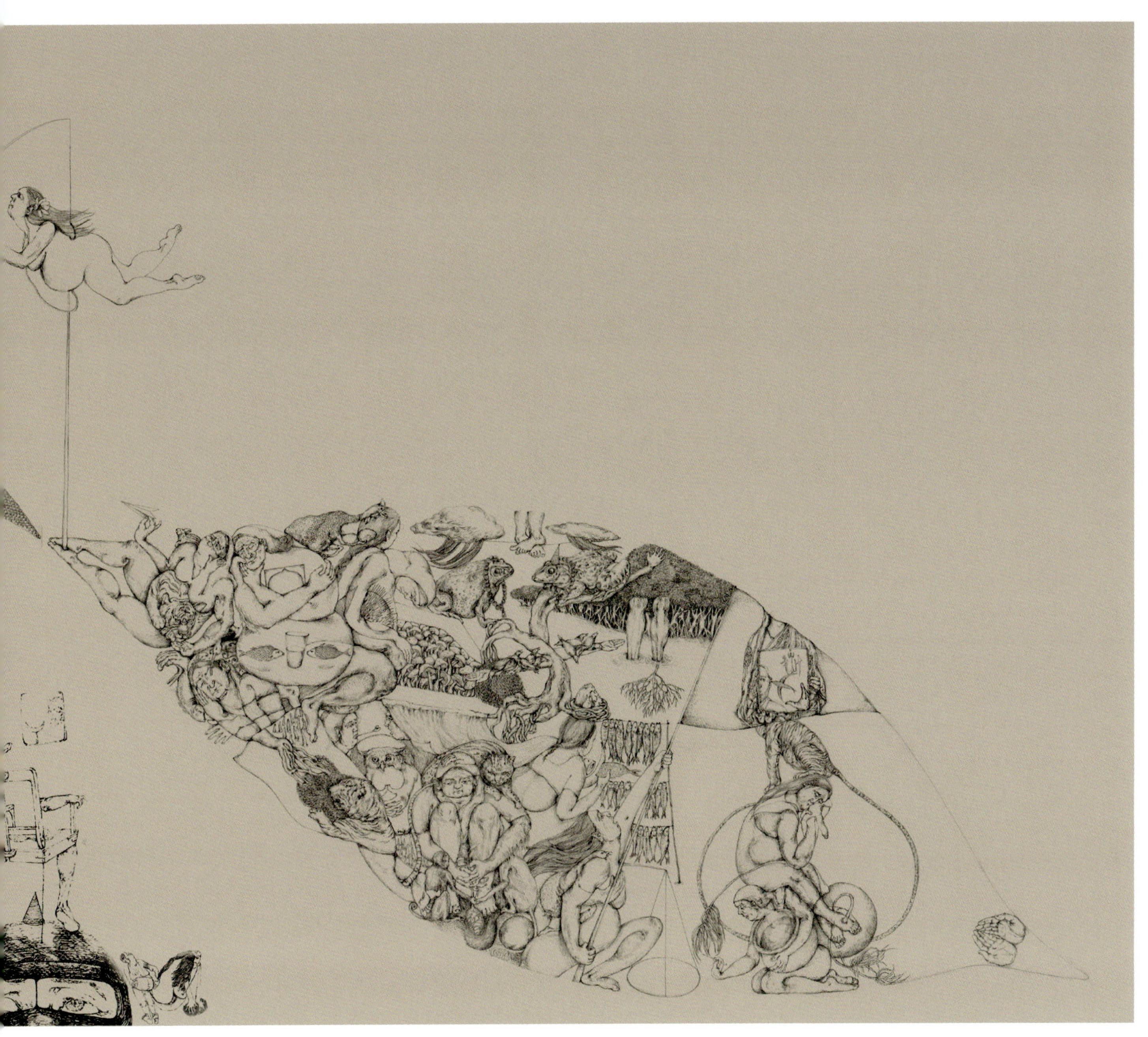

22

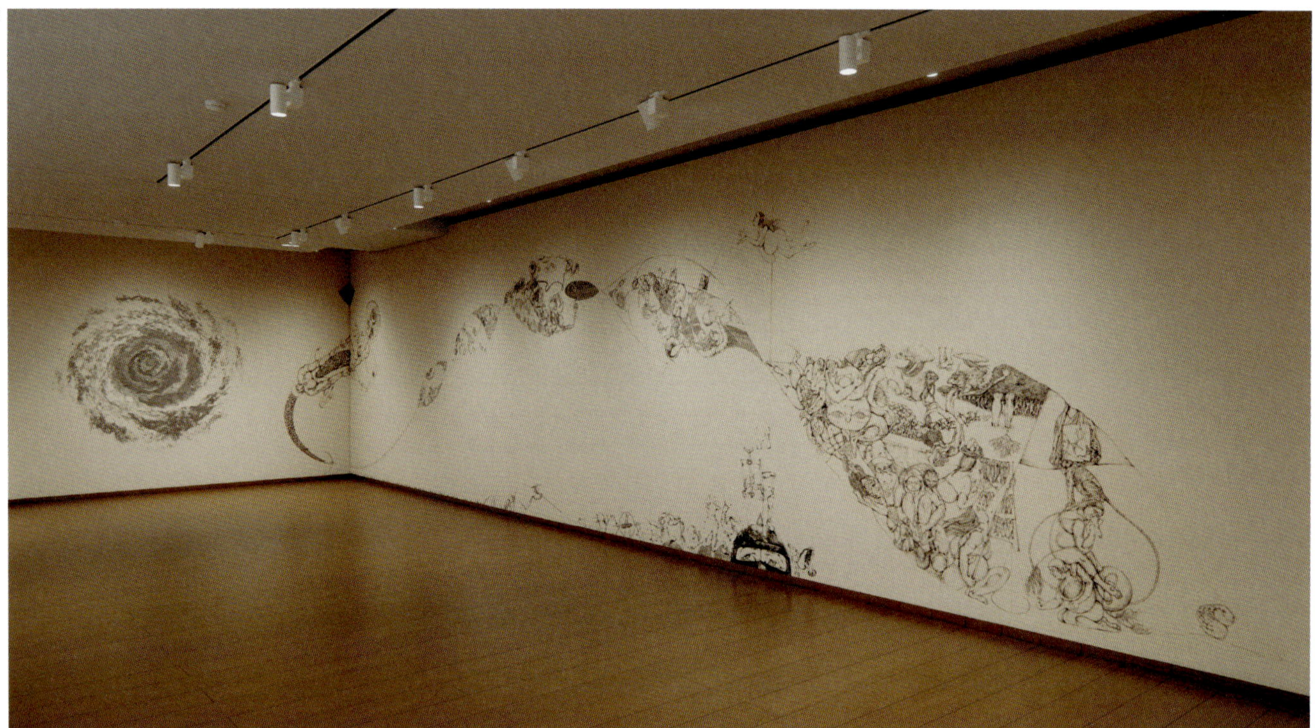

(fig.22) Digital rendition of *She Carries the River in Her Skin*, 2026, drawn directly onto two walls of Gallery 8 (-1 Level), wooden boxes, 1,700 × 300 cm. Ashmolean Museum, University of Oxford. © Soma Surovi Jannat

She Carries the River in Her Skin (fig.22)

In an ephemeral work, drawn directly onto two walls of the exhibition gallery, Surovi explores how climate change profoundly affects women and children, particularly in South Asia. Surovi's work is closely aligned with that of renowned Indian artist Nalini Malani (b.1946), who highlights the challenges faced by marginalised communities and advocates for the significance of women's perspectives in addressing such issues. Malani's influence extends to many young artists across the subcontinent. Surovi drew particular inspiration from Malani's 2004 work, *From Time to Time* (fig. 23). Like Malani, Surovi focuses on the societal disadvantages experienced by women and children, whose ability to advocate for themselves is often hindered by broader political and social systems.

Surovi argues that climate change causes habitat loss, rising sea levels, and crop damage, making life even harder for already vulnerable communities. Her composition, *She Carries the River in Her Skin*, unfolds like a wave, with five distinct boats symbolising various challenges that women face as a result of climate change. The first and largest boat, positioned on the far right, poignantly tells the story of tiger widows (detail 1).

In 2024, Surovi read an article in the *Guardian* by human-rights journalist Thaslima Begum. It included various real-life cases around the plight of widows whose husbands had been killed by tigers. These women were often wrongly blamed, labelled as 'husband eaters', and pushed out of their communities due to superstitions. This injustice is indicative of how gender, myths, and environmental crises intersect. One story in Begum's article told of Shuna Banu, a 43-year-old woman whose life changed dramatically when her husband, Aziz Murad, went fishing one day and never came back. Shuna Banu was devastated by her husband's disappearance, but, unfortunately, her parents-in-law blamed her for the

23

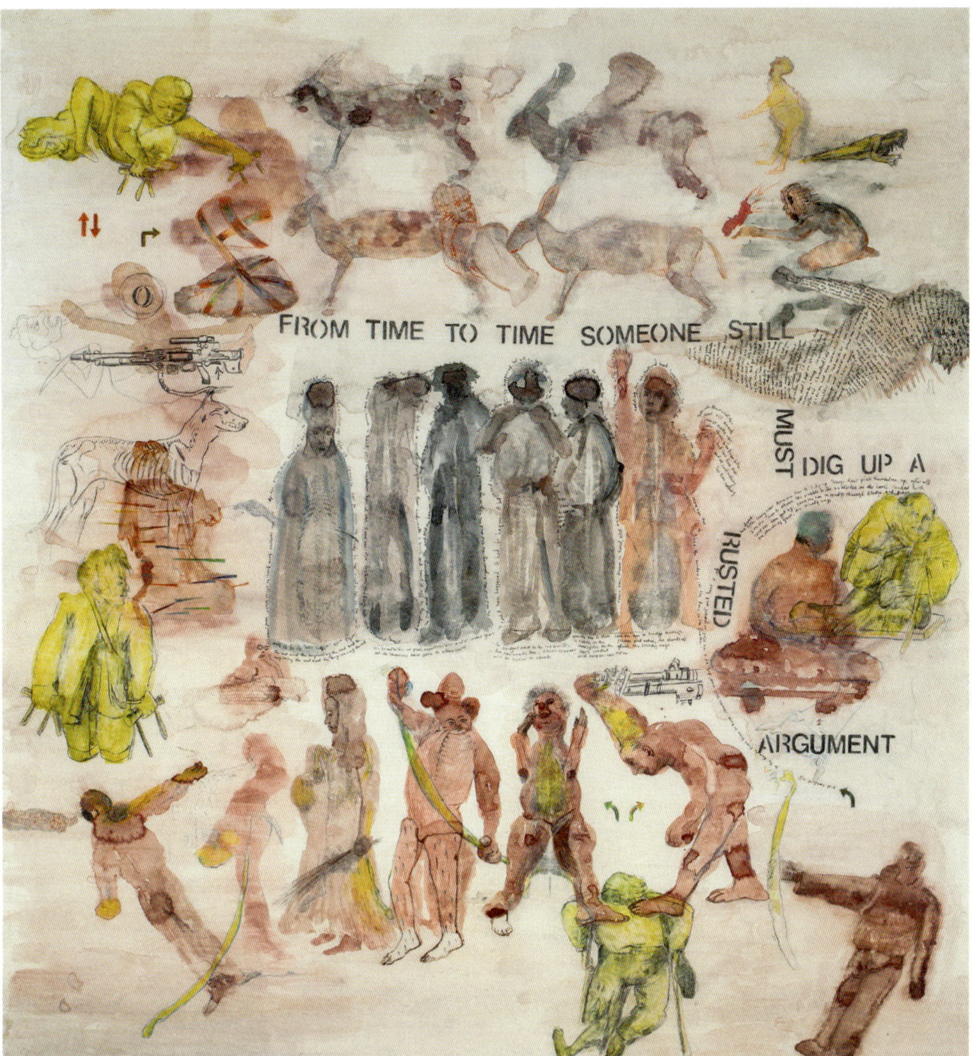

(fig.23) Nalini Malani (b.1946), *From Time to Time*, 2004, mixed media on paper, 109.22 × 104.14 cm. Ashmolean Museum, University of Oxford, EAEN.820. © Nalini Malani

tragedy, insisting she leave their home. With nowhere else to go, she returned to her parents' house. In her village, families relied on fishing and farming, but, as a widow, Shuna Banu found herself unable to engage in these traditional male roles. She expressed her sorrow, saying, 'I didn't just lose my husband – I lost my right to live with dignity'. Another woman, Reshma Khatun, faced a similar fate at 38. Her husband, Abdul Gazi, was attacked by a tiger while collecting honey in the Sundarbans. Left to provide for their two young sons, Reshma faced many challenges. The Bangladeshi government promised around £2,000 in compensation for widows in such situations, but many women either never receive this help or find it insufficient to support their families. Even more troubling, women like Reshma, whose husbands died before a compensation rule was established in 2011, don't qualify for any financial assistance.

Despite their struggles, these widows have formed a supportive community, helping each other care for their children and working to make a living. However, cultural traditions often prevent them from participating in social events or remarrying, leaving them isolated. While some organisations are trying to help by teaching new skills, the support provided is limited. To symbolise the journeys of these women, Surovi depicts a boat, sometimes drifting slowly, sometimes battling strong waves, but always striving to stay afloat amid poverty and social stigma (detail 2).

Through her observations and research, Surovi aims to tell the stories of these women, highlighting a broader issue that extends beyond individual experiences. With thousands of widows across the Indian subcontinent, and many more unrecorded in Bangladesh, Surovi remains dedicated to bringing these narratives to light, focusing on the urgent challenges posed by climate change that disproportionately impact them.

Surovi depicts women on one wall and men on the other. This separation highlights both the connections

22

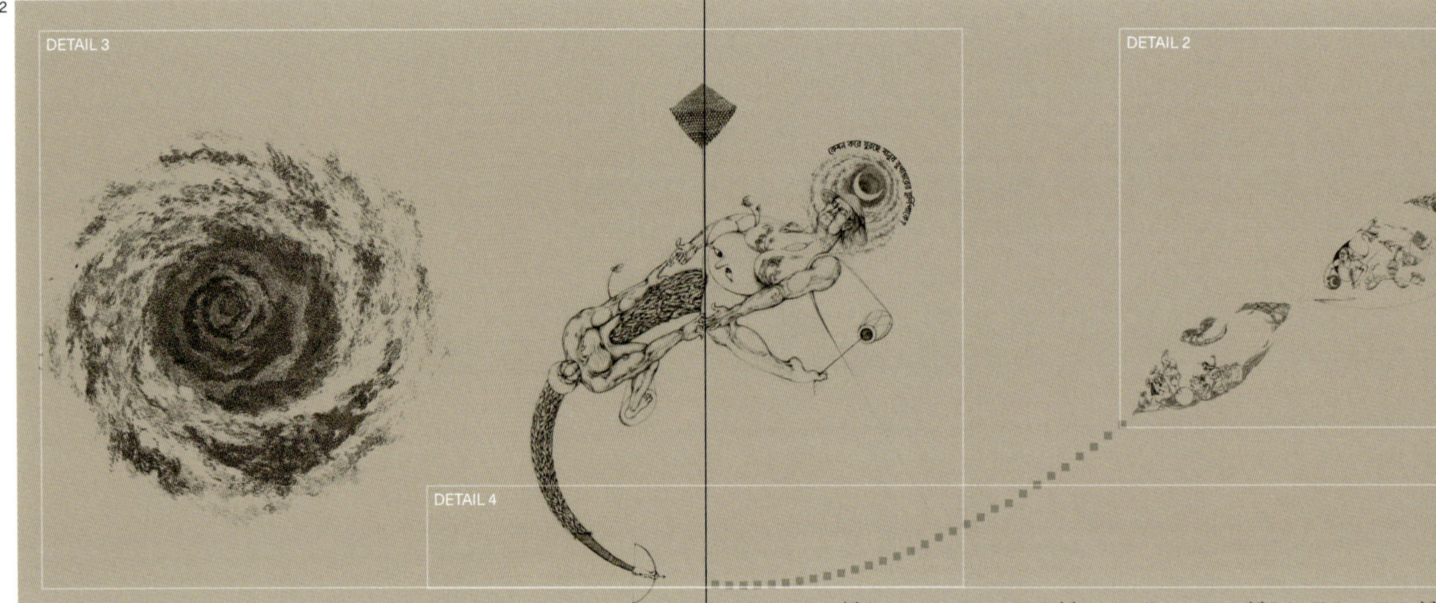

(fig.22) Digital rendition of *She Carries the River in Her Skin*, 2026, drawing on gallery walls, wooden boxes, 1,700 × 300 cm.
© Soma Surovi Jannat

and differences between men and women, inviting viewers to think about gender issues in their own environment (detail 3). The artist also visualises the impact on pregnant women who face many challenges, including access to clean water. In southern Bangladesh, rising sea levels and powerful storms bring salt water into rivers and ponds, making the water unsafe to drink for those who depend on it. Sadly, many women and families are left with no choice but to drink this salty water, which can lead to health issues, particularly for pregnant women, who risk developing high blood pressure during pregnancy. This condition can harm both mothers and their unborn babies, causing complications such as low birth weight and weakened immune systems. As a result, these babies may have ongoing health problems.

Since the 2009 cyclone Aila damaged the main sources of clean water, the Bangladeshi government have tried to help by installing rainwater tanks and other water systems. However, many people still struggle to access clean water and must rely on salty water from wells. This lack of safe drinking water has been linked to various health issues for women and girls, such as infections and menstrual problems. Some girls choose to use birth control to avoid menstruating, fearing the discomfort and infections that could arise. Many are not even aware of the health risks associated with contaminated water. Access to clean drinking water is a basic human right, yet many people in this region still lack it.

Due to disasters, like floods or cyclones, families often lose their homes and sources of income, leading to increased poverty. In these vulnerable situations, girls and women are at a higher risk of being trafficked or forced into early marriages, as desperate individuals take advantage of the chaos that follows. On the far left of this composition, a spiral of seeds, that at first looks like a whirlpool, represents natural disasters like cyclones or tornadoes, as well as life's challenges (detail 3). The seeds, in moving water, could also

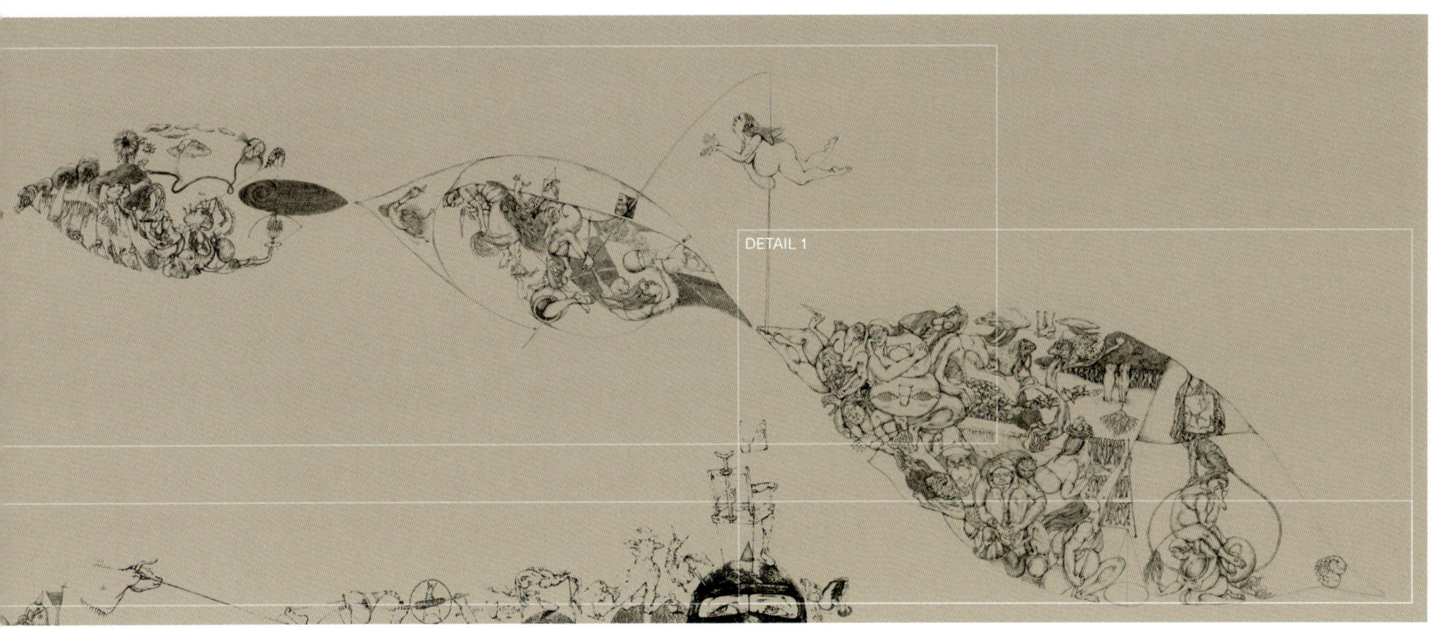

represent dispersal. Near the spiralling seeds, where the two walls in the gallery meet, Surovi portrays a woman and a man holding hands to support and balance one another. Here, around the head of the large female figure (detail 3), she also includes words from the poem 'সংকল্প' ('Sankalpa: Resolution') by Kazi Nazrul Islam (1899–1976). Bangladesh's national poet encourages people to explore and seek knowledge, saying:

থাকব না কো বদ্ধ ঘরে, দেখব এবার জগৎটাকে,
কেমন করে ঘুরছে মানুষ যুগান্তরের ঘুর্ণিপাকে।
I will not remain confined in a cage; now I will see the world
how people are turning in the whirlpool of this changing era.
(Surovi includes the second line in her drawing.)

Viewers are encouraged to step closer to appreciate the details, while stepping back to take in the larger scene. The images invite movement and interaction, allowing audiences to engage with the artwork from different perspectives. In the centre of this piece a blank space provides some breathing room in the design, offering a moment to reflect.

To engage children, Surovi places smaller wooden boxes with drawings along the bottom of the composition, positioned at a child's eye level (detail 4). Meanwhile, she wants adults to physically step back, and bend down, to appreciate the whole work. At the bottom of the wall, lines lead toward the women portrayed, reinforcing the overall narrative. Small boxes resembling boats create a dynamic, circular movement that brings the entire work to life. The transient nature of this site-specific work is perhaps a hope that the future might be more equal, and that the themes explored here might someday be distant memories.

While this work will be carefully documented, it will be removed and destroyed at the end of the Ashmolean exhibition in November 2026.

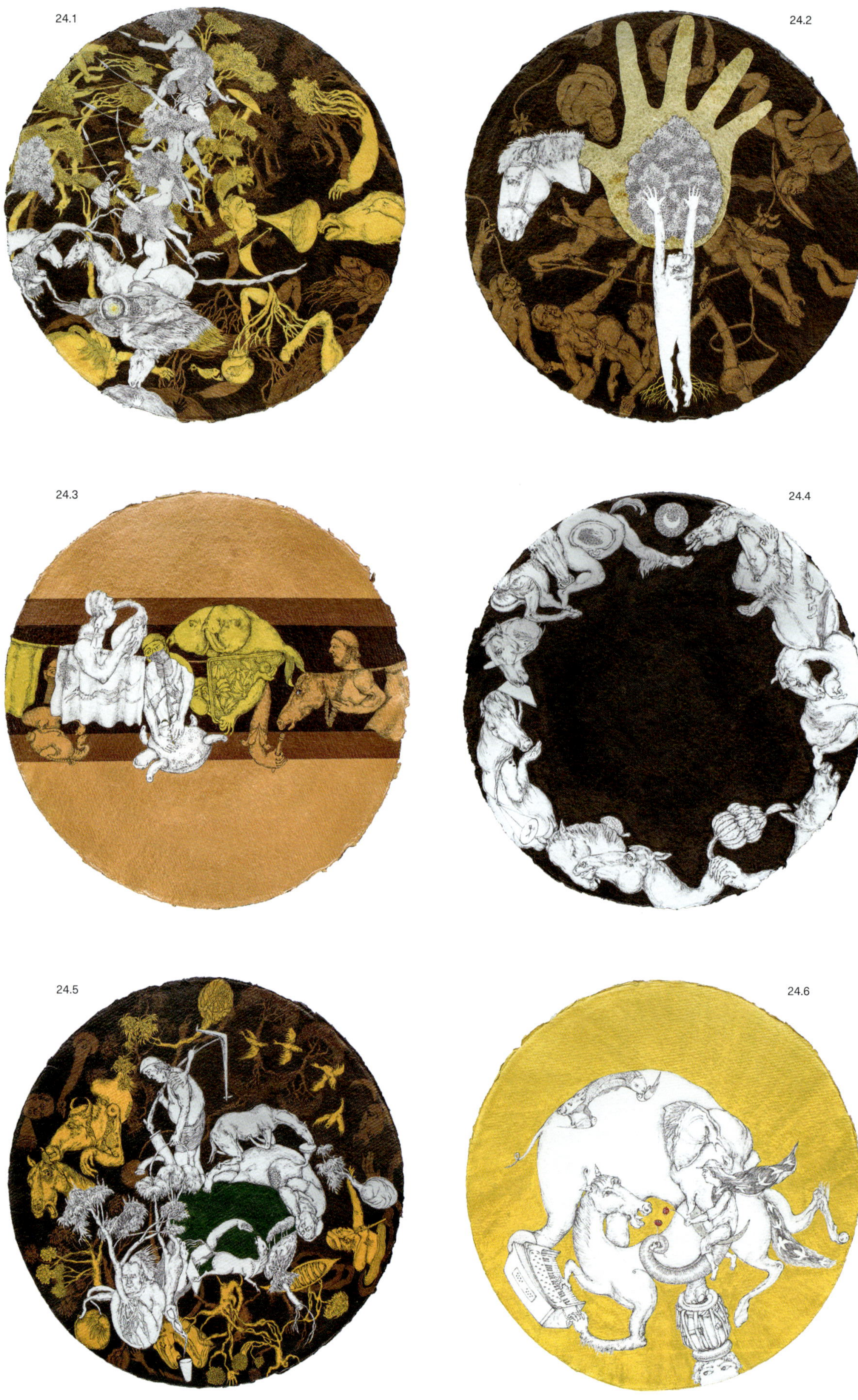
24.1
24.2
24.3
24.4
24.5
24.6

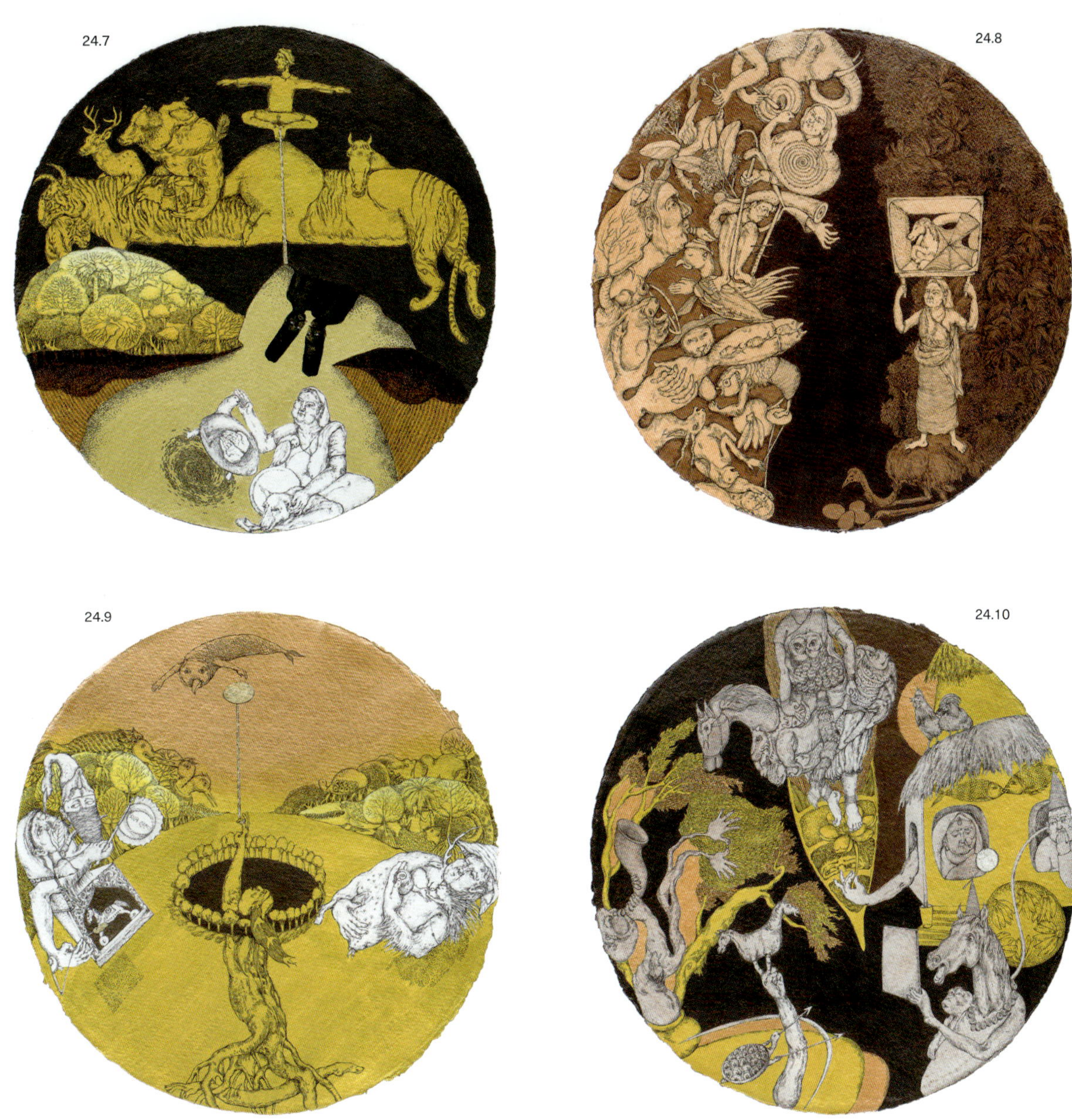

(figs 24.1–24.10) ***Who Carries Whom?*****, 2025, archival ink pen on paper with acrylic colour, gold and silver leaf, 30 cm (diameter).**
Collection of the artist. © Soma Surovi Jannat

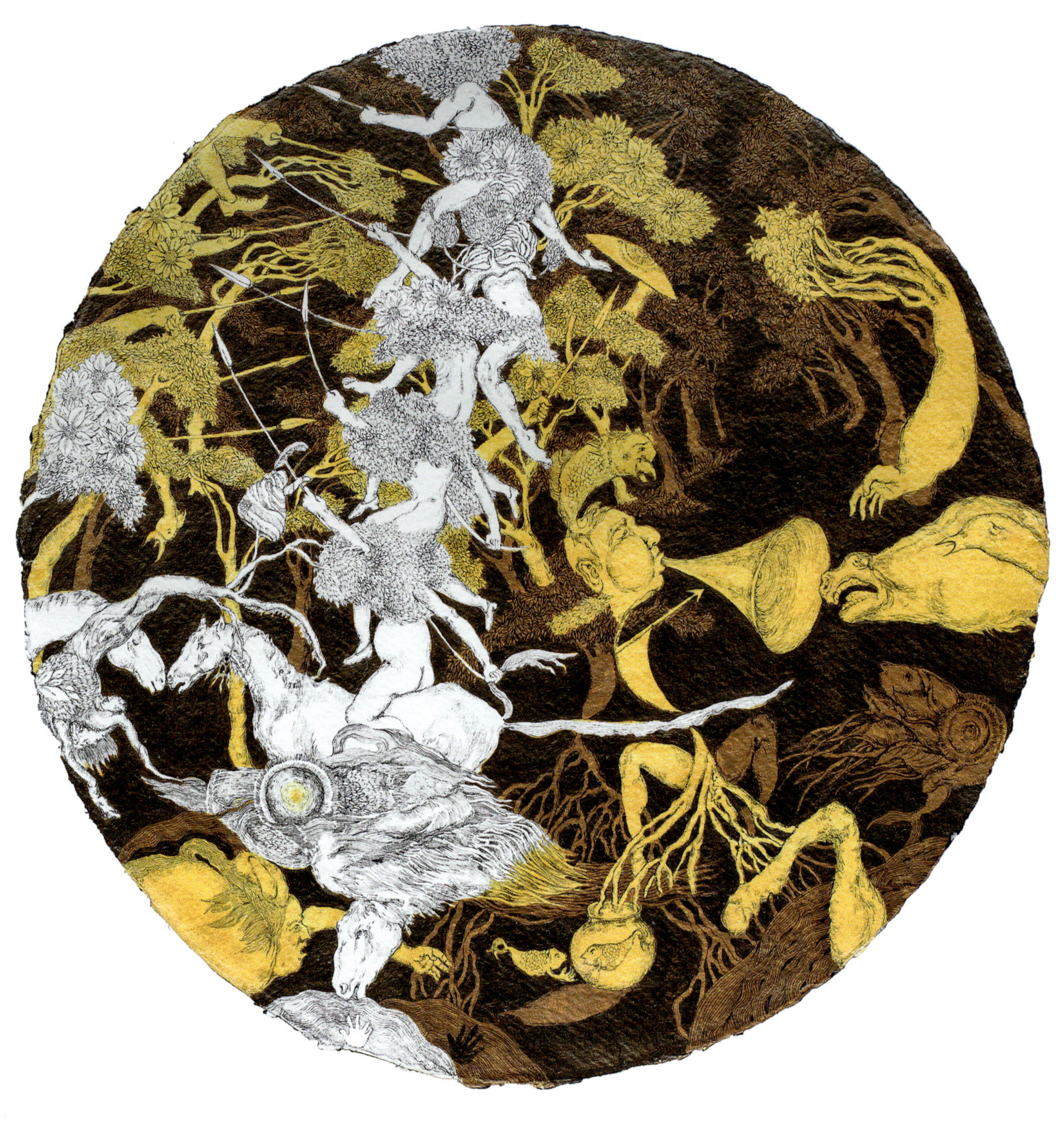

(fig.24.1) ***Who Carries Whom?*****, 2025, archival ink pen on paper with acrylic colour, 30 cm (diameter).** Collection of the artist.

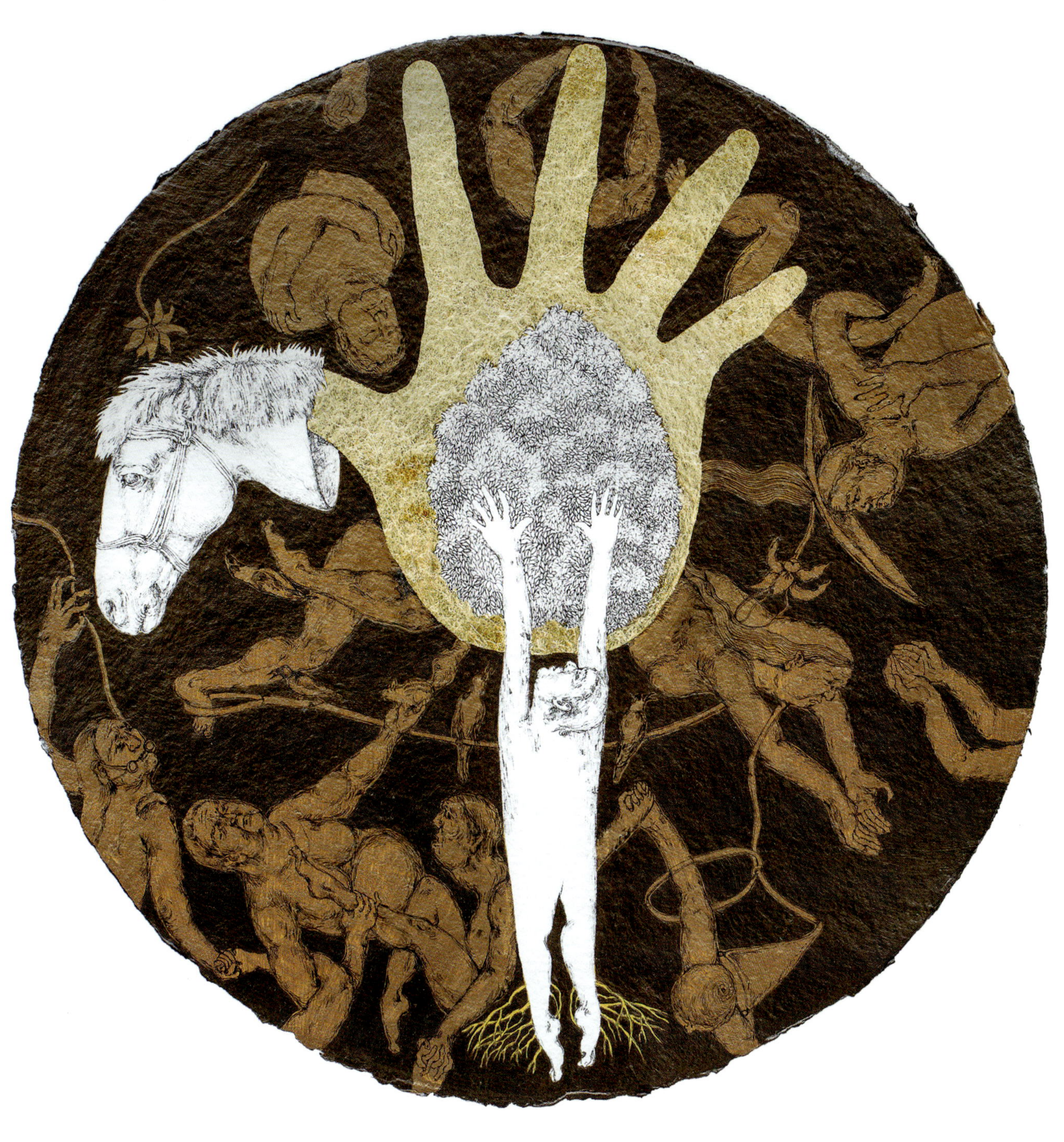

(fig.24.2) ***Who Carries Whom?*****, 2025, archival ink pen on paper with acrylic colour, gold leaf, 30 cm (diameter).** Collection of the artist.

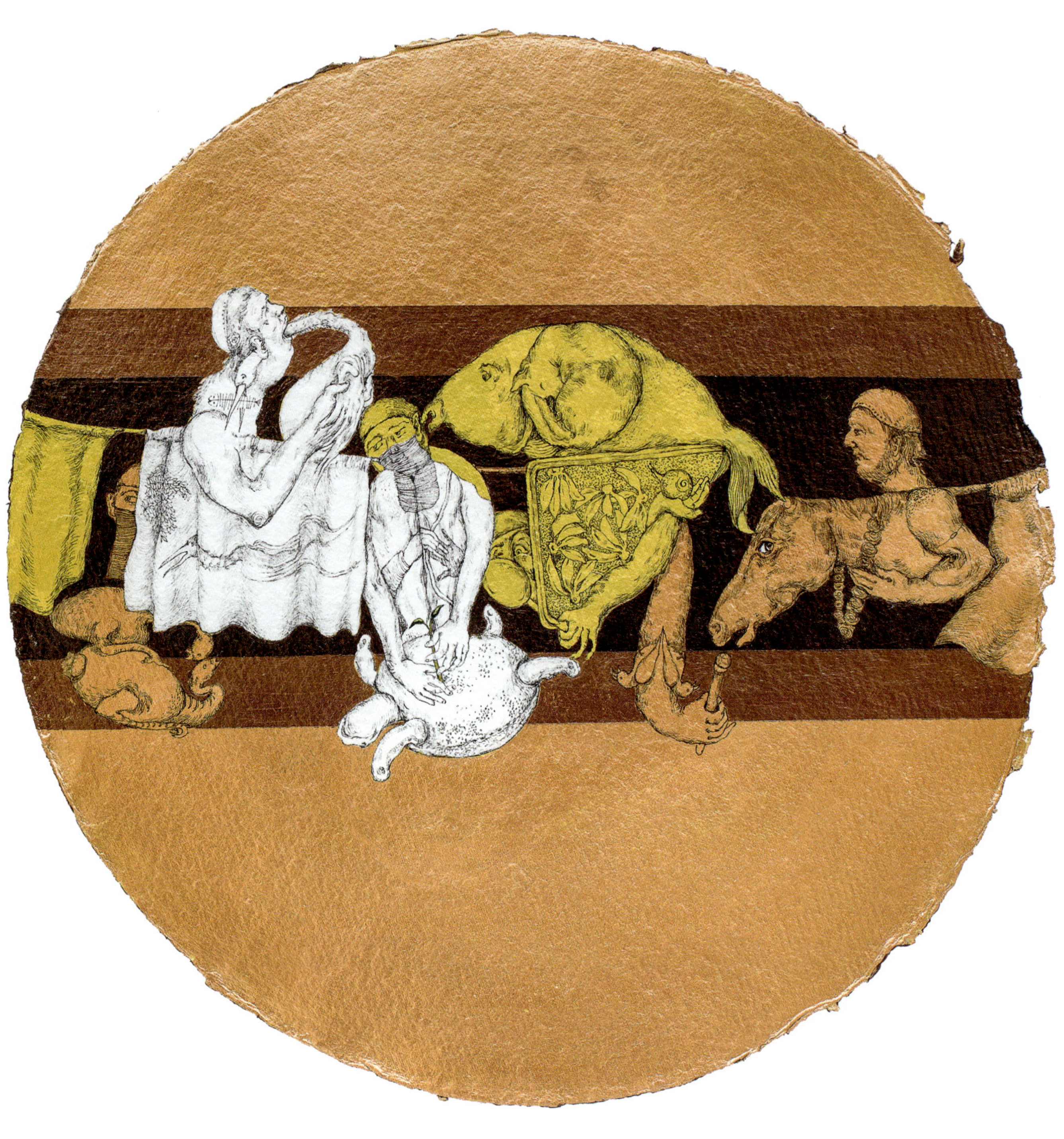

(fig.24.3) ***Who Carries Whom?*****, 2025, archival ink pen on paper with acrylic colour, 30 cm (diameter).** Collection of the artist.

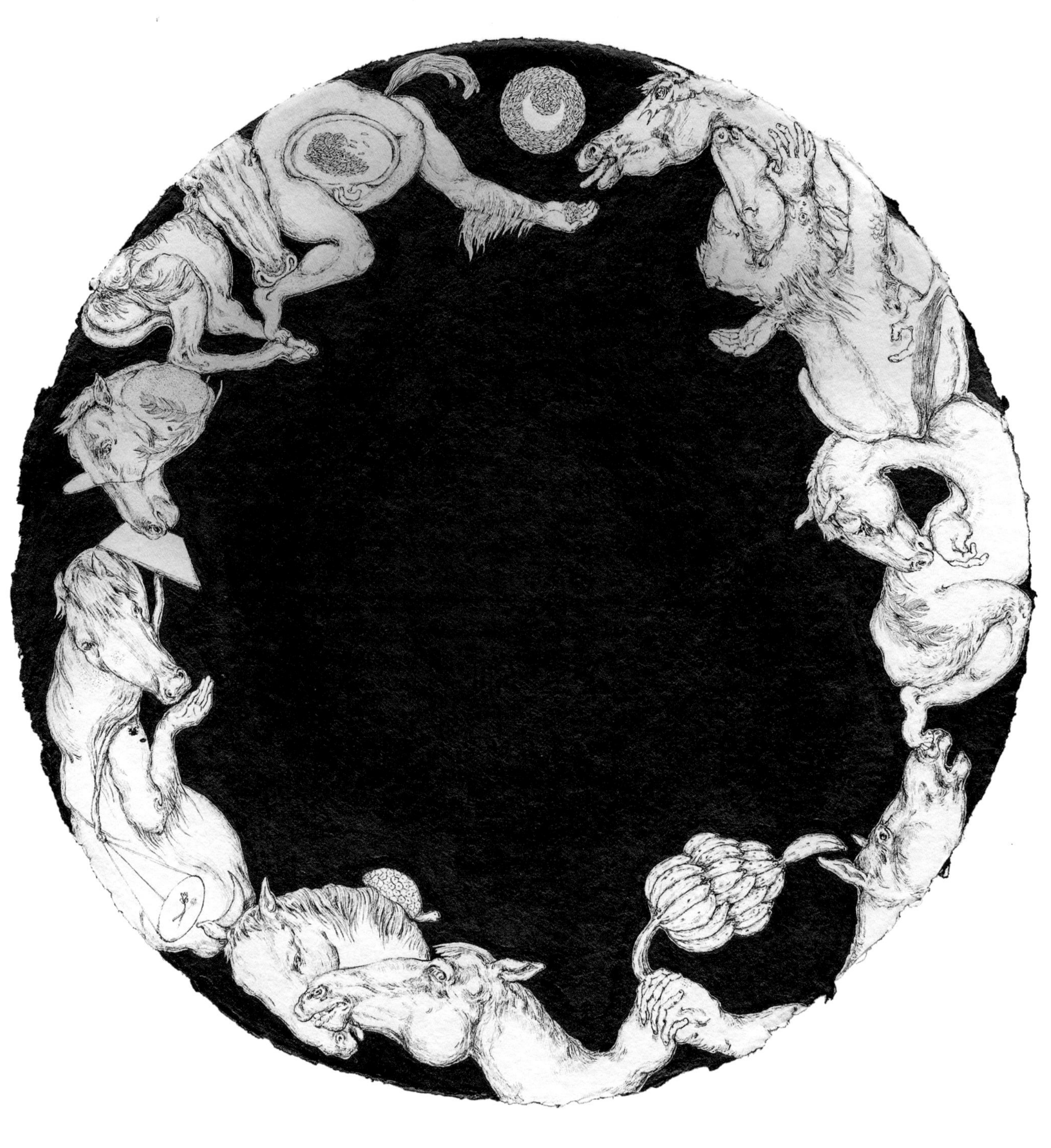

(fig.24.4) ***Who Carries Whom?*****, 2025, archival ink pen on paper with acrylic colour, 30 cm (diameter).** Collection of the artist.

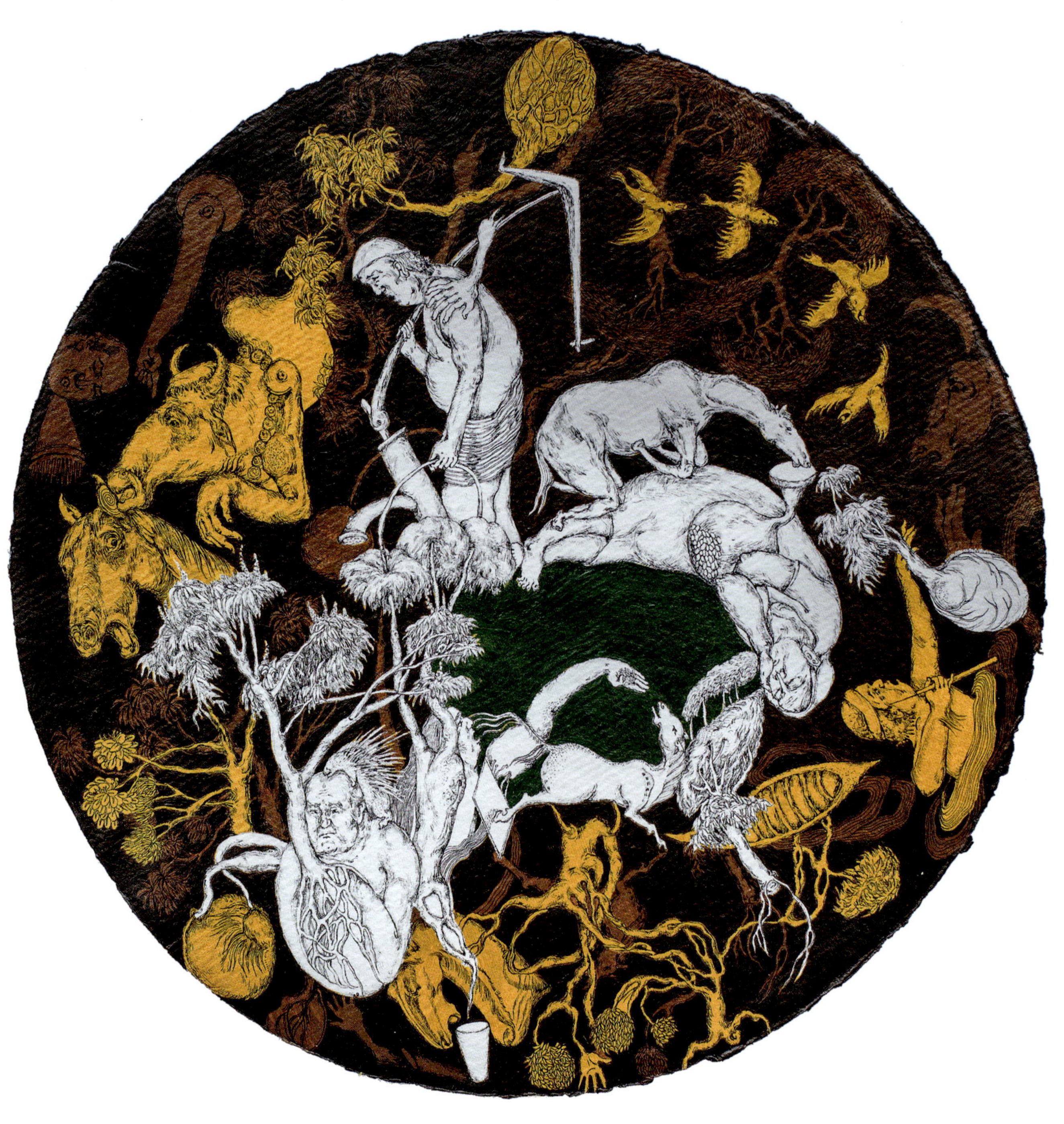

(fig.24.5) ***Who Carries Whom?*****, 2025, archival ink pen on paper with acrylic colour, 30 cm (diameter).** Collection of the artist.

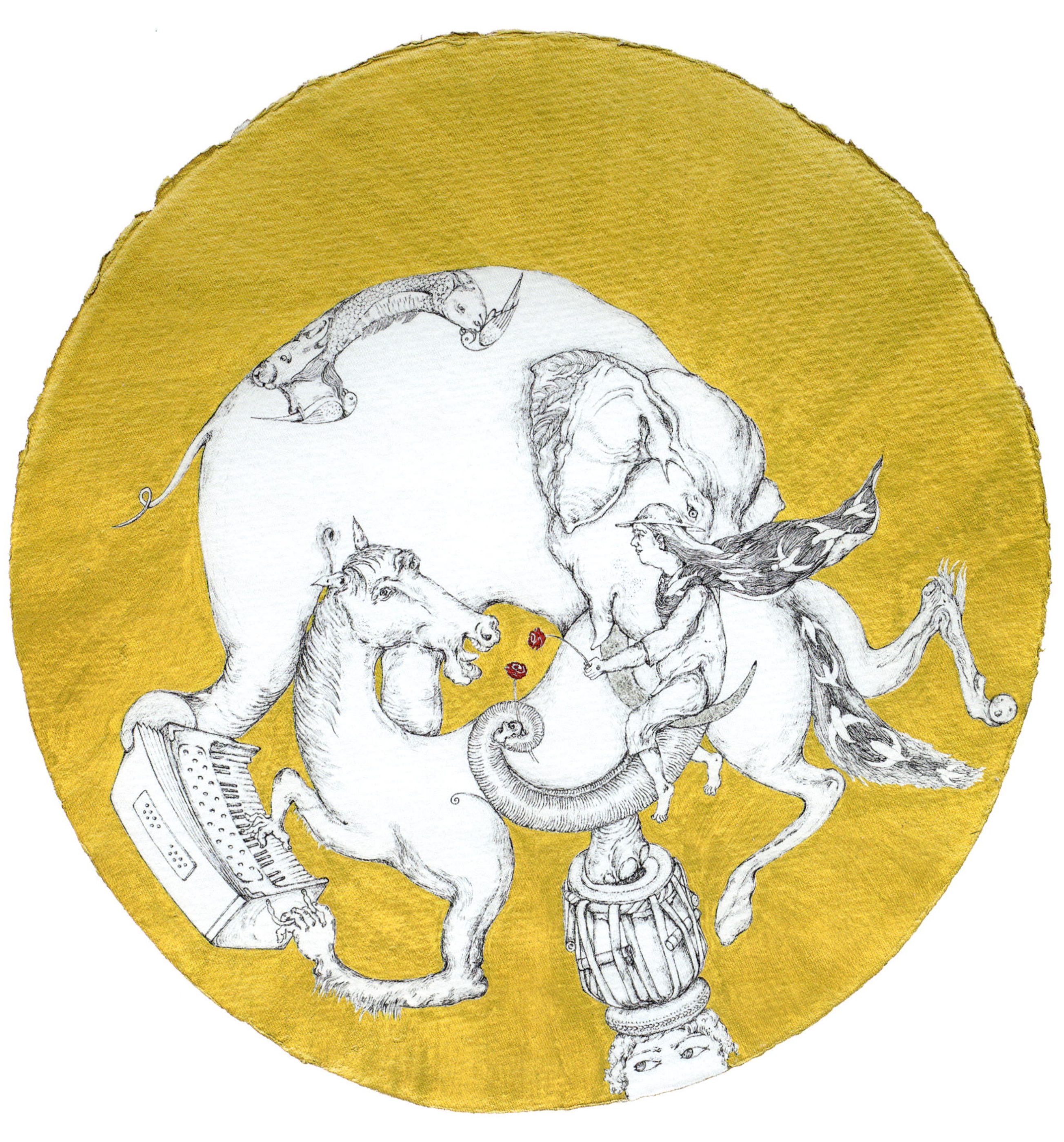

(fig.24.6) ***Who Carries Whom?*****, 2025, archival ink pen on paper with acrylic colour, silver leaf, 30 cm (diameter).** Collection of the artist.

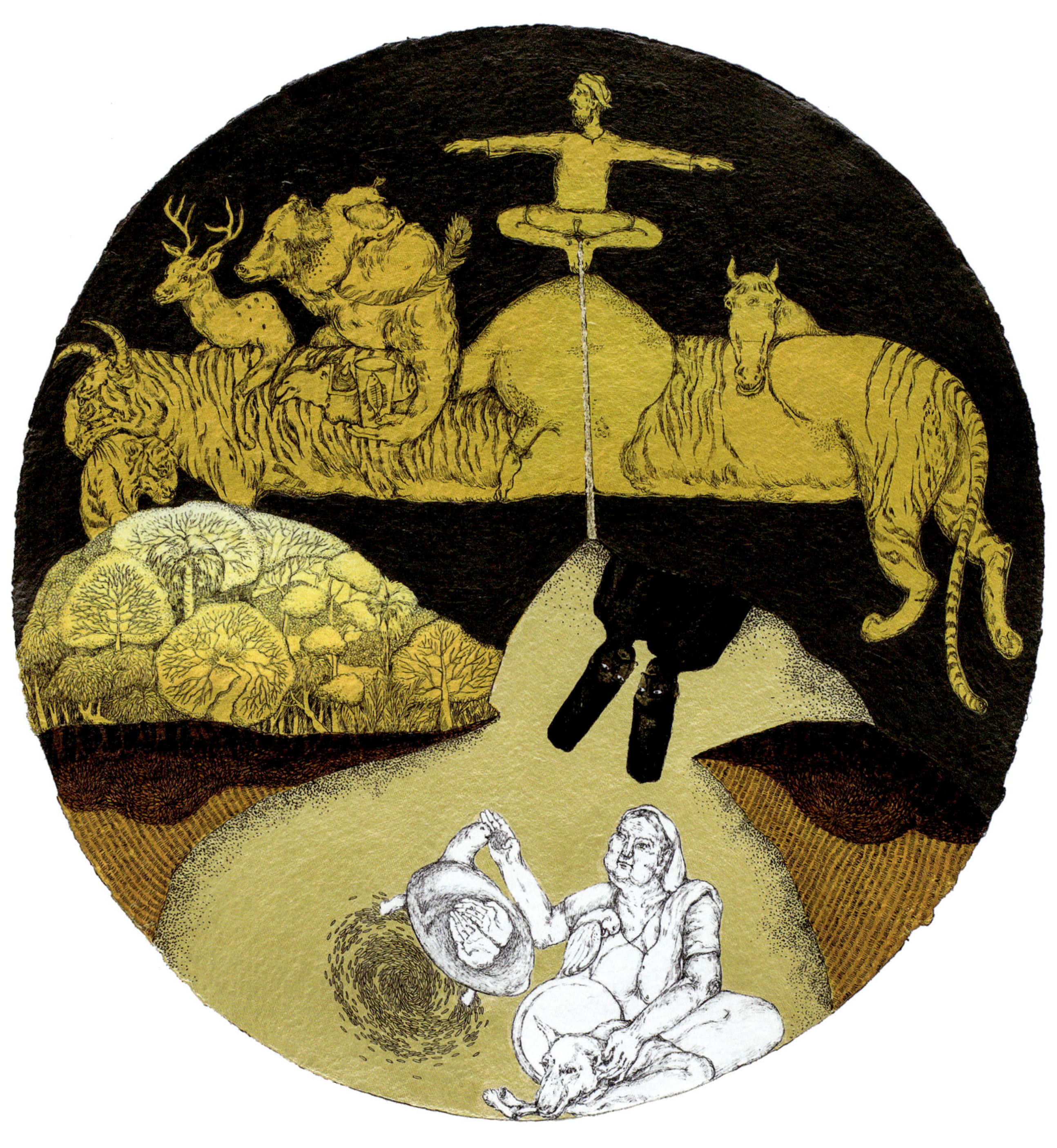

(fig.24.7) *Who Carries Whom?*, 2025, archival ink pen on paper with acrylic colour, gold leaf, 30 cm (diameter). Collection of the artist.

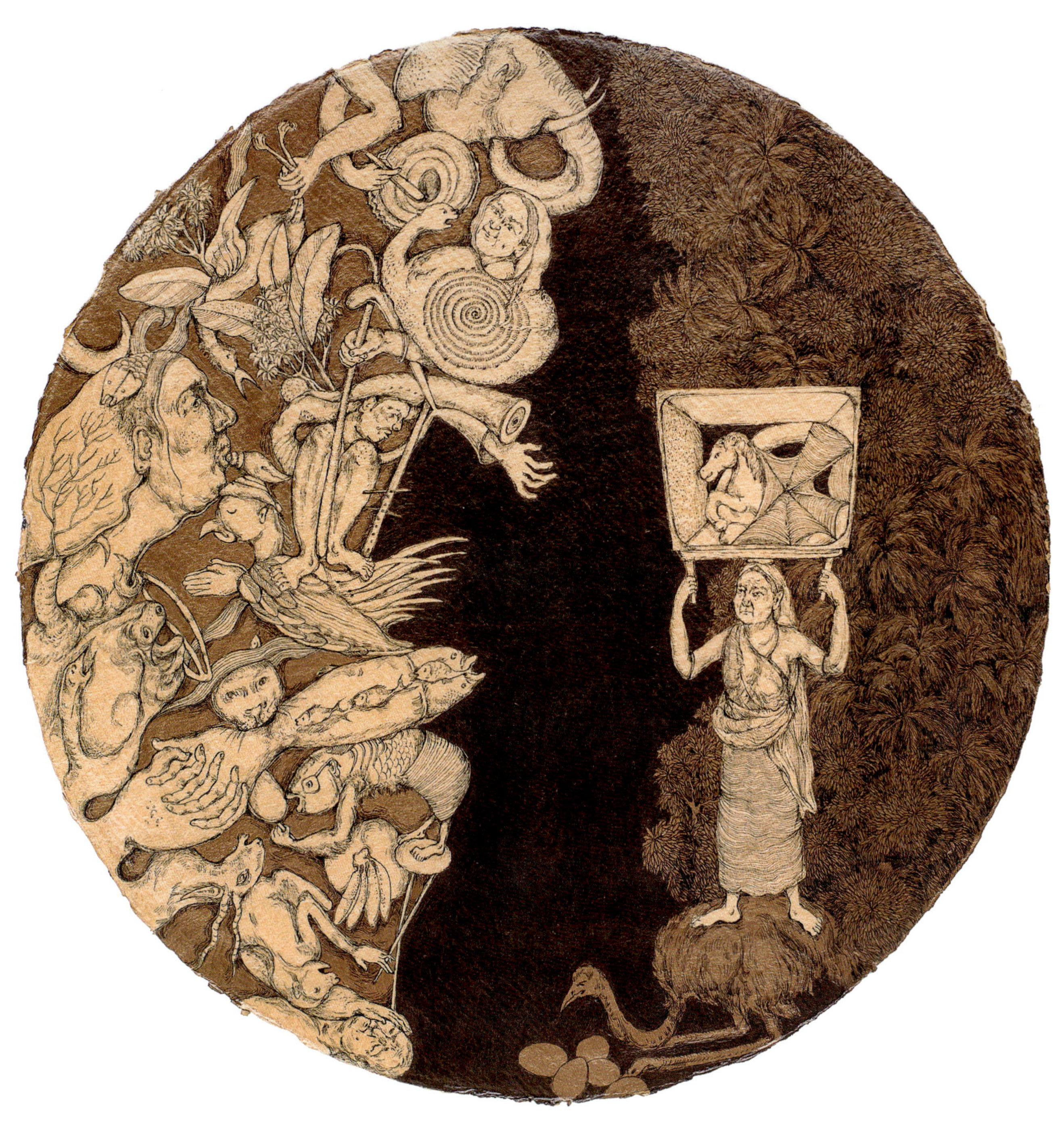

(fig.24.8) ***Who Carries Whom?*****, 2025, archival ink pen on paper with acrylic colour, 30 cm (diameter).** Collection of the artist.

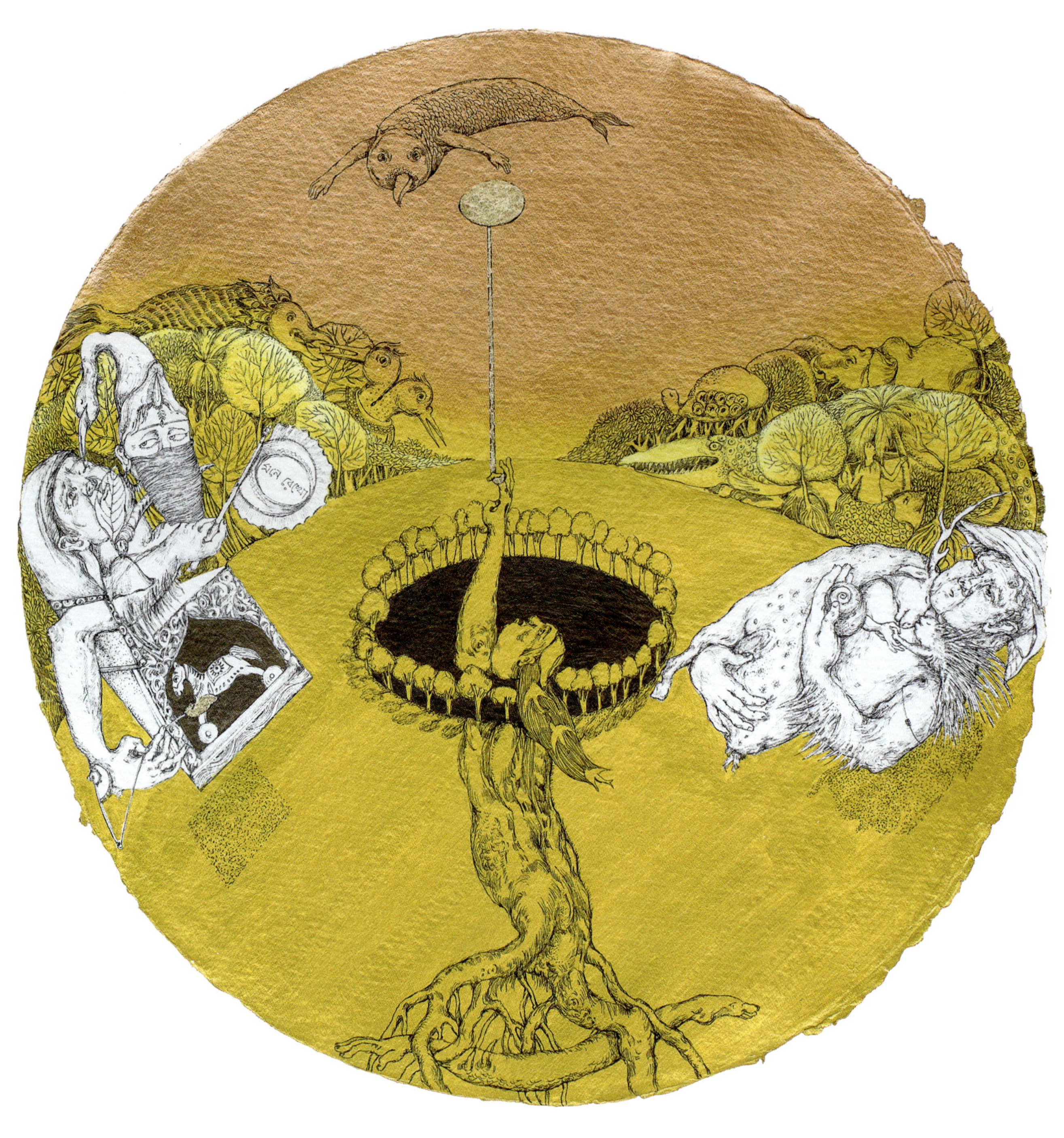

(fig.24.9) *Who Carries Whom?*, 2025, archival ink pen on paper with acrylic colour, gold leaf, 30 cm (diameter). Collection of the artist.
© Soma Surovi Jannat

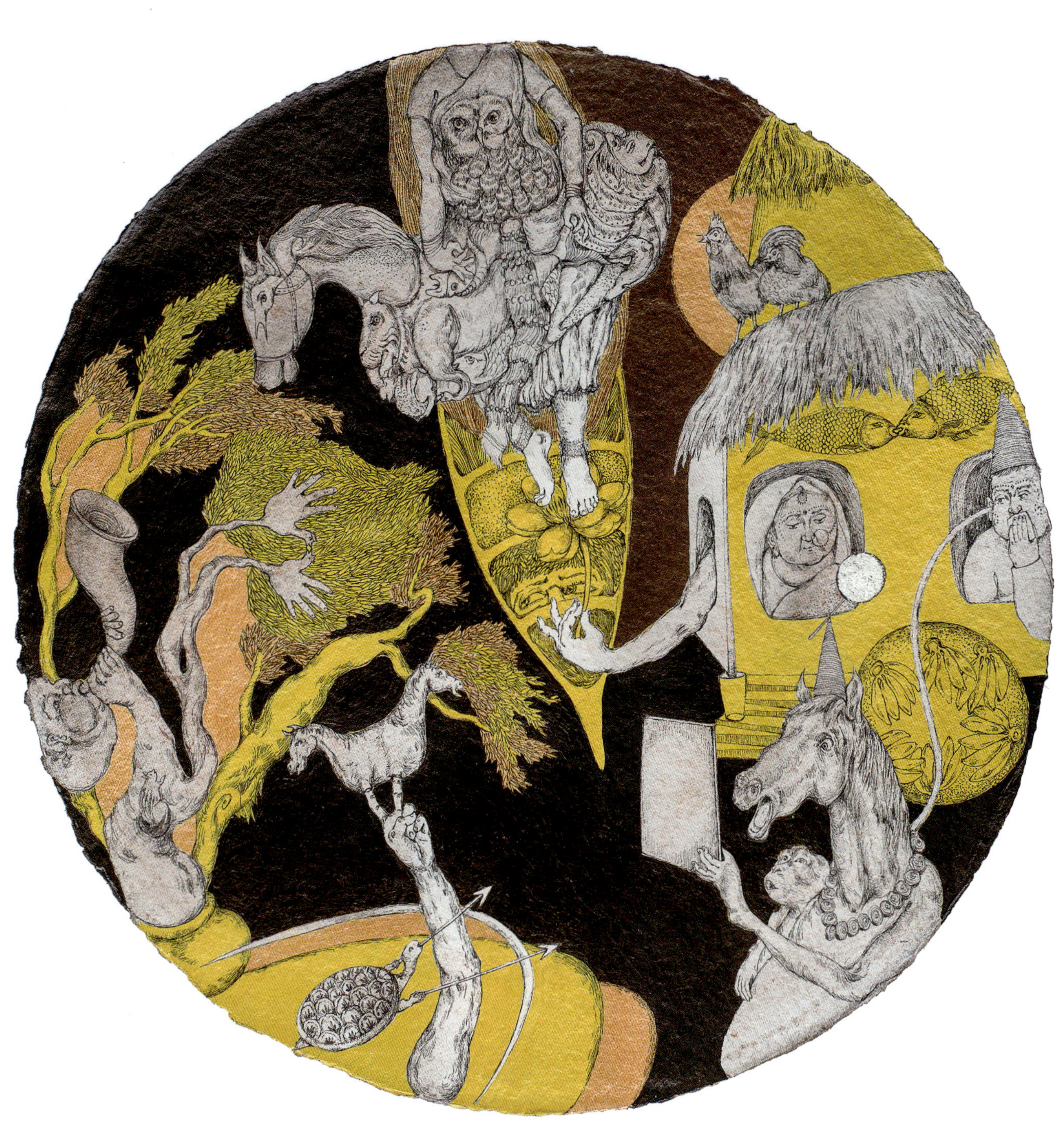

(fig.24.10) ***Who Carries Whom?*****, 2025, archival ink pen on paper with acrylic colour, silver leaf, 30 cm (diameter).** Collection of the artist.

25

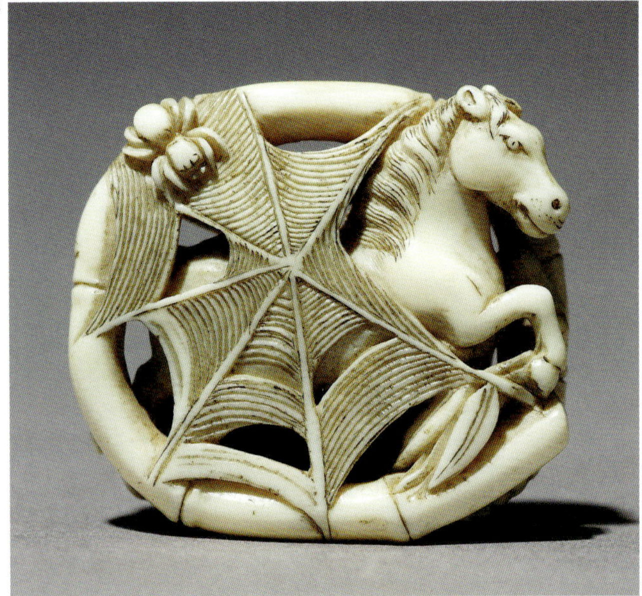

26

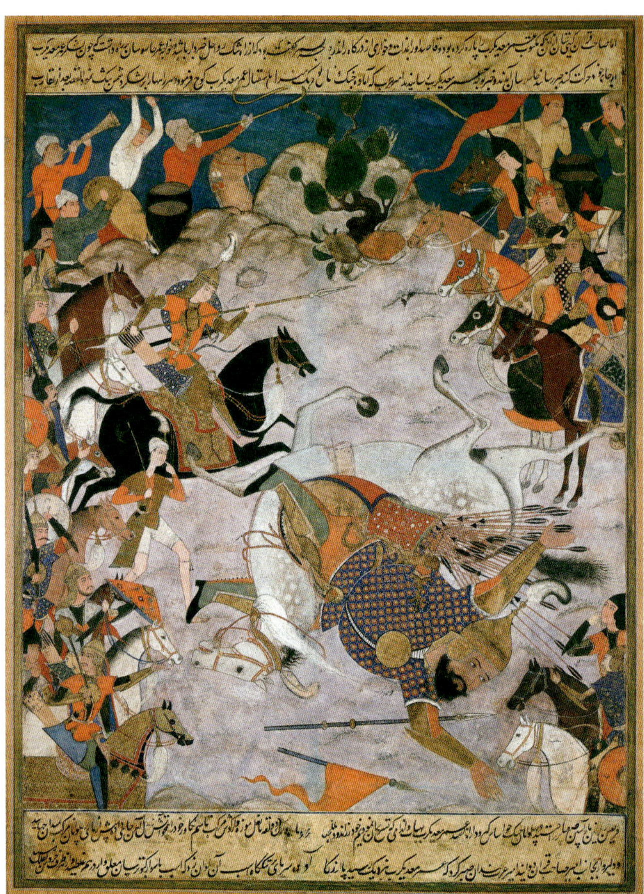

(fig.25) ***Netsuke depicting a horse caught in a spider's web*****, eighteenth century, ivory with carved decoration, 3.6 × 4.1 × 1.3 cm.** Ashmolean Museum, University of Oxford, EA1956.1710

(fig.26) ***Amir Hamza defeats 'Umar-i Ma'di Karab*****, 1562–5, gouache on cotton cloth, and black ink on paper, 69 × 51 cm.** Ashmolean Museum, University of Oxford, EA1978.2596

Who Carries Whom? (fig.24)

In the series *Who Carries Whom?*, Surovi explores the special relationship between humans and animals, particularly horses. She observes that society tends to value animals primarily based on their usefulness to people (figs 25–27). The first work looks at the history of horses in war, highlighting how horses were often left behind and abandoned when the fighting ended. In this piece, we see two horses comforting each other amidst the chaos of war (fig.24.1). The second and third works focus on how humans control horses, which often leads them to lose their natural behaviours as they adapt to living among people and start to imitate human actions (figs 24.2–24.3). In a softer scene, lit by moonlight, Surovi shows the kindness horses can offer one another (fig.24.4). The fifth artwork addresses the role of horses in farming, pointing out the maltreatment they face when they get old or injured and are no longer deemed useful (fig.24.5). The sixth piece is more joyful, featuring a horse playing a harmonium while an elephant dances with a scarf, creating a whimsical and happy moment against a bright yellow backdrop (fig.24.6). The seventh painting dives into the deep emotions of the animal world, showing both compassion and mystery (fig.24.7). In the eighth piece, a woman carries a horse in a box, referencing a small carved Japanese netsuke in the Ashmolean (fig.24.8 is inspired by fig.25). This image represents how horses can feel trapped in the human

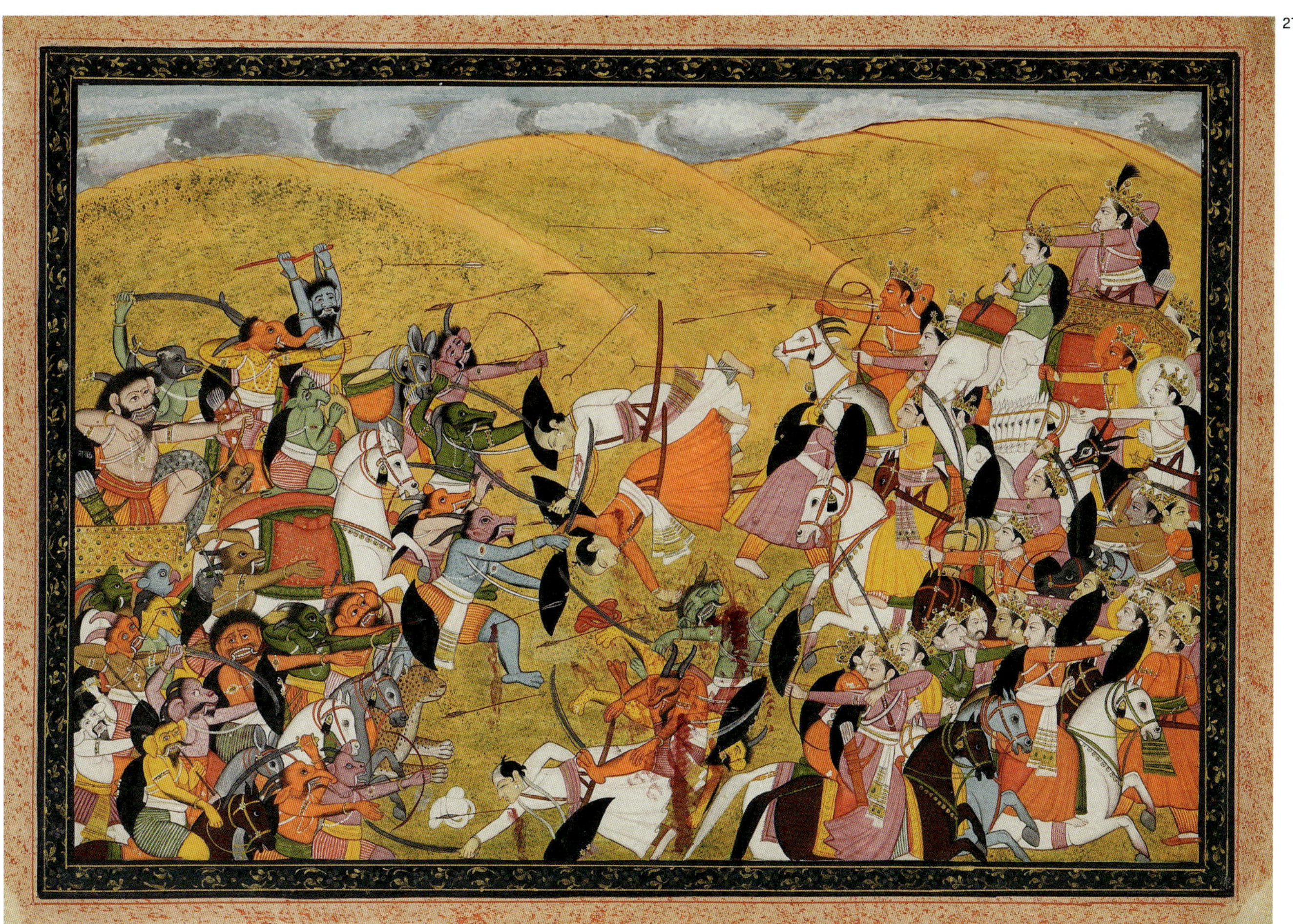

(fig.27) ***Battle scene between armies of devas and asuras*****, first half of the nineteenth century, gouache on paper, 25.2 × 36.6 cm.** Ashmolean Museum, University of Oxford, EA1996.113

world. The ninth work illustrates a journey, symbolising the burdens both horses and humans carry (fig.24.9). The viewer can see the horses struggling to break free and gradually forget who they truly are. In the last piece in this series, Surovi paints a horse surprised by its own reflection in a mirror, a bride with her groom, and a woman holding a horse in a boat; images related to shifts in self-perception and identity. (fig.24.10).

Some years ago, Surovi was particularly moved by the sight of an abandoned horse on a beach in Bangladesh. She called him Badami after his almond-coloured coat. After years of giving children and adults rides, this old and injured horse was left by its owner, who could no longer afford to care for it. While animals in the UK are protected by laws against cruelty, the same cannot be said for much of South Asia, including Bangladesh. Here, animal welfare can be a severely neglected issue, even though animals play an essential role in society and the economy. Sadly, abuse and neglect of animals are common and often ignored by both the authorities and the wider public.

Surovi creates this group of ten works using circular, pre-cut paper. The pieces are small in scale and are displayed back to back in the exhibition. Rather than focusing on a specific narrative, the artist uses the restrictions of the format to explore and experiment with the presentation of the medium.

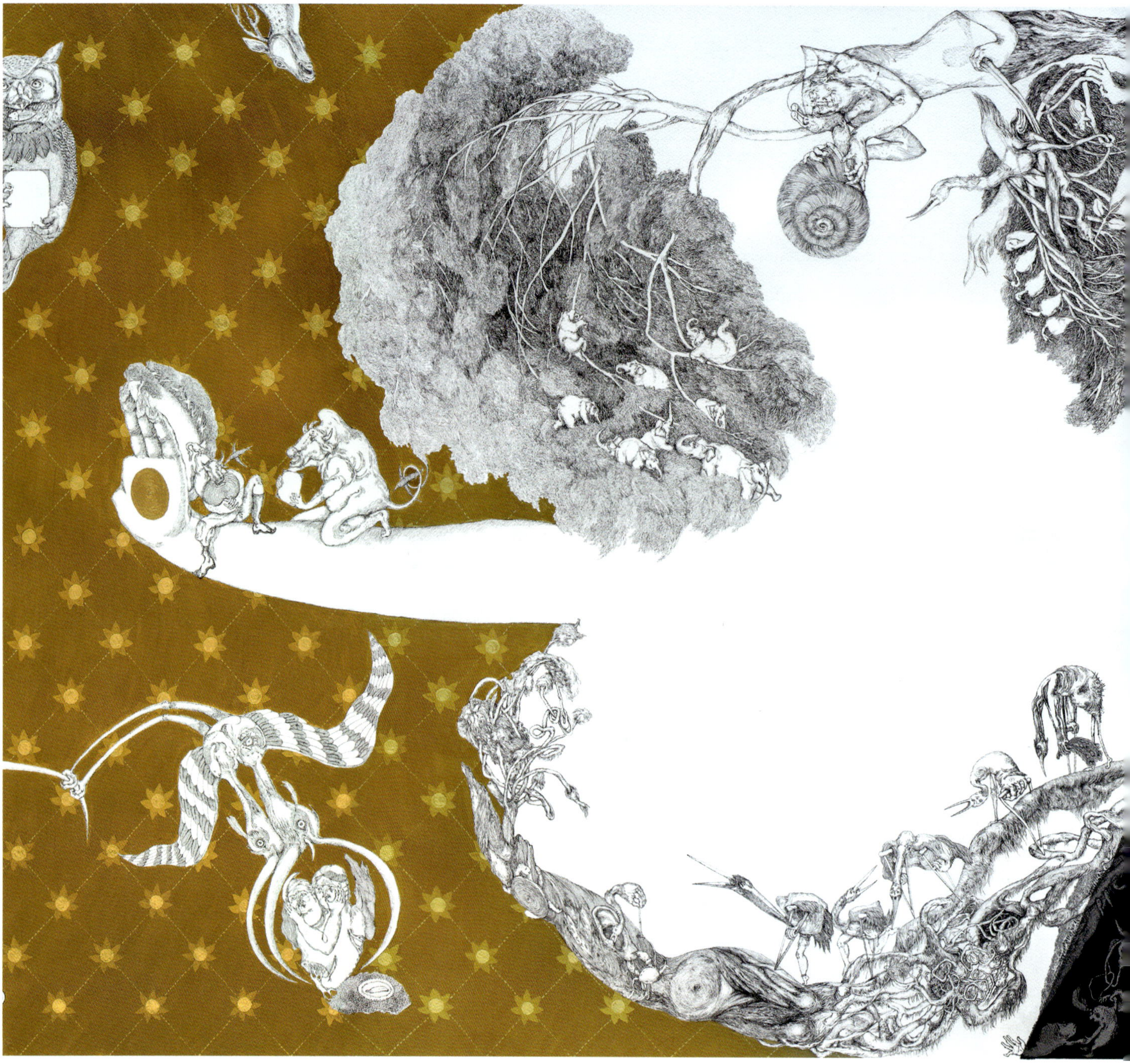

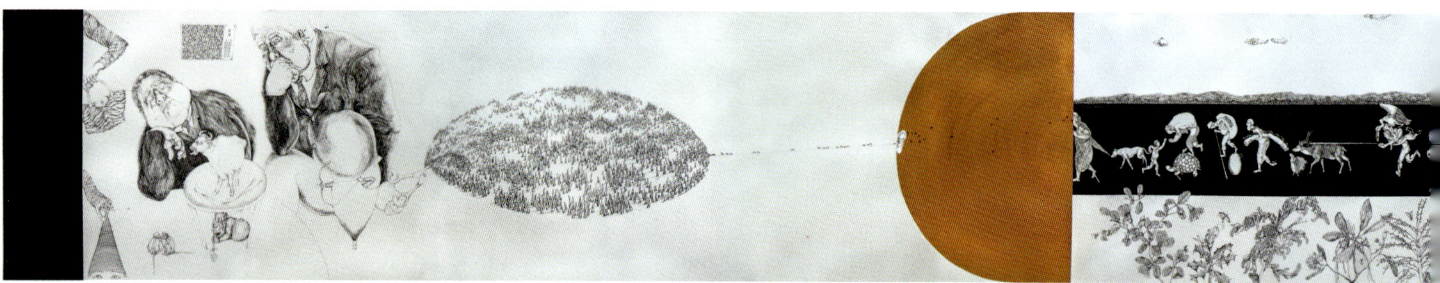

(fig.28) ***Between the Sea and the Sky, Who Holds the Ground?*, 2024–25 (detail), archival ink pen on paper, acrylic colour, gold and silver leaf, 86 × 942 cm.**
Collection of the artist. © Soma Surovi Jannat

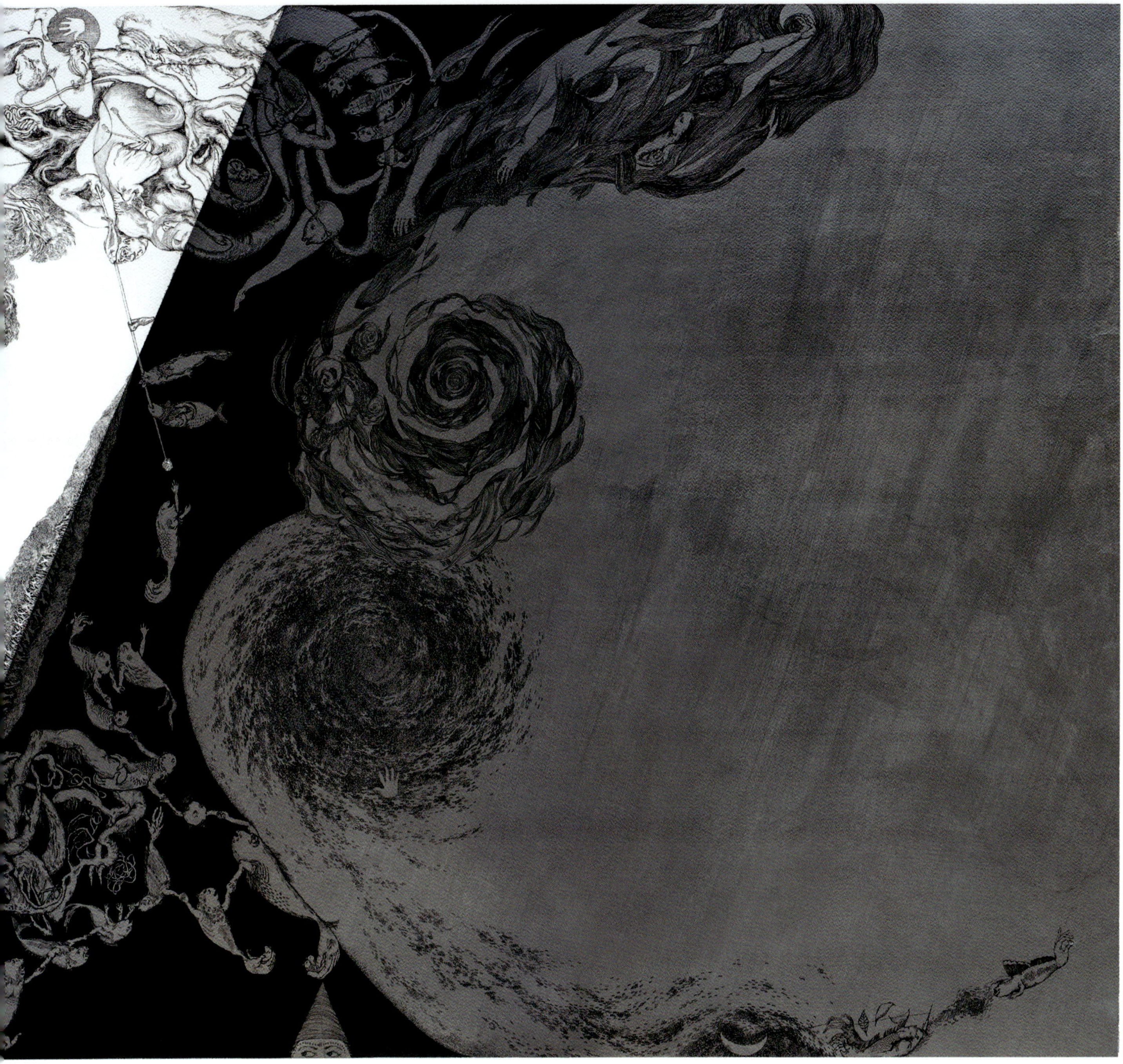

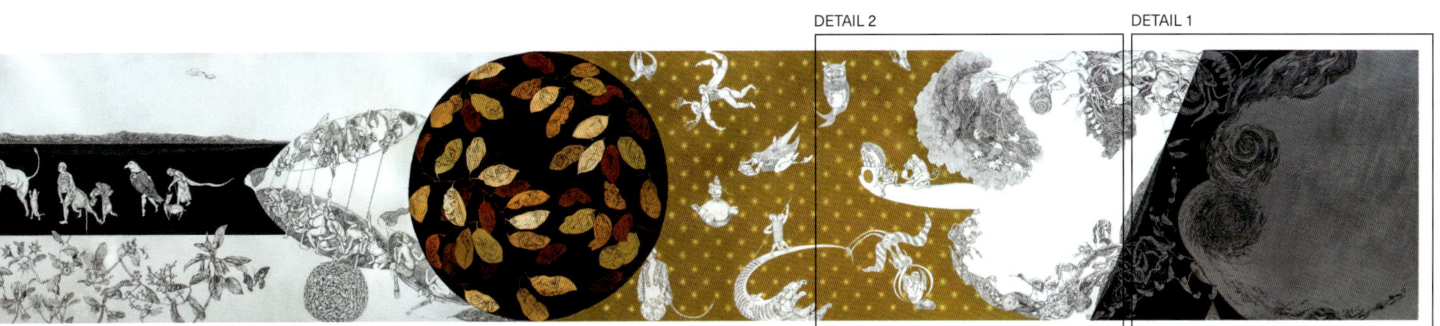
DETAIL 2
DETAIL 1

29

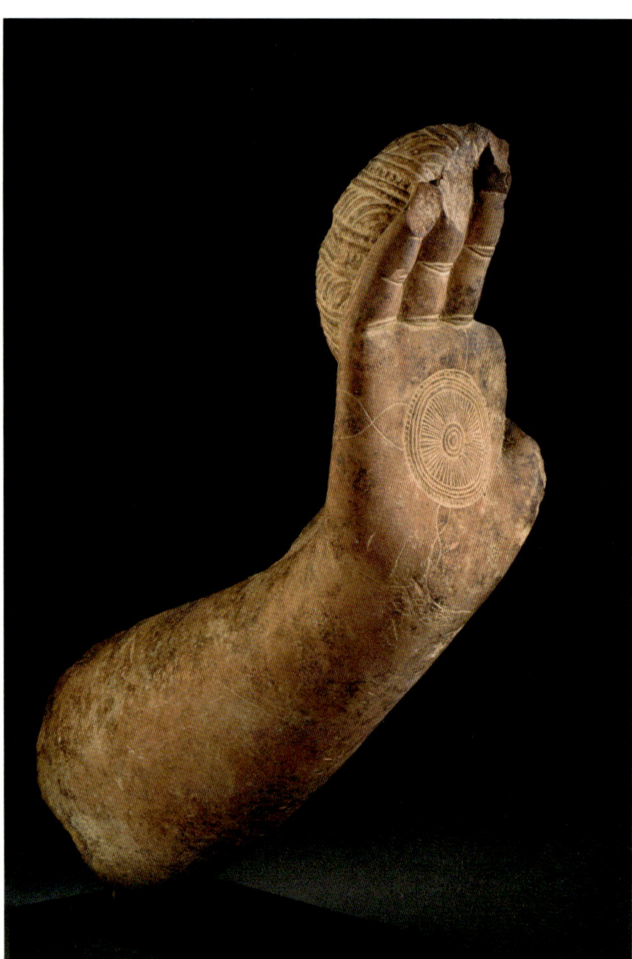

(fig.29) Fragmentary hand and forearm from the Buddha, second century CE, pink sandstone, 55 × 40 × 18 cm. Ashmolean Museum, University of Oxford, EA1997.186

Between the Sea and the Sky, Who Holds the Ground? (fig.28)

This scroll, measuring almost ten metres in length, is divided into several sections, with Surovi portraying everyday plants, animals, insects, and humans. Whereas the series *Where Every Leaf Holds a Tale* (fig.7.1–7.8) focuses on Bonobibi, the forest deity, and the Sundarbans, this scroll addresses the issues of displacement and climate migrants. Aspects from the earlier series, as well as details inspired by various works in the Ashmolean, find their way into this expansive scroll (figs 29–45). Surovi worries that most people still seem unable to envision a more promising future for the planet; and many in the subcontinent still perceive climate change as a natural phenomenon, rather than a consequence of human actions. Although awareness of this issue has increased, with some individuals beginning to acknowledge its urgency, Surovi believes that many struggle to foresee the potential results stemming from current decisions and silence.

On the right-hand side, the artist illustrates rivers merging to form the Bengal delta of Bangladesh (detail 1). While the Bengal delta includes three rivers, the artist shows just two: one flows in wavy, elongated strands, while the other consists of seeds. The two circular images show the method of plant dispersal via moving water, with seeds being transported downstream, caught by flora, or dropped on riverbanks for germination. This natural method of dispersal enables plants to spread to new locations along the river's path. The rivers intertwine with life, death, earth, and the cosmos. The dark underwater imagery features two fish holding fins. The mudskipper fish (or *Chiring Maach* in Bengali) – known for changing its colour in response to its surroundings, or when stressed – was once plentiful in the waters of Bangladesh, but is now increasingly difficult to spot. In an underwater pursuit, a man lures fish with shiny bait while other fish observe in terror. One fish locks eyes with the viewer, prompting questions about its fate. Another dons a hat, performing amid the realms of reality and imagination. Every stroke of the pen and brush tells a story, unveiling beauty in the mundane and the grandeur of nature, reflecting human joy and animal trepidation, but always underlining human impact and its repercussions on the ecosystem.

Surovi applies silver to represent the link between water and land, flanked by mangroves. The empty space

30

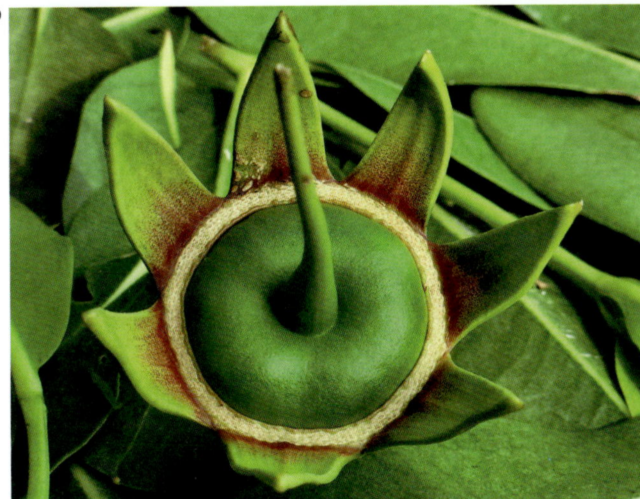

(fig.30) ***Ora flower in the Sundarbans.*** Photographed in September 2025 by the artist. © Soma Surovi Jannat

encourages viewers to ponder, as moonlight glimmers off the image of a hand (detail 2). This hand recalls for Surovi a fragment of a second-century monumental sandstone Buddha from India (fig.29). The Buddha's hand is raised in a gesture intended to dispel fear or convey blessings, with the Wheel of Dharma, symbolising the Buddha's teachings, on the palm.

Seated on the back of the arm, a cow peers into a mirror, as if searching for a missing companion. Her reflection relaxes as she believes she is not alone. This perhaps reminds viewers of the Buddha's teaching, which emphasises that true peace is an inner state, found by cultivating self-awareness and compassion. Various vignettes, including a fisherman with his children and an elderly man holding a snail, highlight emotional connections and empathy.

Central within the composition, elephants walk over treetops. Seemingly endearing at first sight, this displaced group is indicative of the fact that forced migration is crucial for their survival and draws attention to the declining population of elephants in Bangladesh. Below, creatures, such as a peacock displaying its plumage, are perched on a dying tree that resembles a woman. Even within decay and displacement, nature nurtures and supports all living beings, illustrating the intricate relationship between humans, animals, and the environment.

The hand guides the observer towards a saffron-gold backdrop (detail 3), reminiscent of the embroidered flowers and small mirrors found in South Asian textiles. The star shapes on a golden background could symbolise the cosmos, with Surovi's creative figures taking the place of traditional astronomical symbols. The star shape is also similar to the Ora flower (fig.30), which grows in the rich ecosystem of the Sundarbans. This comparison highlights how different elements of nature are connected. Surovi aims to capture the beautiful patterns found in nature, showing that our experiences are often more complex than they seem.

The figures on this backdrop include a double-headed bird with a loving couple caught in its beak. To highlight the fleeting nature of their love and lives, a banana is placed underneath them. Fresh and ripe, it represents their fertility; however, this fruit is temporary and symbolises the impermanence of the couple's lives too. In addition to the human couple, two crocodiles are depicted in an embrace. The crocodile tails morph into fertile land, where two men are tied together, attempting

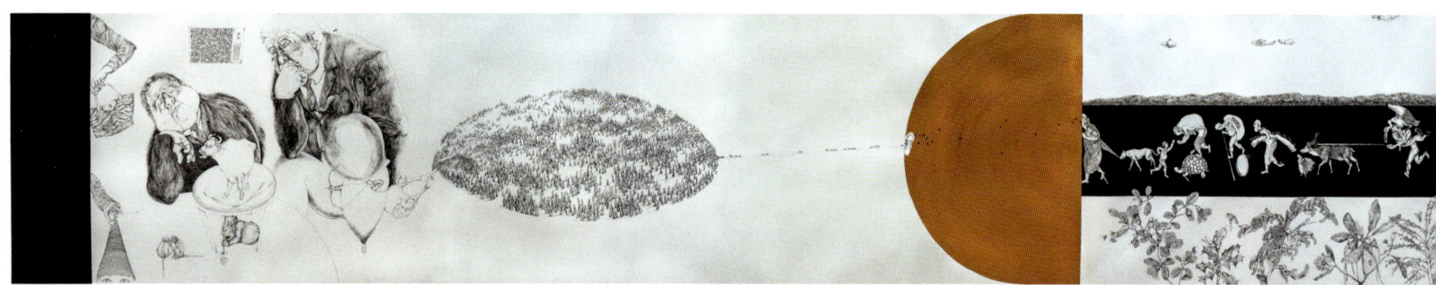

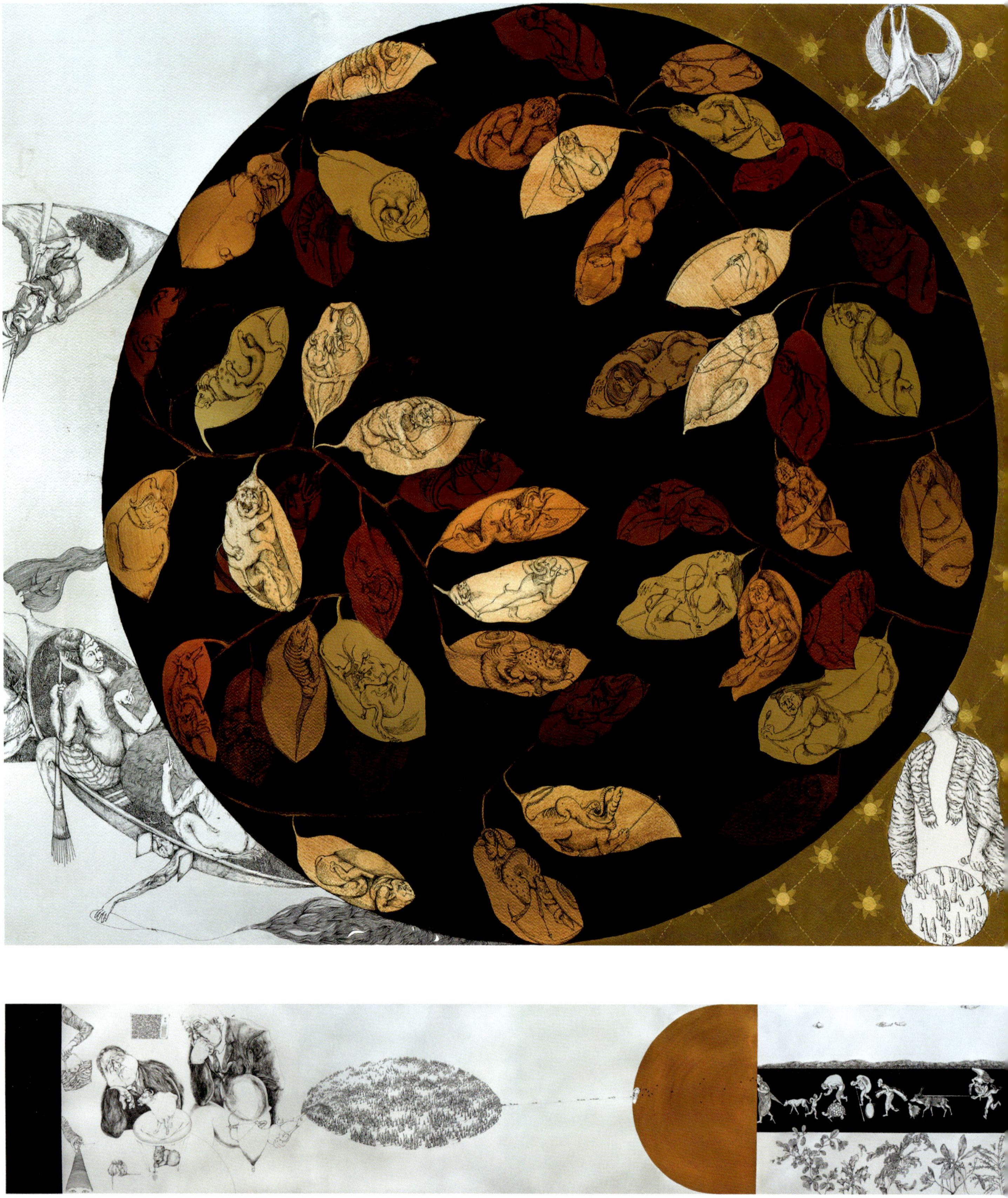

(fig.28) ***Between the Sea and the Sky, Who Holds the Ground?*, 2024–25 (detail), archival ink pen on paper, acrylic colour, gold and silver leaf, 86 × 942 cm.**
Collection of the artist. © Soma Surovi Jannat

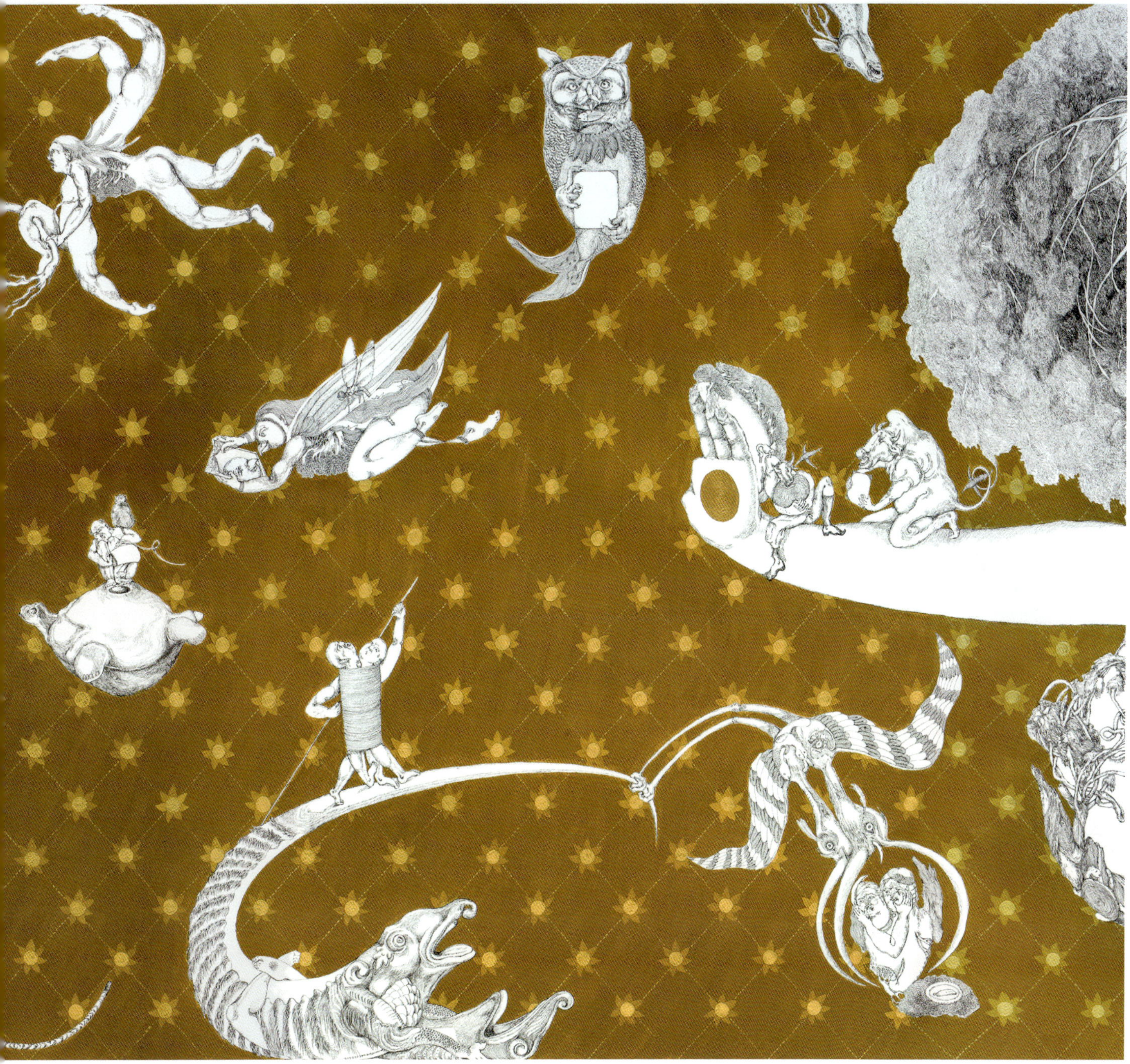

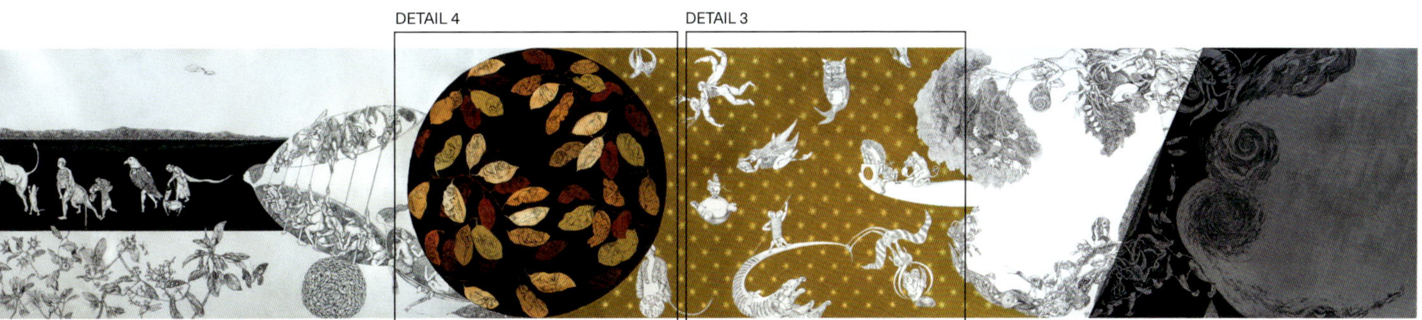
DETAIL 4
DETAIL 3

31

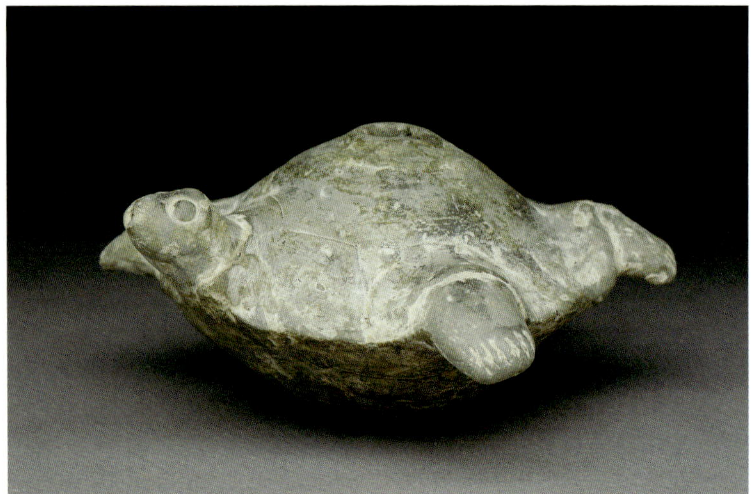

33

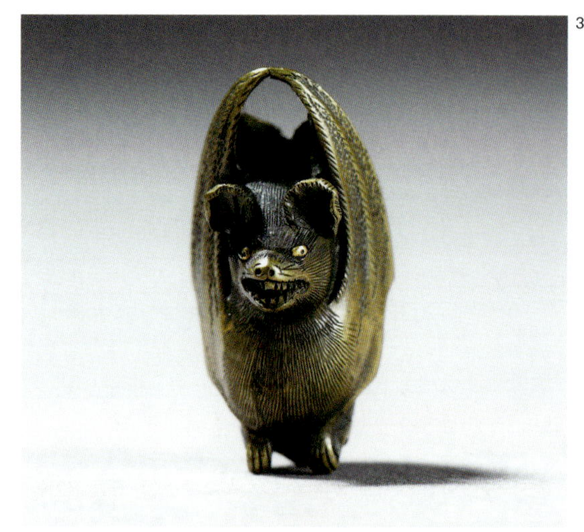

32

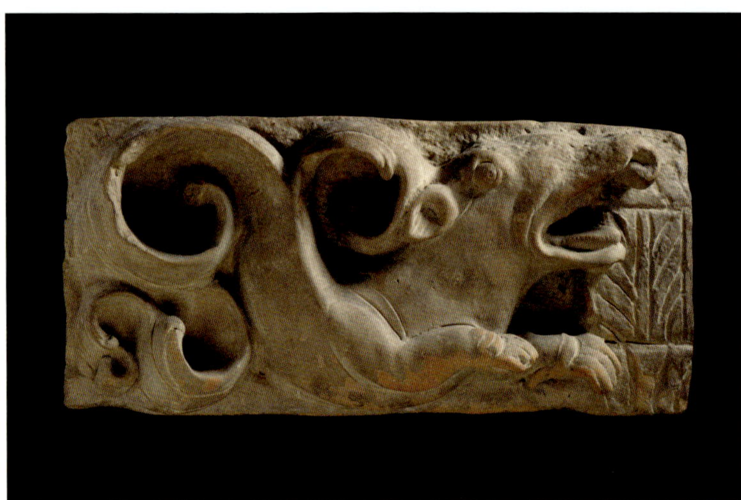

34

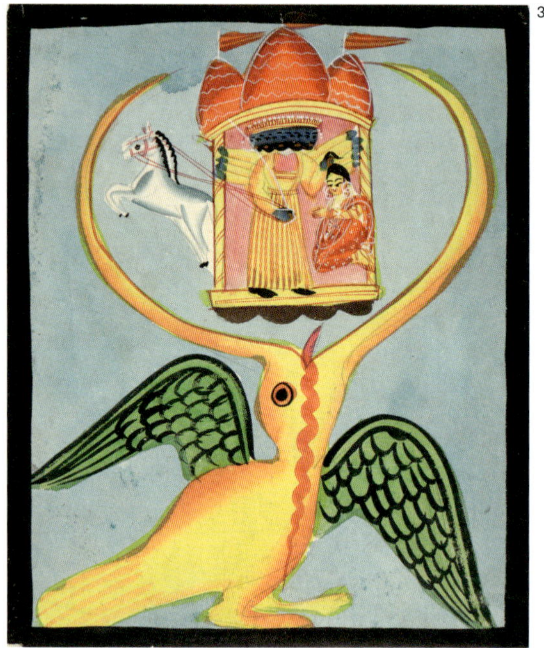

(fig.31) ***Vessel in the form of a turtle*, 230–171 BCE, terracotta, 9.5 × 19 × 19 cm.** Ashmolean Museum, University of Oxford, EA1997.179

(fig.32) ***Plaque with a makara, or aquatic monster*, 320–600, terracotta, 19.7 × 43 × 11 cm.** Ashmolean Museum, University of Oxford, EA1971.13

(fig.33) ***Ojime in the form of a bat*, late nineteenth century, sentoku cast, 2.3 × 1.2 × 1.4 cm.** Ashmolean Museum, University of Oxford, EA1956.3749

(fig.34) ***Baka, the heron demon, mastered by Krishna*, c.1870, gouache with gold on paper, 27.5 × 22 cm.** Ashmolean Museum, University of Oxford, EA1970.137

to balance on this terrain. Surovi illustrates an owl with a mirror and a turtle (detail 3) carrying a man who is watering a plant. These images represent age, resilience, and wisdom. Other figures, such as an inverted bat, three figures sharing a single trunk, and a man adorned in tiger skin, invite viewer interpretations based on their own associations, shaped by personal experiences. Many of these figures draw inspiration from pieces in the Ashmolean (figs 31–39).

The vast expanse of the cosmos turns into a sphere embellished with numerous leaves that cling to branches (detail 4). Each leaf features the expressive faces of human and animal figures. If this sphere represents the earth and the leaves symbolise land, then the planet's waters are polluted, and each leaf holds a tale. A range of emotions, from elation to sorrow, are depicted within the leaves. Closer examination shows that they can be divided into two groups: on one side, different animals, birds, and insects appear anxious as they protect their young; on the other side are the humans.

On the left of the sphere, almost coming out of this space, are two boats converging (detail 5). Surovi showcases a vibrant portrayal of boat racing, a popular activity in Bangladesh. This dynamic scene encapsulates the thrill and beauty of the experience. Some of the boatmen wear masks, reminding the viewer of *Where Every Leaf Holds a Tale* (*Ha Ja Ba Ra La*) (fig.7.3), highlighting contemporary concerns regarding safety

35 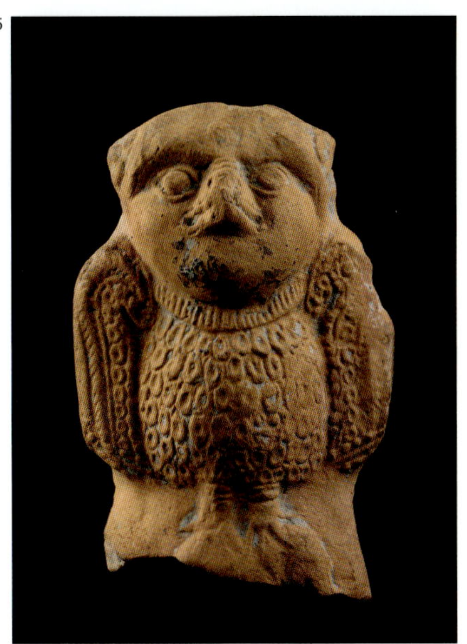

36 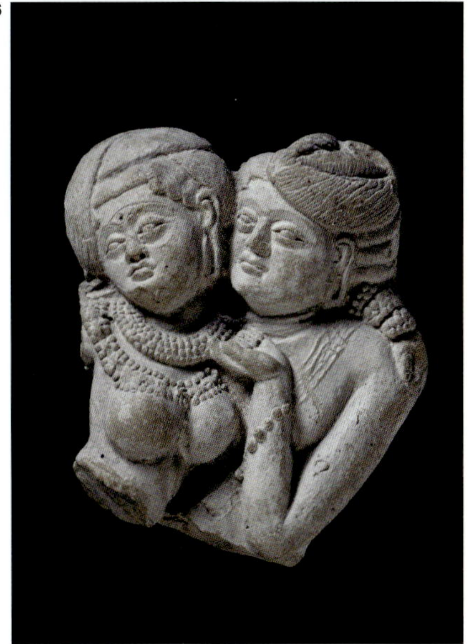

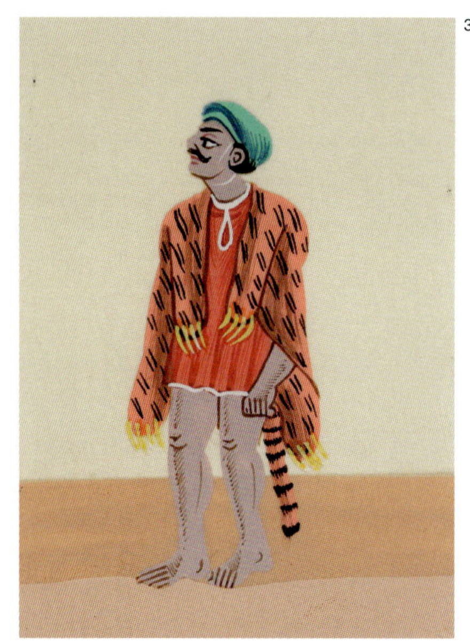 37

38 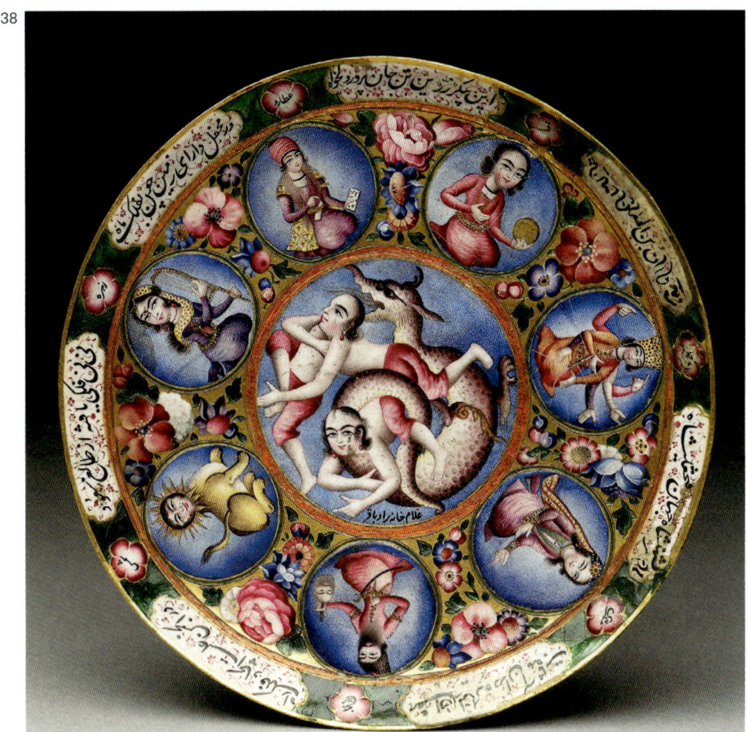

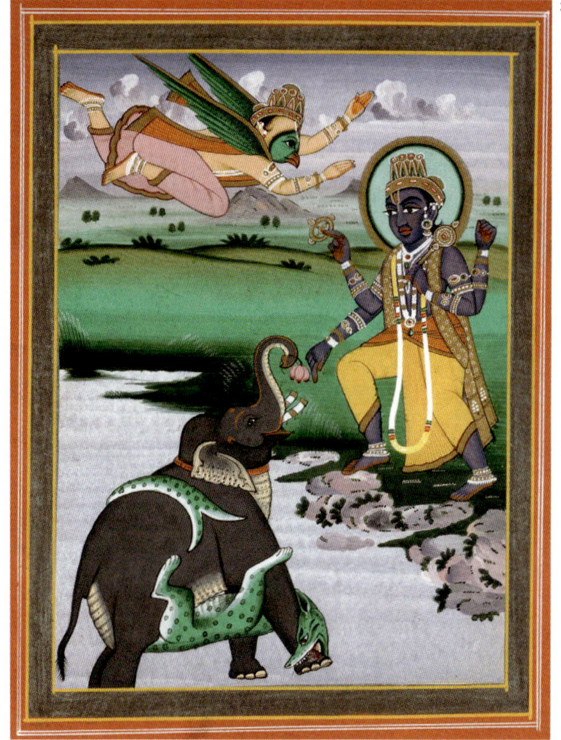 39

(fig.35) ***Owl*****, first century BCE, terracotta, 10.5 cm (height).** Ashmolean Museum, University of Oxford, EA1994.73

(fig.36) ***Plaque fragment with pair of lovers*** **(*****mithuna*****), first century BCE, plaque, 5.8 × 5.5 × 2 cm.** Ashmolean Museum, University of Oxford, EA1993.389

(fig.37) ***Portrait of a man wearing a tiger skin*****, 1800–80, gouache on mica, 10 × 6.6 cm.** Ashmolean Museum, University of Oxford, EA1994.26.iv

(fig.38) Baqir (enameller), ***Saucer with astrological decoration*****, early 1800s, gold, enamelled, 12.7 cm (diameter).** Ashmolean Museum, University of Oxford, EA2009.3

(fig.39) ***Krishna, Garuda and the elephant*****,** ***c.*****1800s, gouache on cardboard, 28 × 21 cm.** Ashmolean Museum, University of Oxford, EAX.2012

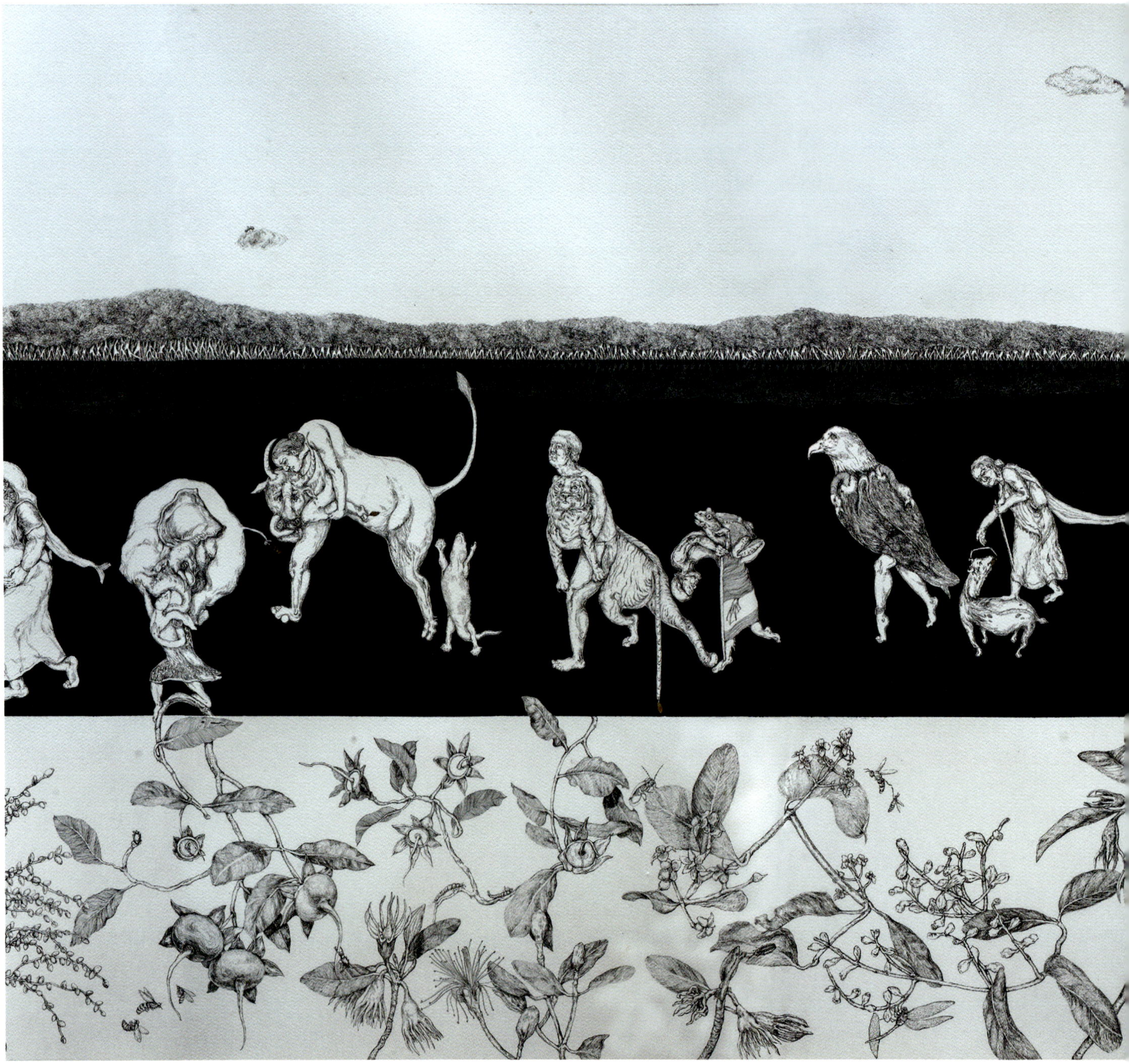

DETAIL 6 (AND FOLLOWING SPREAD)

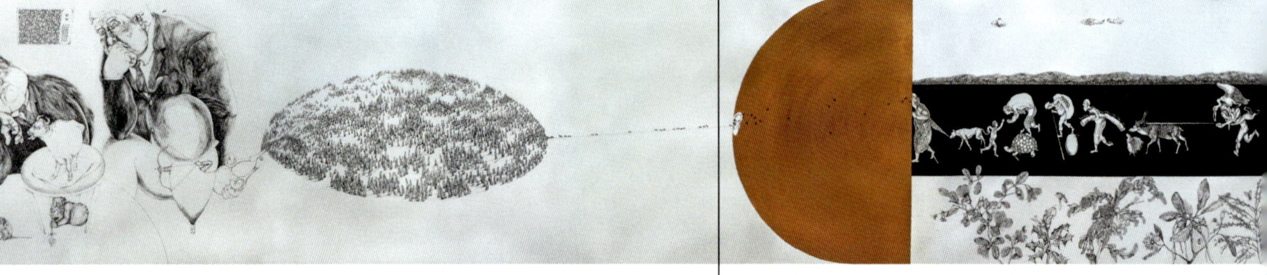

(fig.28) ***Between the Sea and the Sky, Who Holds the Ground?*, 2024–25 (detail), archival ink pen on paper, acrylic colour, gold and silver leaf, 86 × 942 cm.**
Collection of the artist. © Soma Surovi Jannat

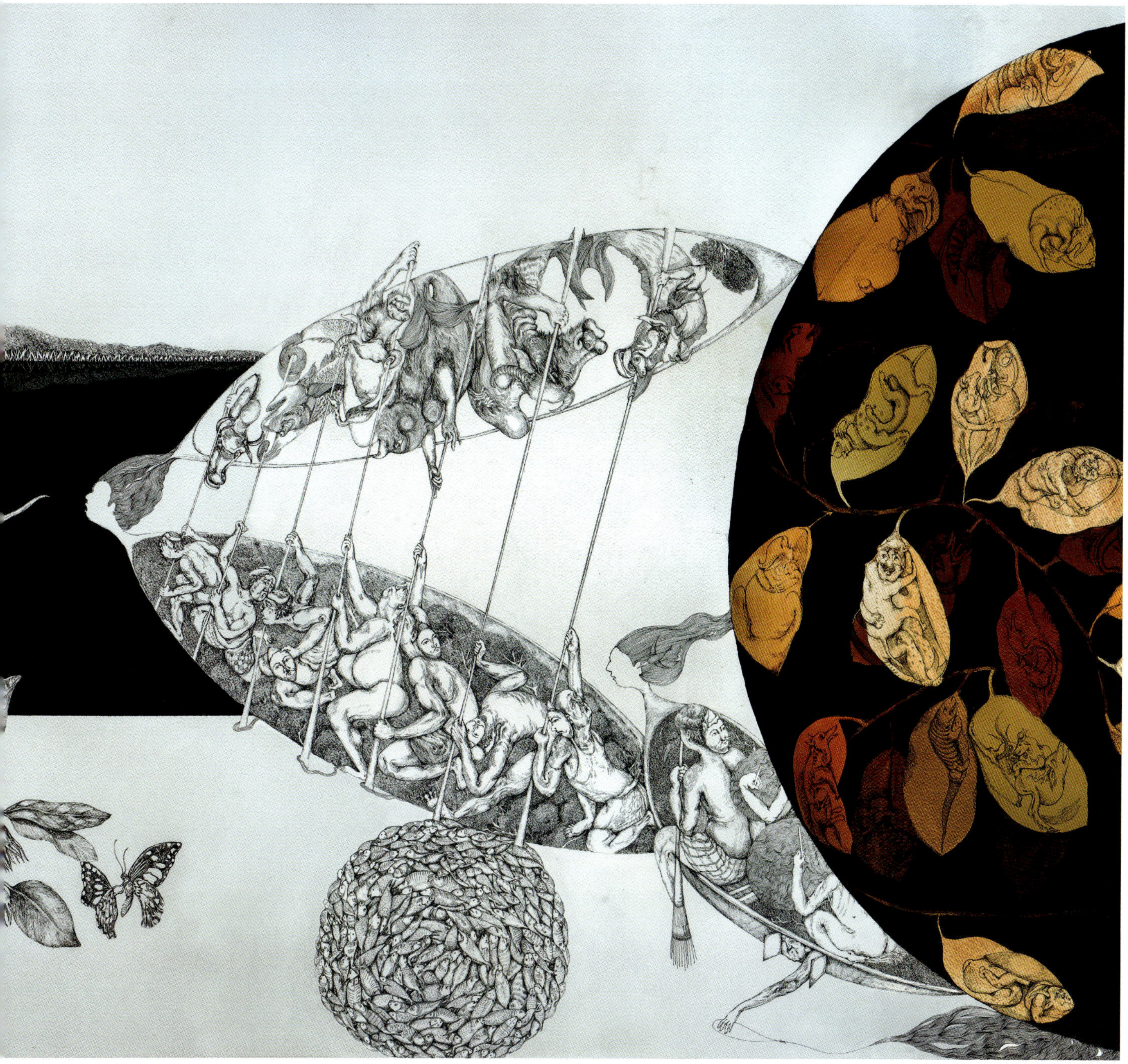

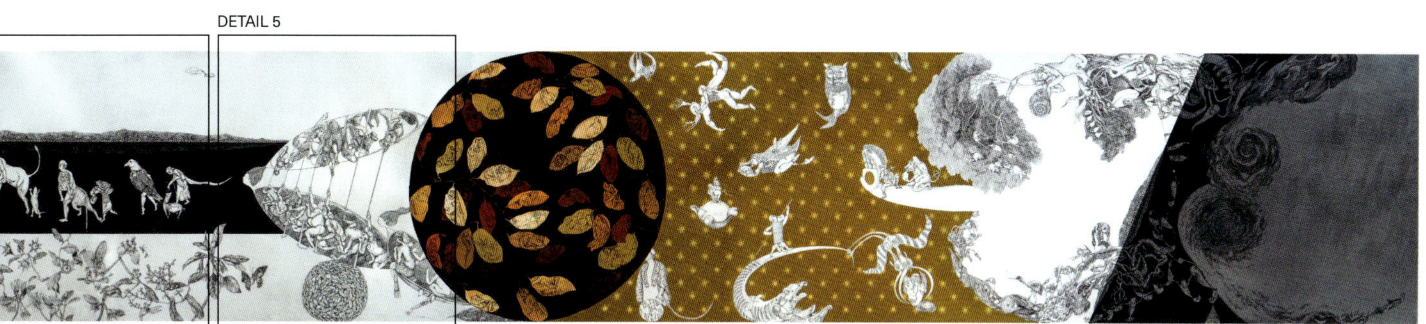
DETAIL 5

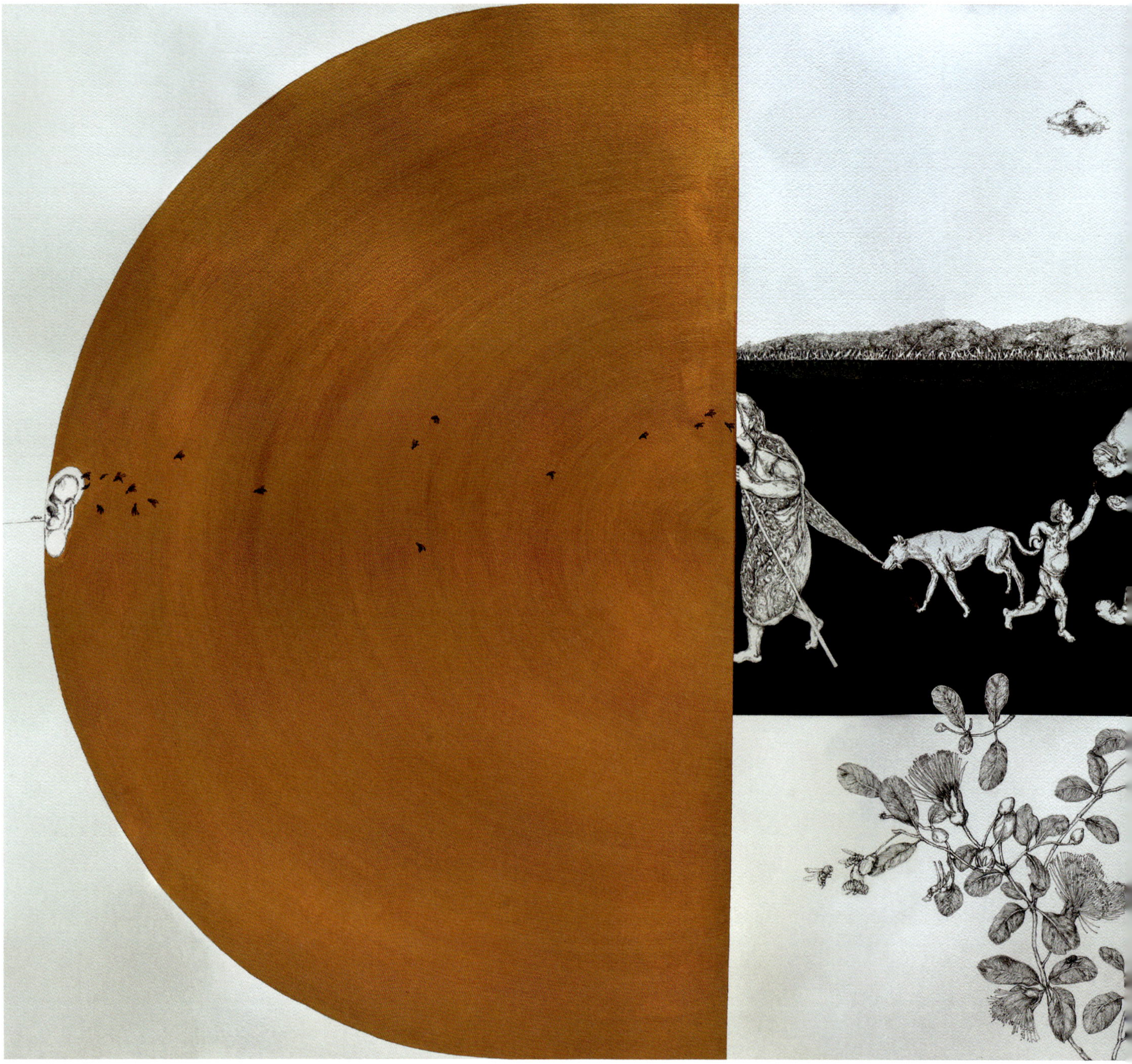

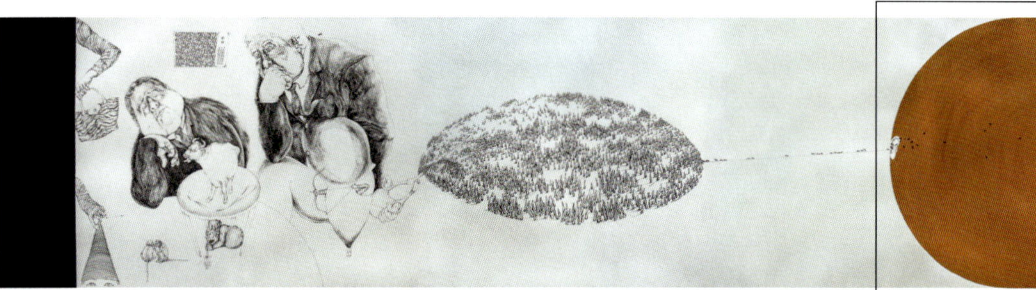

DETAIL 6 (AND PREVIOUS SPREAD)

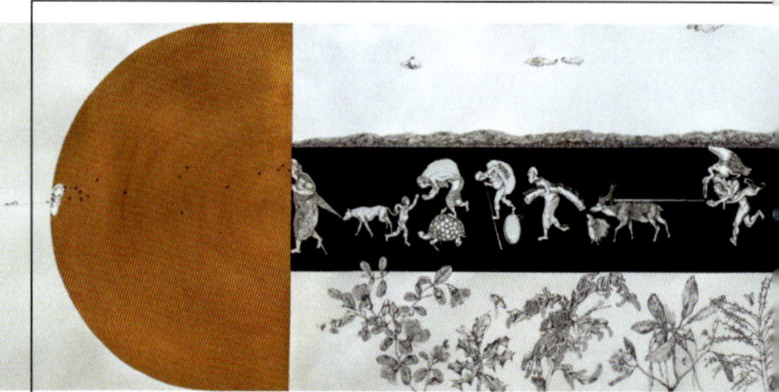

(fig.28) ***Between the Sea and the Sky, Who Holds the Ground?*, 2024–25 (detail), archival ink pen on paper, acrylic colour, gold and silver leaf, 86 × 942 cm.**
Collection of the artist. © Soma Surovi Jannat

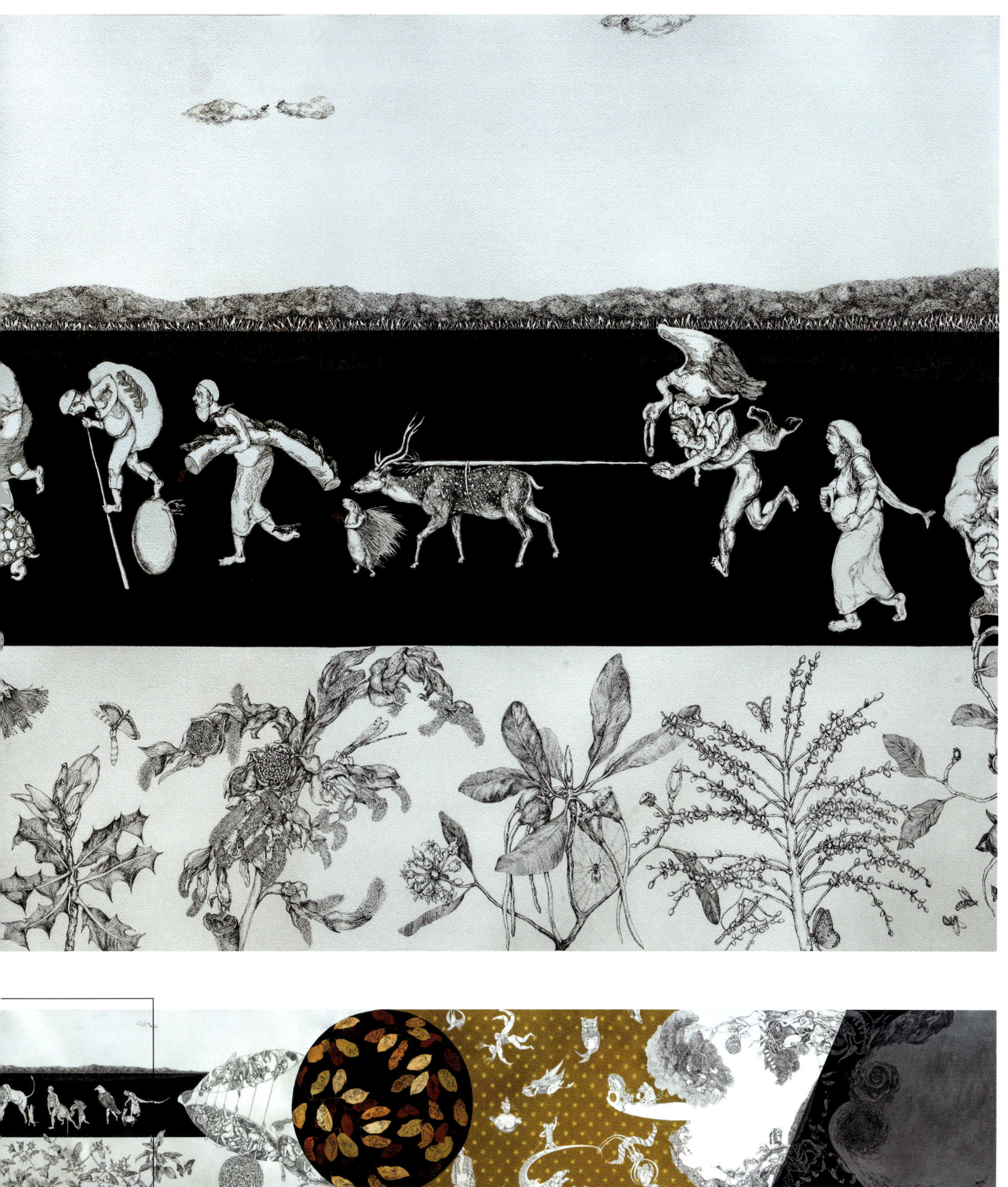

40

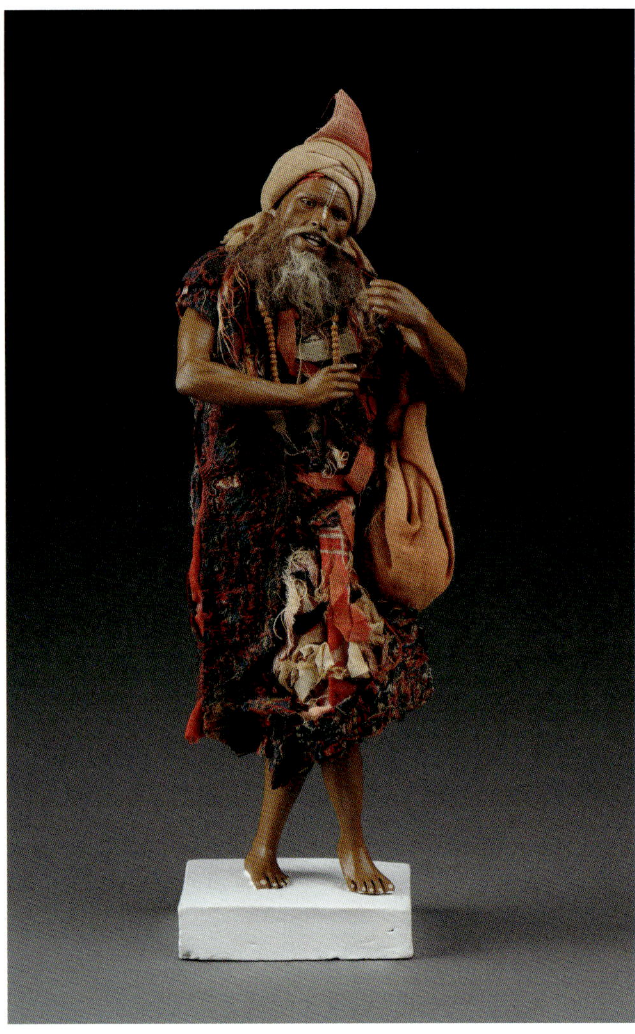

41

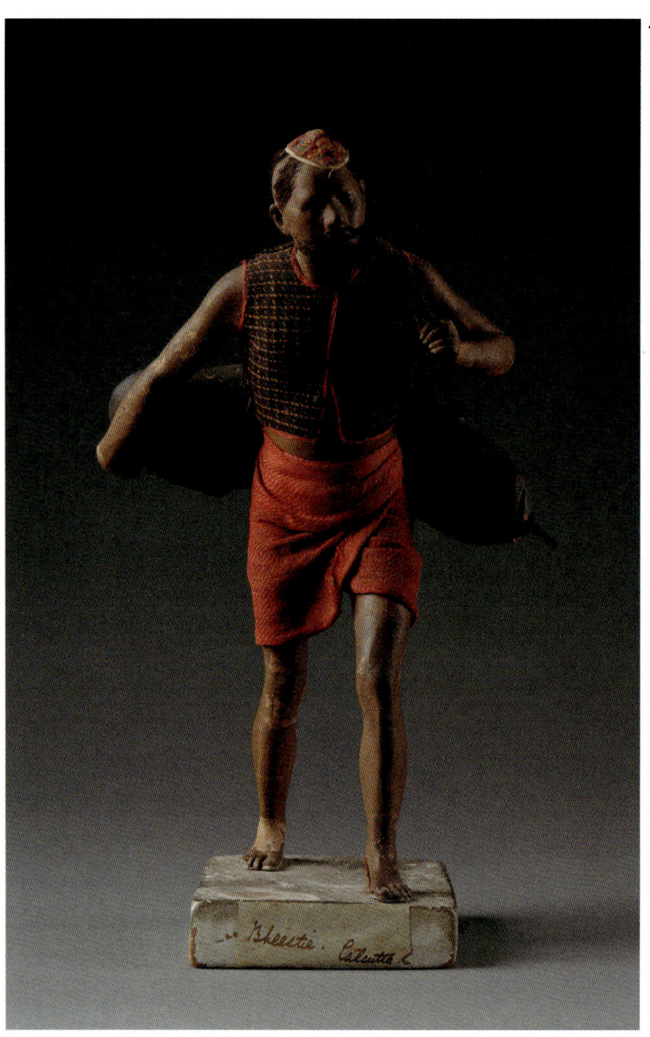

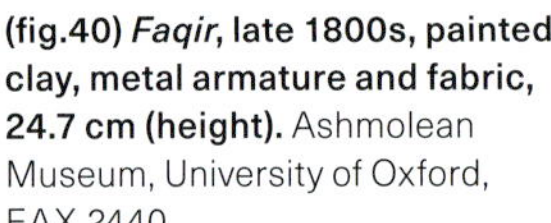

(fig.40) ***Faqir*****, late 1800s, painted clay, metal armature and fabric, 24.7 cm (height).** Ashmolean Museum, University of Oxford, EAX.2440

(fig.41) ***Bheesti*** **(water carrier), late 1800s, painted clay, metal armature and fabric, 22.3 cm (height).** Ashmolean Museum, University of Oxford, EAX.7056

and the environment. One figure takes off his mask, as if to confront the pressing environmental challenges ahead. Beneath one of the vessels a sizable net brimming with fish represents the interdependency of various life forms and overfishing.

The dark hues in this section of the artwork signify rising sea levels, a critical problem that leads to flooding and displacement of humans and animals in the area. The polluted waters in the Sundarbans look dark due to soot, chemicals, sewage, and other poisonous substances.

The boat on the dark waters points towards a migration of human and animal refugees (detail 6). It seems that they are travelling together quietly and supportively. Surovi was inspired by the Ashmolean's numerous nineteenth-century clay figures (figs 40–43), depicting the fortitude of everyday people living on the subcontinent. She recreated the spirit of these figures in this section of the scroll, portraying ordinary individuals exhibiting extraordinary determination, emphasising their struggle and survival during migration. Included are: an old woman with a goat; a human-legged eagle; an elderly man with a frog; a man carrying an injured tiger; a woman holding a cow and an otter; a little girl carrying a baby elephant; a pregnant woman carrying a fish, a leaf, and a butterfly; a man with a child on his shoulder and a heron with feathers of a peacock; an antelope; an elderly man hauling a tree trunk accompanied by crows; a porcupine; a young boy with a boulder; an old lady upon a tortoise; a boy holding the tail of a dog; and finally, a woman leading the group,

42

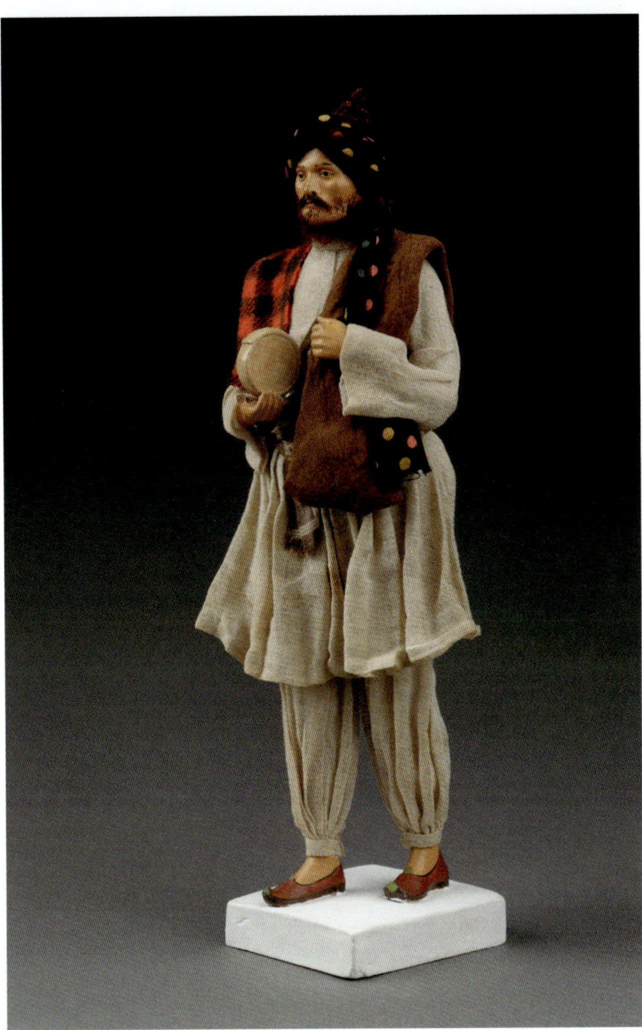

(fig.42) ***Pathan*, late 1800s, painted clay, metal armature and fabric, 25.3 cm (height).** Ashmolean Museum, University of Oxford, EAX.2437

43

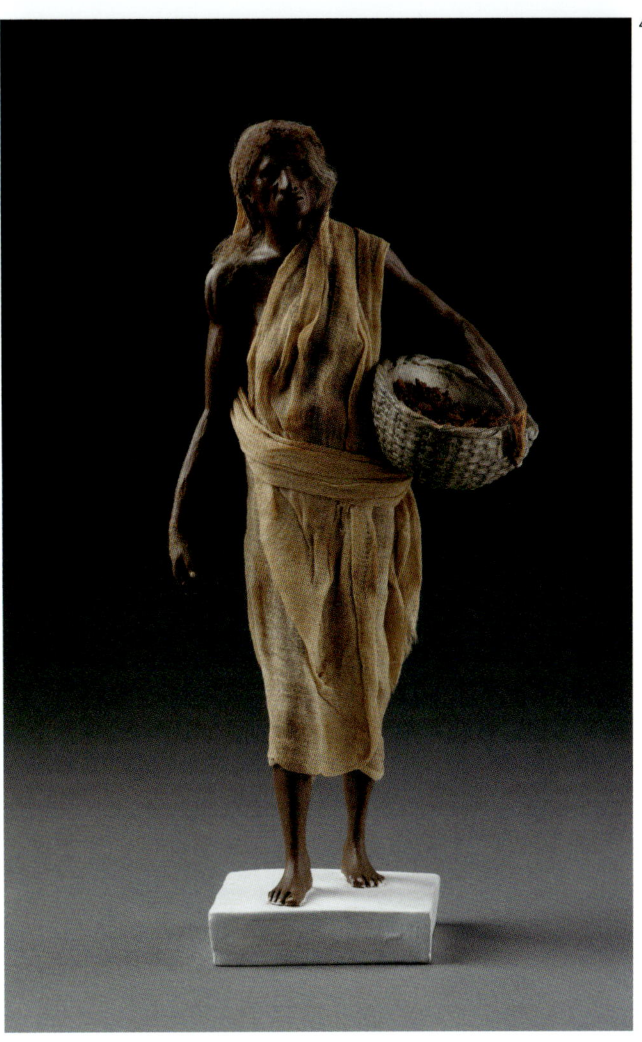

(fig.43) ***Widow*, late 1800s, painted clay, metal armature and fabric, 23.5 cm (height).** Ashmolean Museum, University of Oxford, EAX.2439

with the same dog holding her saree. Each individual is clutching a leaf, as if putting their faith in nature.

Above the migration scene, mangroves extend their roots deep into the earth, seeking sustenance and offering stability, while underneath lie various plants and flowers. A closer examination may spotlight the insects. For example, a butterfly with its wings beautifully displayed; a bee interacting with another accompanied by a dragonfly; a beetle; and fireflies. These highlight the often-underappreciated world of insects. The ants on the clouds denote the insects' response to environmental changes; when threatened, they instinctively seek higher ground. Two ants are presented together, showcasing their collaboration and resilience. Each illustration narrates a story that warrants attention, prompting the audience to recognise the complex world of insects and the profound connections in nature.

Many migrants and refugees dream of reaching a brighter future, a land full of promise. However, when they arrive, they often feel overlooked and unwelcome in a large, unfamiliar place. The artist encourages the viewer to look closely at the migrants morphing into bees. The bees subsequently transform into ants. These small insect details signify the disregard for those seen as insignificant and inconsequential. Like a buzzing fly, seen as a nuisance, migrants are often recognised as an annoyance, a headache. However, migrants continue to exist and contribute to an ecosystem, where they are often unheard and unseen by politicians, and neglected by most.

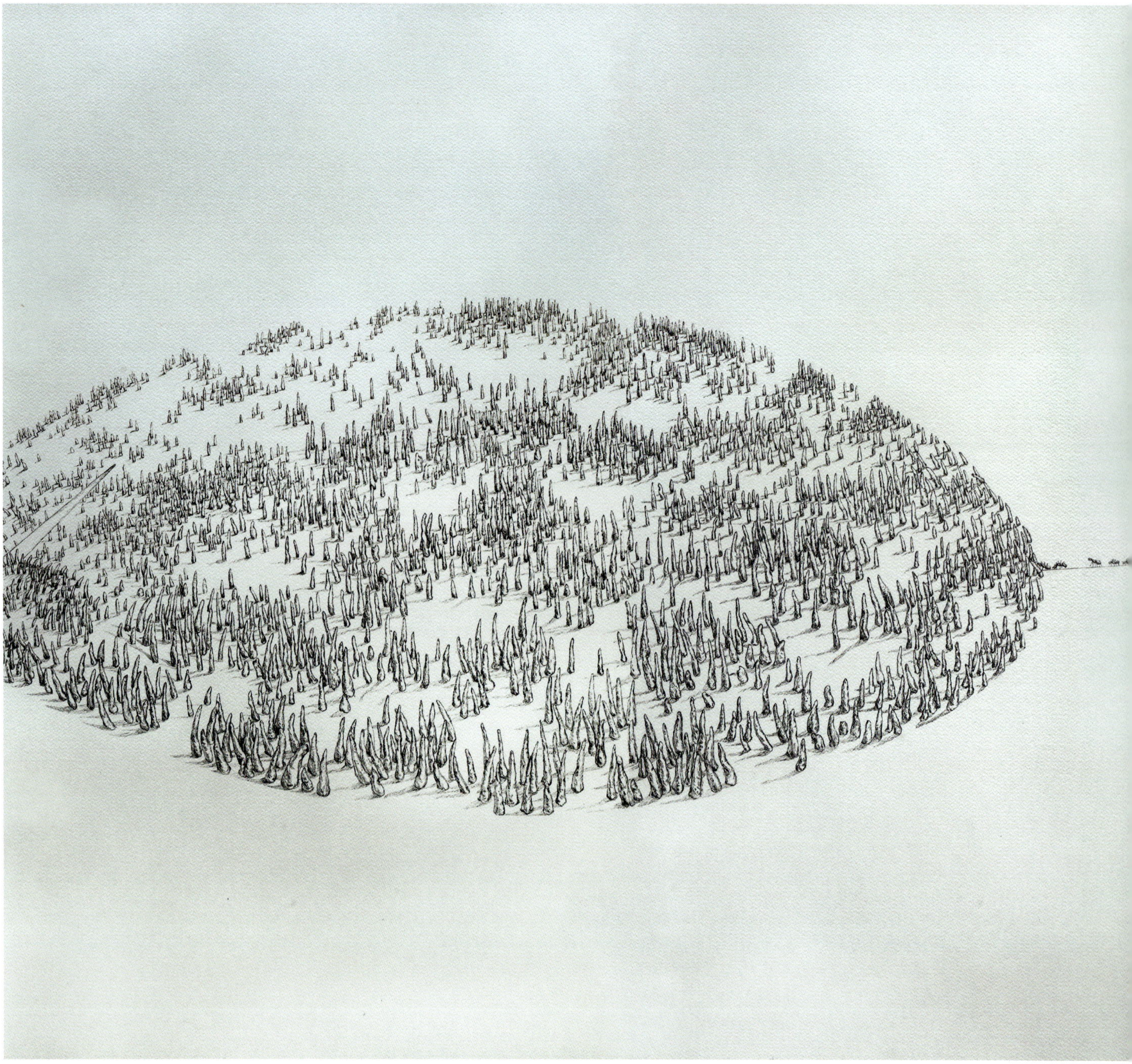

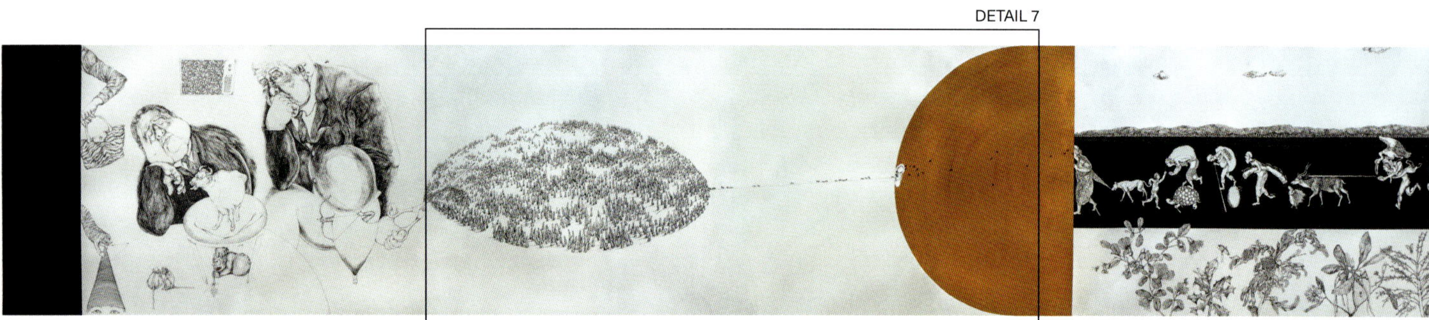

(fig.28) ***Between the Sea and the Sky, Who Holds the Ground?*****, 2024–25 (detail), archival ink pen on paper, acrylic colour, gold and silver leaf, 86 × 942 cm.**
Collection of the artist © Soma Surovi Jannat

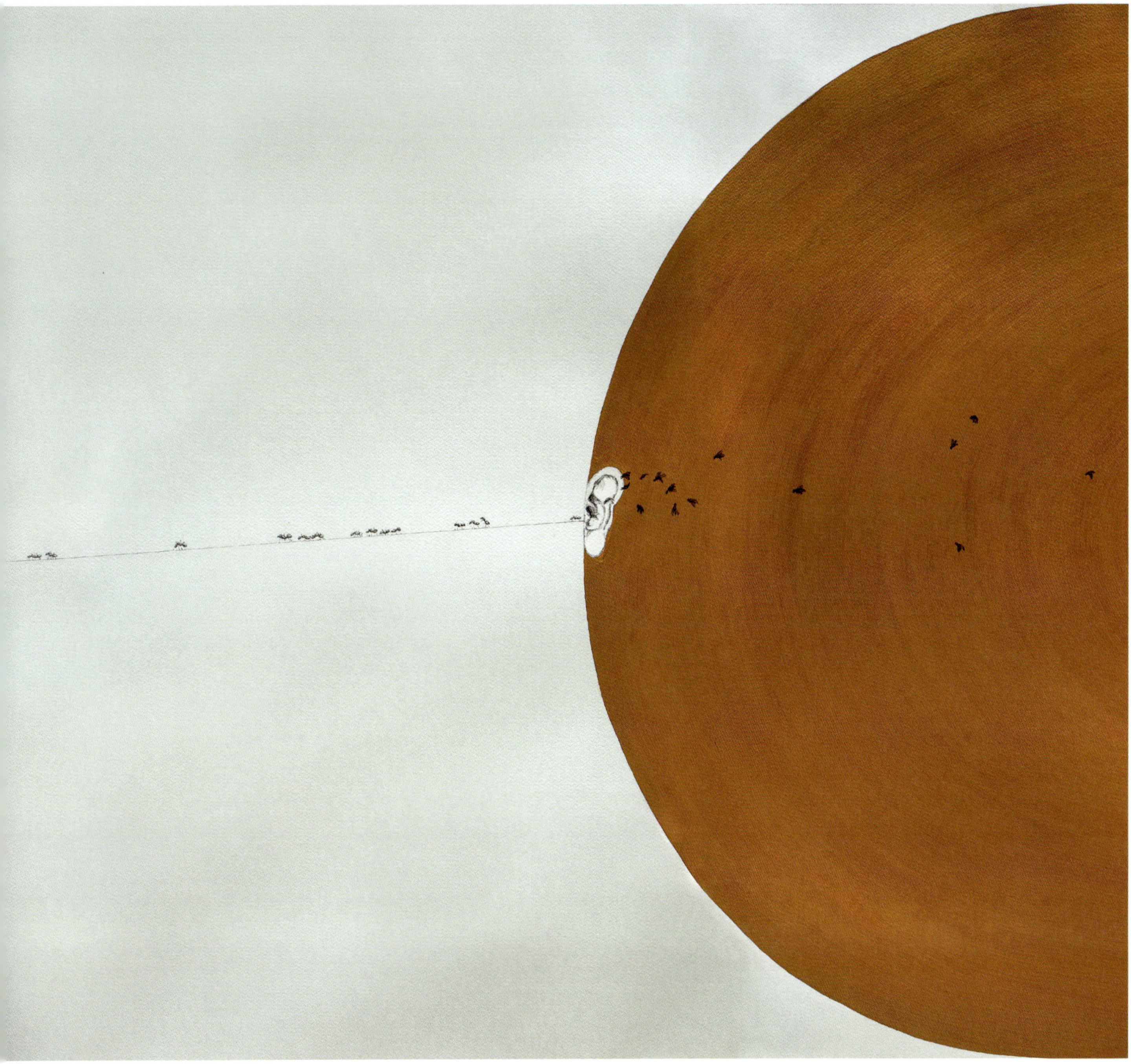

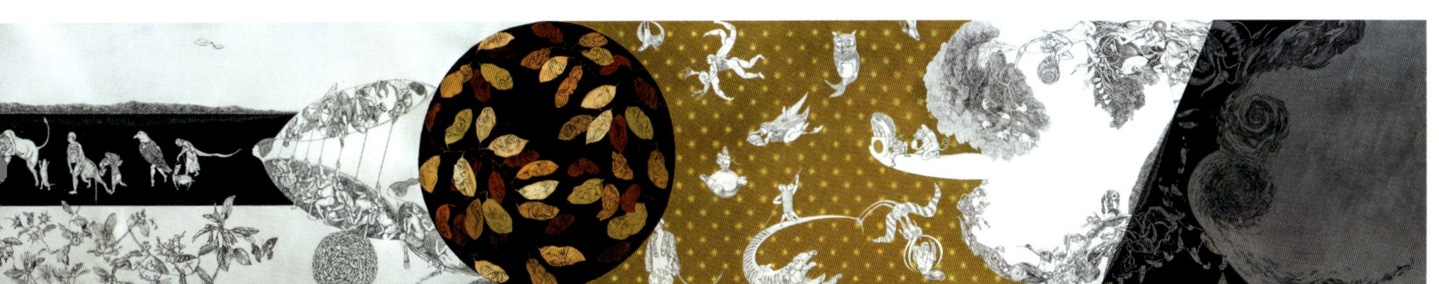

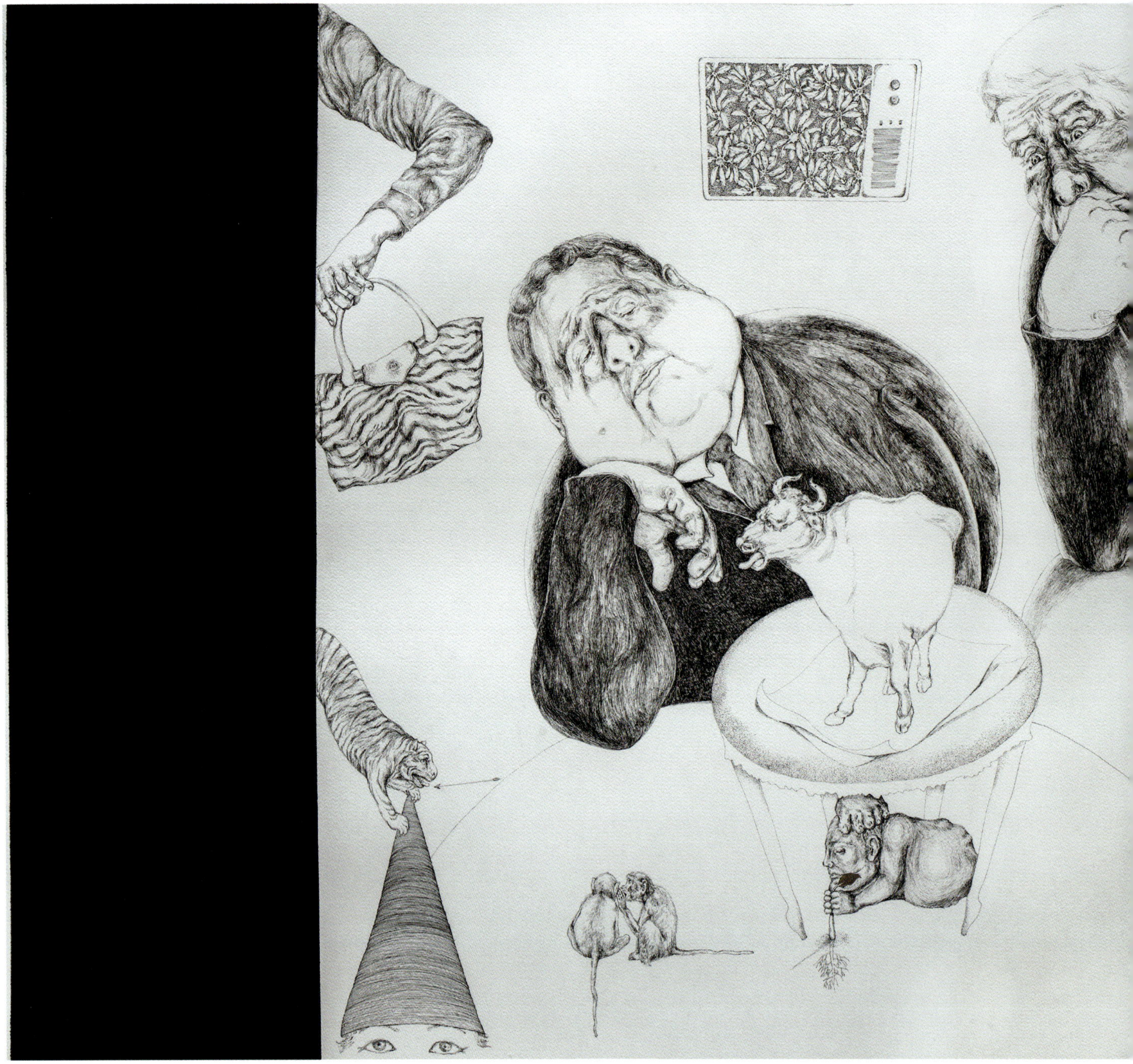

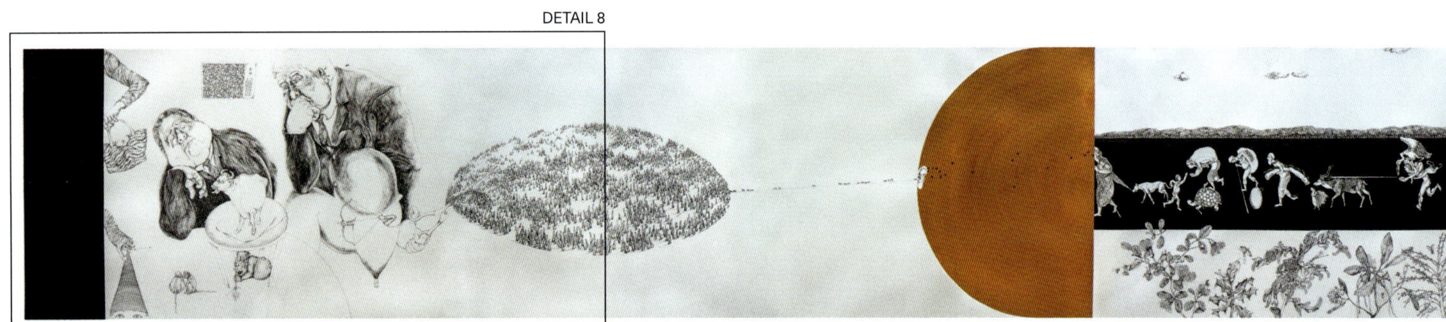

(fig.28) ***Between the Sea and the Sky, Who Holds the Ground?***, **2024–25 (detail), archival ink pen on paper, acrylic colour, gold and silver leaf, 86 × 942 cm.**
Collection of the artist © Soma Surovi Jannat

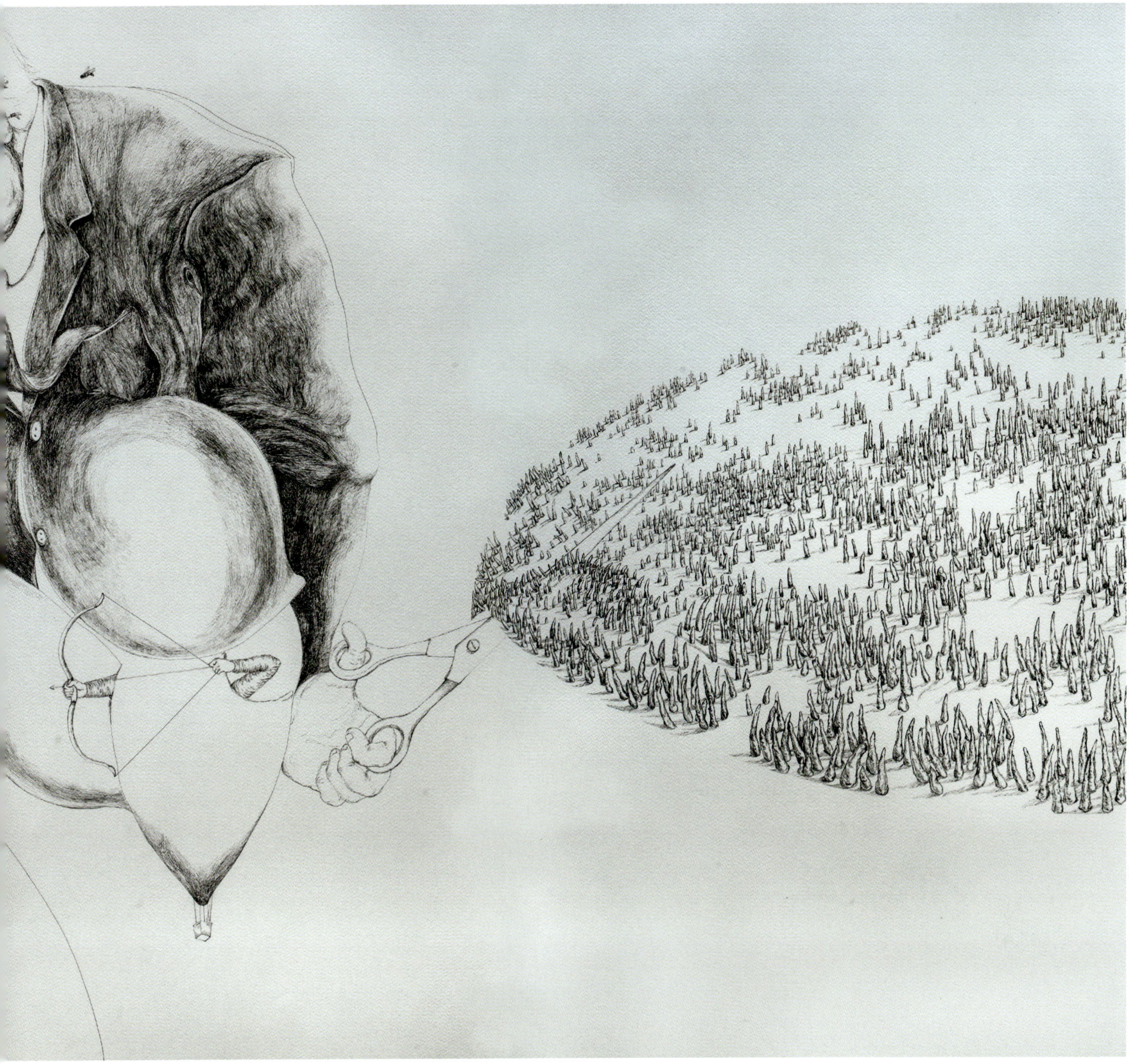

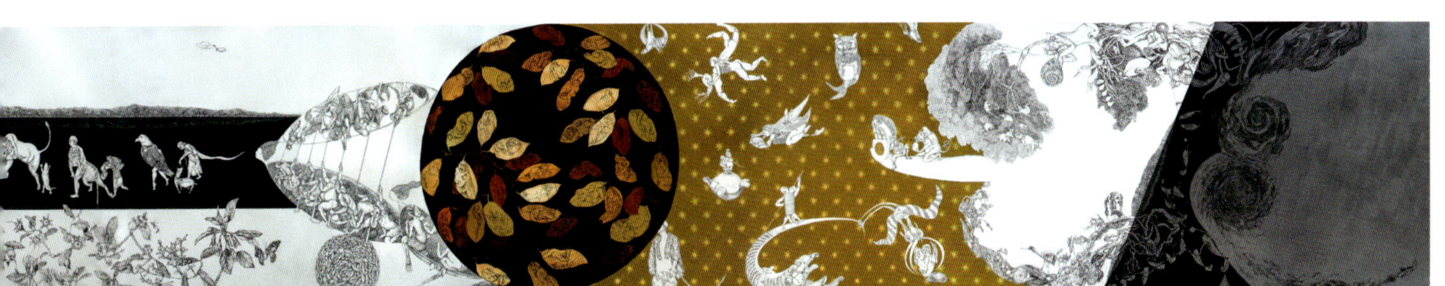

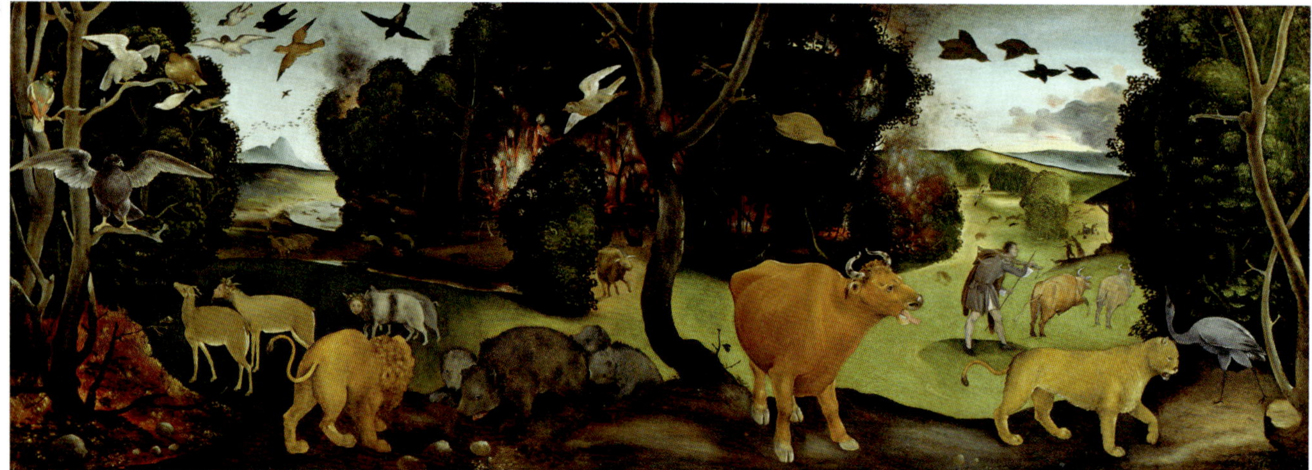

44

(fig.44) Piero di Cosimo (1462–1522), *The Forest Fire*, *c.*1505, oil on panel, 71.2 × 202 cm. Ashmolean Museum, University of Oxford, WA1933.2

(fig.45) *Yaksha*, second century CE, pink sandstone, 28 × 32 × 13 cm. Ashmolean Museum, University of Oxford, EA1996.76

The insects, like humans and animals, gain their strength from the sun. Surovi intends to showcase the beauty of nature's interdependence with humans, and its crucial role in sustaining life. The focus should not only be on individual efforts for climate care; it must also tackle the root causes of ecological challenges. The ants lead to roots, which, even when underwater, persist in their quest for air and growth (detail 7). By emphasising the roots, rather than trees in this space, Surovi focuses on hidden, yet vital, aspects of the environment, elements that nurture and inspire hope and life.

This work invites viewers to embark on a journey from darkness to light or vice versa, encouraging them to examine their own perspectives. Surovi intentionally leaves certain areas blank, offering room for contemplation about what might happen next, or what has already taken place. She invites questions and deeper thought from anyone engaging with the artwork. In the final image, shadows play a crucial role, highlighting spaces.

Surovi was struck by a painting in the Ashmolean's Italian Renaissance gallery, depicting a cow with its mouth wide open as it flees a burning forest (detail 8 and fig.44). The work, by Piero di Cosimo (1462–1522), compares well with Surovi's own ideas about illustrating humanity's relationship with nature, and the consequences of unrestrained actions. The painting, created around 1505, portrays a chaotic scene of a forest fire with animals, birds, and humans fleeing from the heat and danger. It serves as a reminder of the destructive power of nature and the importance of balance and preservation.

Under the cow, Surovi depicts a Yaksha figure, also inspired by an object in the Ashmolean collection (fig.45).

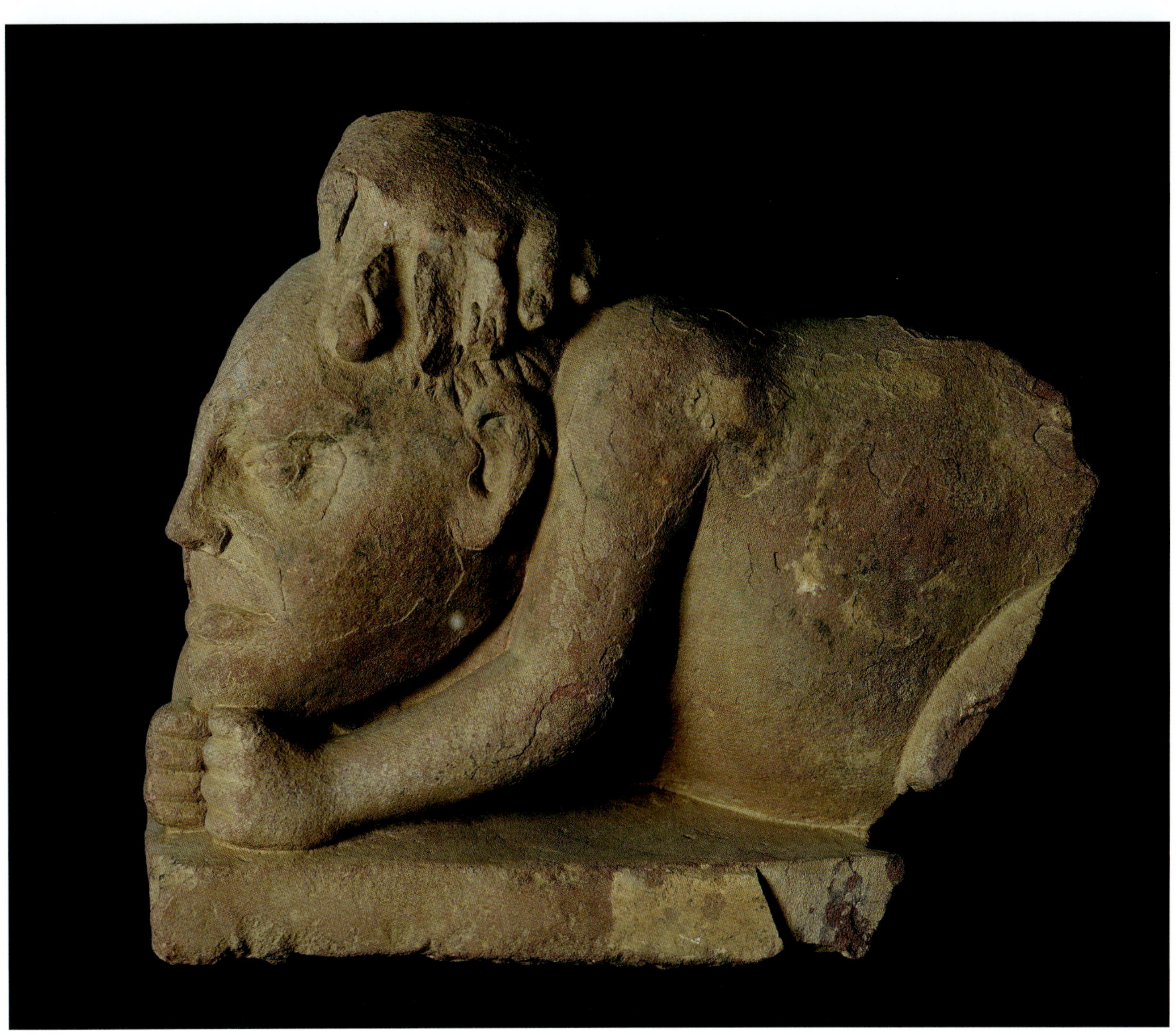

45

Like the female Yakshi, the Yaksha is a personified male nature spirit, a guardian figure with the power to protect and destroy. To the left is a politican and, upon closer inspection, one might spot a version of *The Thinker* (cast 1901) by Auguste Rodin (1840–1917), contemplating actively to engage with his environment. The two male figures represent politicians, who inflict damage by hindering collaboration and encouraging unrest through self-serving policies and nationalist priorities, which lead to economic and social harm. One of the figures is seen cutting a portion of the mangroves.

Another recurring motif in Surovi's work is bananas. Here the bananas appear on a television screen just above the two figures, a comment on the digital era, where the tangible seems just out of reach. At the bottom, a playful scene features two monkeys quietly exchanging thoughts, perhaps about real bananas, which in this picture exist solely in the digital world. Nearby, a woman holds a bag made from tiger skin, while a tiger is shown in a vulnerable moment, running, facing inevitable misfortune.

A significant portion of the world's challenges stem from decisions made by those in power. Many individuals share the feeling of helplessness in the face of these decisions. Surovi aims to convey enduring themes, urging the audience to look beyond particular historical scenarios, to not assign blame but to concentrate on the positive changes that can be made today. In the end, the focus should be on discovering hope, resilience, and the interconnectedness of life, while also addressing the more profound issue of inequality, which confronts society at present. Surovi ends the work with a definite void; a silence; a space for reflection.

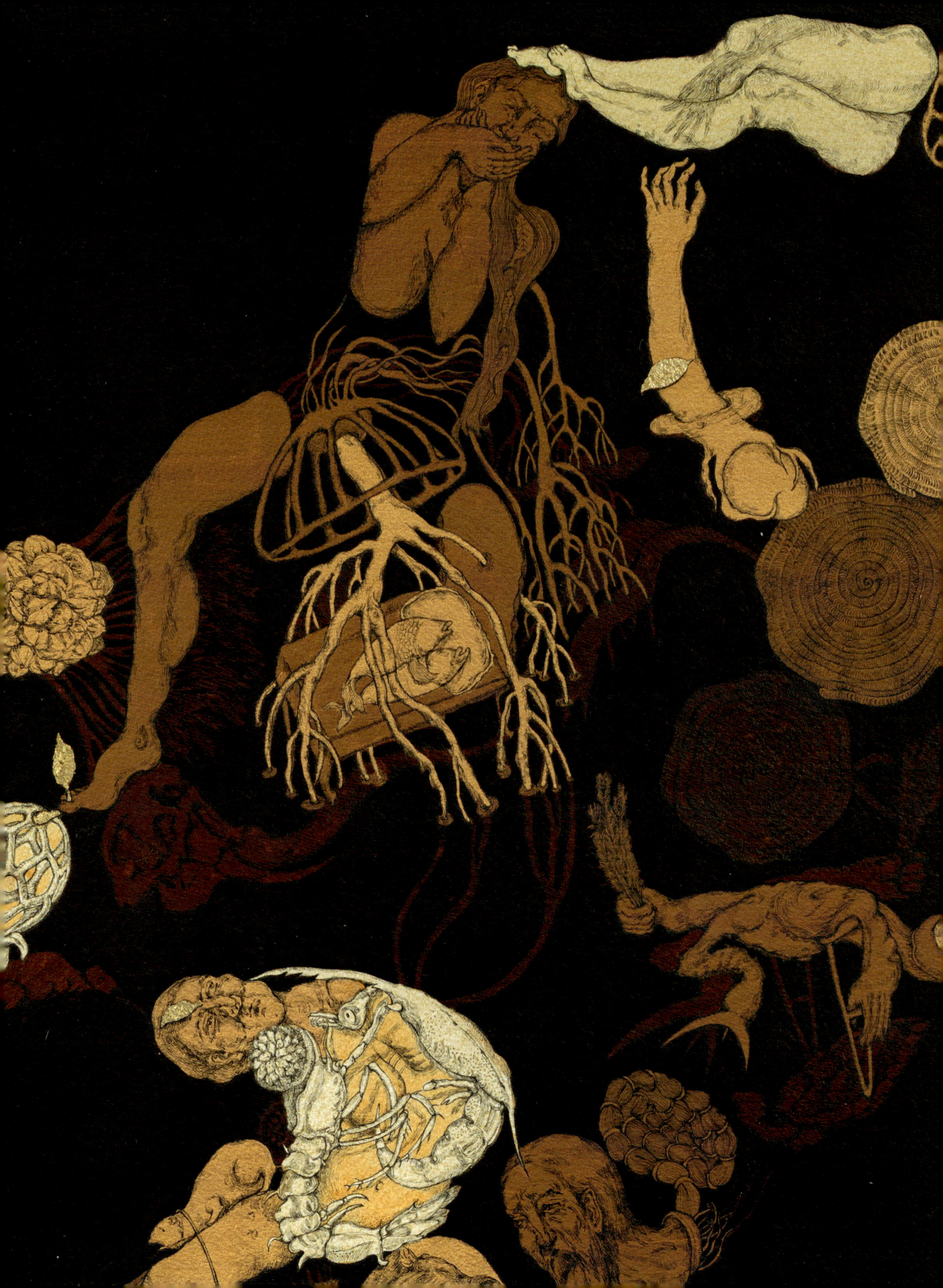

IN CONVERSATION

A series of conversations between the artist Soma Surovi Jannat (SSJ) and the curator Mallica Kumbera Landrus (MKL) took place between 2023 and 2025, in Oxford and Colombo, as well as online. What follows are excerpts from those various conversations.

Mallica Kumbera Landrus: I've always called you Surovi, since the moment we met in 2023, but I realise many people, especially in the art world, refer to you as Soma. Do you have a preference?

Soma Surovi Jannat: In my family, I'm called Surovi, which I mostly prefer, but I'm fine with both names. In the exhibition publication I would prefer Surovi, rather than Soma, and not my last name Jannat.

MKL: Let's dive into some of your earliest memories.

SSJ: I was born in 1990 at my maternal grandparents' home – a red-brick railway quarter in Lalmonirhat, a beautiful region in northern Bangladesh where my grandfather worked as a railway officer. Back then, Lalmonirhat still carried whispers of its past as a vibrant railway hub, though by my childhood it had grown quieter.

Some of my happiest memories are from long school breaks spent there. In the 1990s, without mobile phones or modern distractions, life felt slower, softer. My cousins, neighbourhood friends, and I would spend our days playing under the open sky – chasing each other through fields, fishing in ponds, and sharing picnic meals under shady trees.

Winter was my favourite. Evenings would draw us to the courtyard, where we sat huddled around a crackling fire. My grandparents and aunts would tell stories – some real, some magical – their voices weaving warmth into the cold night air. Those moments were pure, simple, and rich with love.

When I paint now, I find myself reaching back to that world; trying to hold on to the innocence, the unspoken closeness, and the quiet joy of a life rooted in genuine relationships.

MKL: Have there been any particular family traditions or practices that have influenced the way you think?

SSJ: My grandmother and mother had a strong ethic of resourcefulness and sustainability, never wasting anything. Their homes were filled with repurposed items such as old bottles, frames, and fabric pieces. They would often sew with leftover materials long before recycling gained popularity. Even now, my mother continues this practice, reusing many things instead of discarding them. My father also has an immense love for planting trees; in an area of our village that was once just sandy ground, my father and mother together planted nearly 1,000 trees. This approach has instilled in me a deep appreciation of caring for our environment.

MKL: Have the places and things around you changed a lot since you were a kid?

SSJ: I fondly remember that, in the 1990s, we experienced six distinct seasons: summer, monsoon, autumn, late autumn, winter, and spring, each beautiful in its own way. Spending time in my village allowed me to truly appreciate these seasons. However, today in Bangladesh, it seems we only have two main seasons, a long summer and a short rainy period, with winter lasting just a few days.

Thinking back to my childhood, I recall that my school had spacious play areas, unlike many schools today, which are just buildings. In Dhaka, there are still a few fields and playgrounds where children can enjoy outdoor

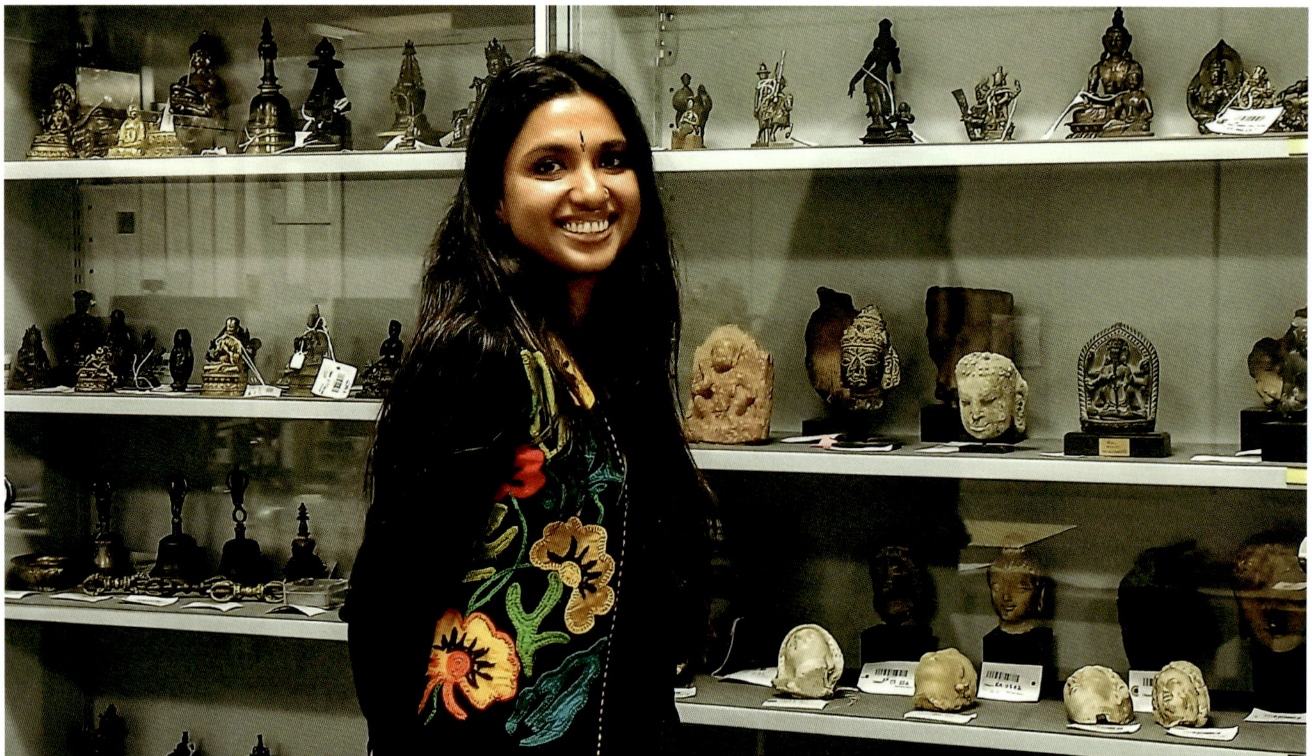

Soma Surovi Jannat in the Jameel Centre, Eastern Art Department, Ashmolean Museum, University of Oxford, 2023.

activities, but they are becoming increasingly rare – like the last pages of an old story, slowly disappearing.

MKL: When you were a child, was there a specific moment or experience that made you interested in art?

SSJ: Since I was very little, even before I realised it, I loved to draw. I believe drawing is a natural way for children to express what they feel inside. I remember drawing not only in my drawing books but also on the walls of our home, which didn't please our landlord very much! Seeing how much I enjoyed drawing, my parents enrolled me in a weekend art school, Dhanmondi Art School, where my love for art grew even stronger.

One of my most cherished memories is receiving the book *Abol Tabol* from my uncle for my tenth birthday. This collection of Bengali nonsense poems and whimsical illustrations by Sukumar Ray (1887–1923) captivated me, and inspired me to explore drawing and storytelling even more. Those early days – full of fun, creativity, and support – remain some of my happiest childhood memories.

MKL: Can you say a little more about what it was like for you at the weekend art classes?

SSJ: After completing a three-year course at Dhanmondi Art School, my mother discovered a Russian cultural centre that offered advanced art classes, and she enrolled me there, placing me in the senior group despite me being only eleven, the youngest in the class. Most of the other students were older adults, either in college or already working. It was a diverse group, but my mother had faith in my skills. At that age, I didn't fully understand the significance of being among older students; I simply wanted to draw and paint.

We would go outdoors to study nature, and we experimented with various mediums like watercolours, oil paints, wood, clay, and even sculpture. I loved everything we did during that time; it became the highlight of my life. At my regular school, I was just an average student, particularly struggling in subjects like mathematics. However, in art class, I truly thrived. Both my art teacher and my mother encouraged me to develop my talent further and believed in my potential.

MKL: Having your mother support your interests, especially in the beginning, seems like it was really important.

SSJ: My mother encouraged me to enter various competitions and, thanks to her support, I won over twenty awards as a young artist. This achievement gave me confidence and solidified my desire to pursue art. I noticed that many of my classmates wanted to be artists too, but their parents didn't support their dreams, leading them to treat art as a mere hobby while focusing on their studies. I felt for them, but I was determined to avoid that same regret. I aimed to attend art college instead.

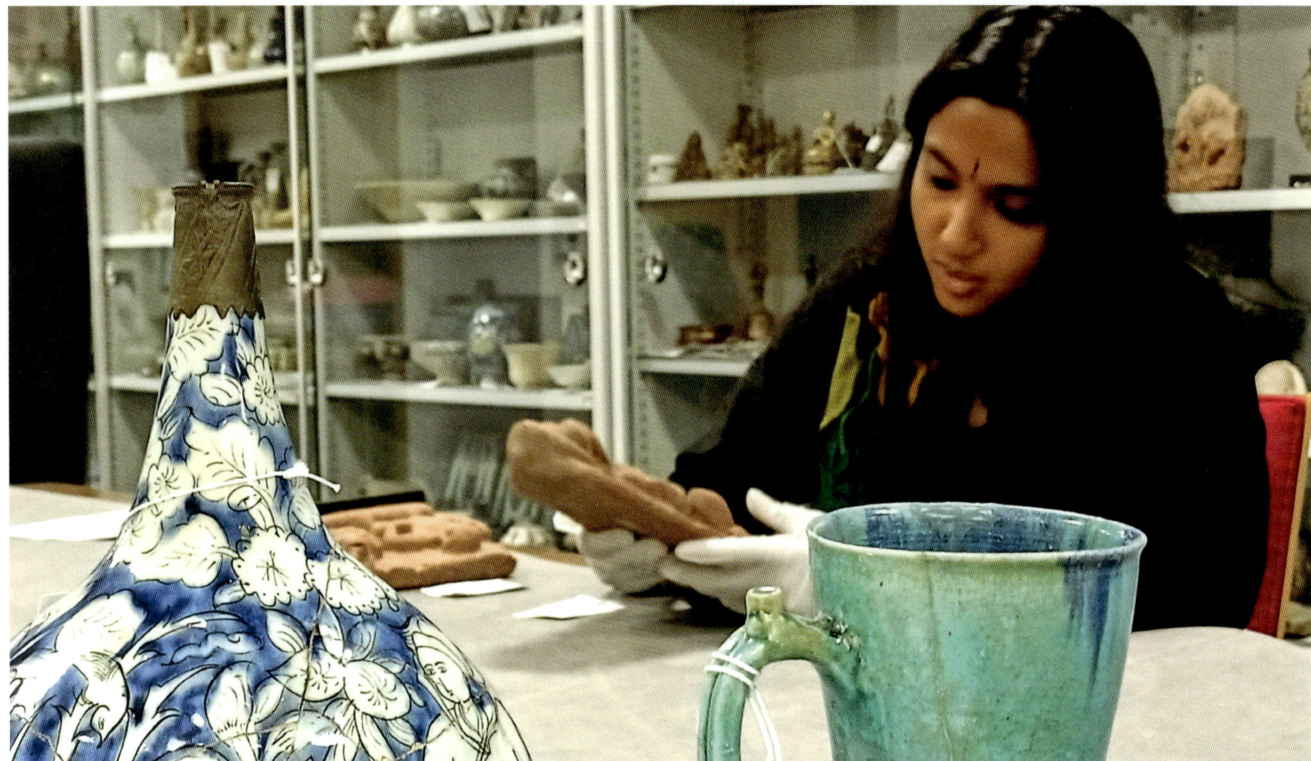

Soma Surovi Jannat in the Jameel Centre, Eastern Art Department, Ashmolean Museum, University of Oxford, 2023.

One day in 2002, I came across an article in the *Prothom Alo* newspaper about a sculpture exhibition, featuring an artist named Ferdousi Priyabhashini (1947–2018). There was a stunning image of the artist, with a large bindi on her forehead, standing beside her work. Excited, I shared this with my mother; she took me to see the exhibition, where I had the chance to meet the artist in person. The sculptures deeply moved me, and I thought I wanted to become a sculptor like Priyabhashini. Later I also learned about her experiences through her powerful autobiography, which spoke about her struggles in life and her work as a Bangladeshi freedom fighter.

MKL: What aspects of Priyabhashini's work and life do you find most inspiring?

SSJ: While many in Bangladesh believed the struggle for freedom ended after 1971, for Priyabhashini, that was just the beginning. She became a prominent social activist, fighting for the rights of women, children, and especially rape victims. She spoke publicly about her own experiences, using her voice to advocate for those in need. Her sculptures, often created from simple materials like bamboo or tree branches, demonstrated how everyday objects could be transformed into something extraordinary. This inspired me to pursue sculpting as well.

MKL: Did your parents have an interest in the arts themselves?

SSJ: Yes, they had and have an immense interest in art. My mother, Halima Rashid, who studied Islamic history, had a passion for singing and dancing. She also enjoyed framing old photographs. Our home has always felt like a gallery. Whenever my mother discovered my drawings, she would cut them out and proudly display them on our walls. Even now, my mother is the first person I show my artwork to after completing it, and she has a very natural eye for critiquing art.

My father, Mohammed Harun ur Rashid, was a pioneering engineer who personally designed and manufactured medical equipment by hand in Bangladesh. He was among the first in his field to combine technical skill with hands-on craftsmanship in creating these machines. My first art teachers were my *Abbu* (father) and *Ammu* (mother), who taught me how to draw simple objects like mangoes and trees, as well as scenes from the freedom fighting of Bangladesh. They were my initial guides on this artistic journey.

MKL: Your parents seem to be very kind, caring, and always there for you.

SSJ: Yes, I feel very lucky to have such supportive parents. Growing up in a middle-class family, my parents quietly made many sacrifices to encourage my passion for art. My mother was always vocal and proud of my work. My father was more reserved, but his quiet support was just as strong – he always prioritised giving us the best, even if it meant making sacrifices for himself.

I remember in seventh grade, when I wanted expensive art supplies like oil paints, many people around us thought it was wasteful. But my parents understood how important it was to me and did their best to provide what I needed. My mother even sewed my clothes larger so they would last longer, saving money in other ways so I could have what I wanted.

They never made me feel guilty for dreaming big, which really helped me grow confident in pursuing my art. Their support was a constant presence in my life, even if it was quiet at times.

I also feel grateful that my family encouraged all of us equally – my brothers are talented musicians and have followed their own creative paths, and I've always felt free to chase mine.

When I hear stories from others about the struggles girls face to be artists, I realise how fortunate I've been to have parents who stood by me so firmly. Their kindness and care shaped not only my art but also who I am today.

MKL: What difficulties do girls in Bangladesh face today?

SSJ: Girls in Bangladesh face many challenges today that deeply affect their childhood and dreams. In cities like Dhaka, safe places to play and be carefree are scarce, and this worries me a lot. Safety is a constant concern because so many children, especially girls, suffer violence and abuse – often from people they trust. It breaks my heart to think how these hardships force children to grow up too fast, losing the simple joys and freedom every child deserves.

Education, which should be a gateway to a better future, is often cut short by poverty, early marriage, and social pressures. On top of that, many girls face attitudes that discourage them from following their passions or expressing themselves creatively.

MKL: Did you have art classes as part of your regular school subjects too?

SSJ: Yes, I had art classes until grade eight. I remember one time when a craftsman came to our school and asked us to draw lines on the board. From those lines, he made all kinds of interesting pictures. It was fun and really sparked my imagination. After that, I kept playing with lines at home, trying to make new shapes, and my brothers and friends joined in too. Even though I switched to science in high school, art has always been close to my heart.

MKL: Given the intense pressure children often face to excel in their studies, especially on the subcontinent where there's a strong emphasis on science, how did you persuade your parents to let you attend a fine arts college instead?

SSJ: At the time of my admission, I was feeling quite unhappy with the idea of following the usual path my parents had in mind, like architecture. Secretly, I reached out to my weekend art teacher, Kakon didi, for guidance on how to get into art college. She encouraged me to join a coaching programme and promised to speak to my mother if I did well.

When my mother noticed I was often away, I shared my plans with her. She was supportive, though a bit unsure at first. But, when I ranked first in the admission test, her hesitation vanished, and she wholeheartedly supported my decision.

With Kakon didi's advice, I chose painting at Dhaka University, which allowed me to explore many creative fields. Getting into fine arts in 2007 was a proud and life-changing moment, made possible by my parents' quiet but strong support.

MKL: Could you share some of your experiences as an undergraduate studying fine arts at Dhaka University?

SSJ: Due to a session jam (a delay in completing university studies on time, often due to political unrest, strikes, or administrative delays in Bangladesh), my first year at Dhaka University stretched to eighteen months. This gave me the unexpected chance to really dive deep into improving my drawings. During this time, I was fortunate to study under Shishir Bhattacharjee (b.1960), a renowned artist and political cartoonist whose work and passion inspired me and shaped my artistic vision.

In 2008, I found myself drawn into a powerful moment for artistic freedom when I actively joined protests against the demolition of the Lalon sculpture. That experience opened my eyes to the importance of protecting our cultural heritage. Shahbagh, where our campus is located, has always been alive with political energy, and I often felt both the excitement and responsibility of being part of these movements.

IN 2008, I FOUND MYSELF DRAWN INTO A POWERFUL MOMENT FOR ARTISTIC FREEDOM WHEN I ACTIVELY JOINED PROTESTS AGAINST THE DEMOLITION OF THE LALON SCULPTURE.

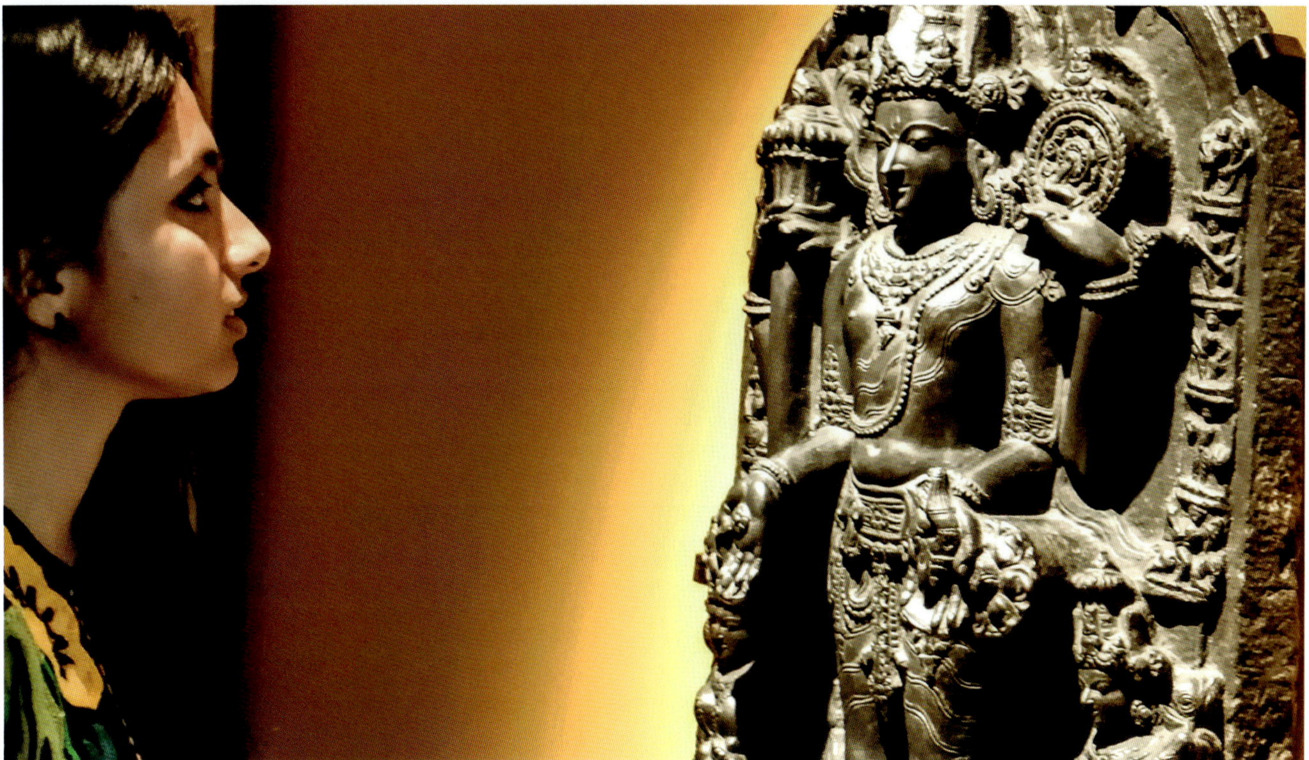

Soma Surovi Jannat in the Indian Gallery, Ashmolean Museum, University of Oxford, 2023.

Then, in 2013, the Shahbagh Movement erupted across the country, demanding justice – capital punishment for the war criminals of 1971 and the banning of Jamaat-e-Islami. Alongside my fellow fine arts students, I marched with flags and candles, driven not just by a political cause, but by a deep, personal commitment to justice and the freedom to express ourselves through art.

MKL: How did these interruptions affect your time at university?

SSJ: They shaped my experience at Dhaka University in good ways. Because of the session jam, my bachelor's degree ultimately took six years instead of four. The delays, mainly caused by student political activities disrupting exams and academic sessions, could have been frustrating, but they also gave me unexpected time to focus deeply on my art and personal growth.

Much of our learning was practical, i.e. drawing and hands-on projects both inside the classroom and in outdoor locations like parks, zoos, riverbanks, and even busy hubs like Kamalapur railway station. Working in these spaces, observing life and the struggles of the people around me, gave me a unique perspective and a deeper understanding of society. Some male classmates stayed late into the night to draw, and though I didn't join them, I often imagined what it would feel like to sketch freely in the city at midnight – a freedom I hope future generations of girls in Bangladesh will enjoy.

Overall, these interruptions taught me patience, resilience, and the value of engaging fully with both my art and my surroundings. While the journey was longer than expected, it made my university experience immersive, reflective, and deeply meaningful, shaping how I approach creativity and life even today.

MKL: What types of social activities were you involved in?

SSJ: At university, I tried to be involved in a variety of social and cultural activities that made campus life lively and engaging. One of the biggest was *Pohela Boishakh*, the Bengali New Year. We organised a colourful Shobha Jatra rally, made masks and decorations, and invited local artisans to showcase their art and crafts. It was a wonderful way to come together, learn from each other, and enjoy the spirit of the community.

We also celebrated smaller seasonal events, like a Mango Festival, where we gathered mangoes, made juice and pickles, and shared food with everyone – simple joys that brought us closer as a group.

Outside of festivals, I often worked on figure drawing and other art projects with classmates, mostly in outdoor locations like Suhrawardy Udyan. These informal sessions were just as important to my artistic growth as classroom

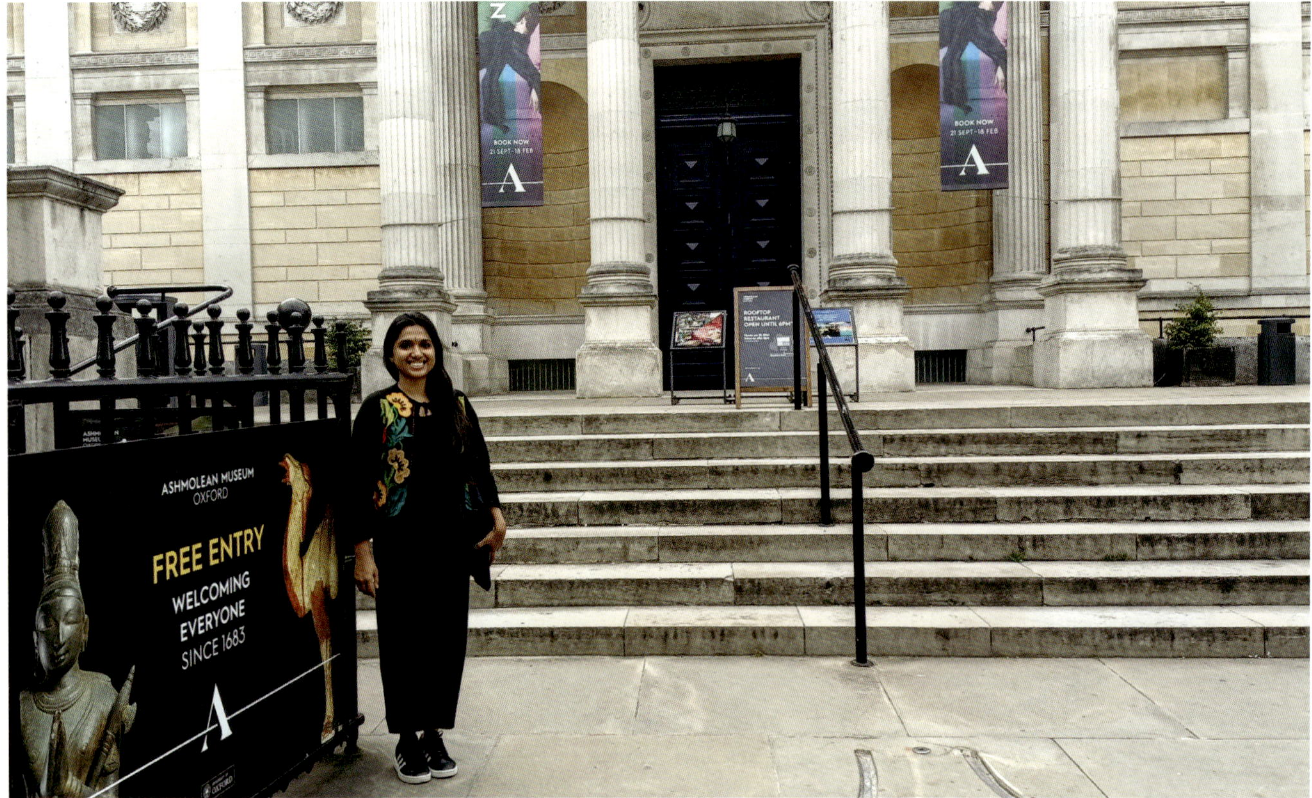

Soma Surovi Jannat, Ashmolean Museum, University of Oxford, August 2023.

lessons. I also taught weekend art classes to children, which allowed me to share my skills and connect with others while earning a bit of pocket money. Participating in these activities not only enriched my university experience, but also helped me develop a sense of community, collaboration, and creative expression.

MKL: Could you provide some additional information about the institute?

SSJ: The institute I attended, known as the Faculty of Fine Arts at Dhaka University, was established in 1948 under the leadership of Shilpacharya Zainul Abedin (1914–1976). Recognised as the pioneer of modern art education in Bangladesh, Zainul Abedin played a pivotal role in shaping the institution's direction. Initially named the Government Institute of Art, it began with just six teachers and eighteen students, focusing on nurturing traditional and modern artistic practices.

In 1963, the curriculum expanded to include theoretical subjects alongside practical training, marking a significant development in the institute's academic structure. However, during my time there, the emphasis remained predominantly on realism and technical skills, with limited encouragement for experimental or contemporary approaches. This westernised focus sometimes felt restrictive, especially for students eager to explore diverse artistic expressions.

Despite these constraints, the institute's rich history and the legacy of its founders provided a solid foundation for artistic development. Over time, I've observed a shift towards greater openness to innovation and experimentation, reflecting the evolving landscape of art education in Bangladesh.

MKL: You were quite young back then, and I'm curious about how you managed your work, friendships, and family life. Did these years have a big impact on your life or your future career?

SSJ: Growing up, I had experiences that made me feel unsafe and later, in 2010, my family faced financial difficulties that profoundly affected me. During that time, I found solace in religion, listening to Islamic scholars, praying, and developing a love for Arabic calligraphy. I even started learning Arabic at Dhaka University, though I didn't complete the course. I often felt out of place in public, and came to believe that wearing a hijab and dressing modestly would help me be treated with respect in Bangladesh, rather than judged by stereotypes.

I've always respected the hijab as a personal choice, a way for women to express and protect themselves.

I chose to wear it myself and without any pressure from my family. While my parents treated me equally, society often didn't.

University was a liberating space where I met diverse people and maintained my religious practices. Wearing a hijab helped me focus on prayer, though some peers misunderstood my intentions, assuming I had become more conservative or even joined extremist groups. This led to feelings of isolation, but I saw it as a challenge to prove that a girl in a hijab could thrive while feeling comfortable in her clothing.

I also sensed subtle misjudgements from some professors, particularly during the selection process for a residency at the Slade in London. I had the chance to participate in a drawing workshop led by Lisa Milroy (b.1959), who taught me the power of metaphor in art – a lesson that has stayed with me. Excited to be the top student eligible for the one-month Slade residency, I was heartbroken when, during a short holiday in my village, the opportunity was given to another male student. Despite my efforts and achievements, the selection process felt vague and unfair, leaving an impression on me.

MKL: Did you express your feelings about what happened or ask your teachers for clarification?

SSJ: I didn't voice my disappointment at the time. I kept it to myself. When I was at Shantiniketan in India, there was a system where students who excelled in the first semester had the opportunity to study briefly in France. One student had excellent grades, but due to his disability, he struggled to communicate effectively with his peers. Several students approached our teachers, seeking the opportunity to be awarded to them instead. However, my teachers at Shantiniketan were fair and decided to give the chance to that student, recognising his hard work despite his disabilities. I thought this was fair and appropriate, which contrasted sharply with my experience in Dhaka.

MKL: You've stopped wearing a hijab. When did you make that decision?

SSJ: My perspective began to shift when I moved to Santiniketan. Over time, I felt a sense of safety and freedom from judgement there, which gave me the confidence to remove it. It's not that I am against wearing the hijab; in fact, I have great respect for it. But that experience made me realise something important, that clothing by itself cannot protect you from harm; it's ultimately people's attitudes and behaviours that shape how safe you feel. From that point onward, I decided to wear clothing that made me feel comfortable. In Bangladesh, there is a saying that encourages us to dress appropriately for different places. I noticed that many Europeans visiting the subcontinent wore sarees or kurtas, which showed respect for our culture.

While dressing in a way that is comfortable for me is important, I am also aware of the judgements I might face. In certain neighbourhoods in Dhaka, I feel more comfortable wearing a t-shirt and trousers. However, I often find it necessary to wear a dupatta to cover my head when I'm out, primarily due to the way people look at me. Women are frequently judged for their clothing choices, and this attention can be uncomfortable, often coming from other women.

ULTIMATELY, I'VE LEARNED THAT COVERING UP DOESN'T GUARANTEE SAFETY, AND IT IS ESSENTIAL TO BE TRUE TO ONESELF.

Ultimately, I've learned that covering up doesn't guarantee safety, and it is essential to be true to oneself. These days, though now rare, I choose to wear a hijab out of cultural and religious respect, but I also dress in a way that makes me feel at ease. I am incredibly grateful that my family has accepted me as I am, regardless of how I choose to dress. They have never judged me based on whether I wear a hijab or not.

MKL: There was a moment when I thought about studying art history in Shantiniketan. I even had the chance to visit Shantiniketan and meet K. G. Subramanyam (1924–2016). Ultimately, I chose to go to Baroda before heading to the United States in 1995. When did you decide you wanted to study in India? Did you find the experiences of living in Dhaka/Bangladesh and Shantiniketan/India, to be very different?

SSJ: The difference between Dhaka and Shantiniketan was striking, especially in terms of noise; Dhaka was chaotic and loud, while Shantiniketan offered a serene atmosphere. Over time, even Shantiniketan has become a bit noisier with more auto rickshaws, but the contrast remains.

I decided to study in India quite unexpectedly. Inspired by the Indian Council for Cultural Relations (ICCR) scholarship, I applied despite only having eighteen days and no passport or ID. With my mother's calm encouragement and the help of a friend, I received my acceptance from Shantiniketan, along with a generous scholarship.

Life there was a significant change. I lived in an ashram, ate mostly vegetarian meals without ginger, garlic, or onion, and travelled by bicycle. Each student had their own studio, and I was fortunate to have the largest, which allowed me to work on a 70-foot-long canvas; something impossible in the cramped classrooms of Dhaka.

Academically, Shantiniketan was transformative. Instead of memorising facts and dates, we engaged in discussions with peers and visiting artists, deepening our

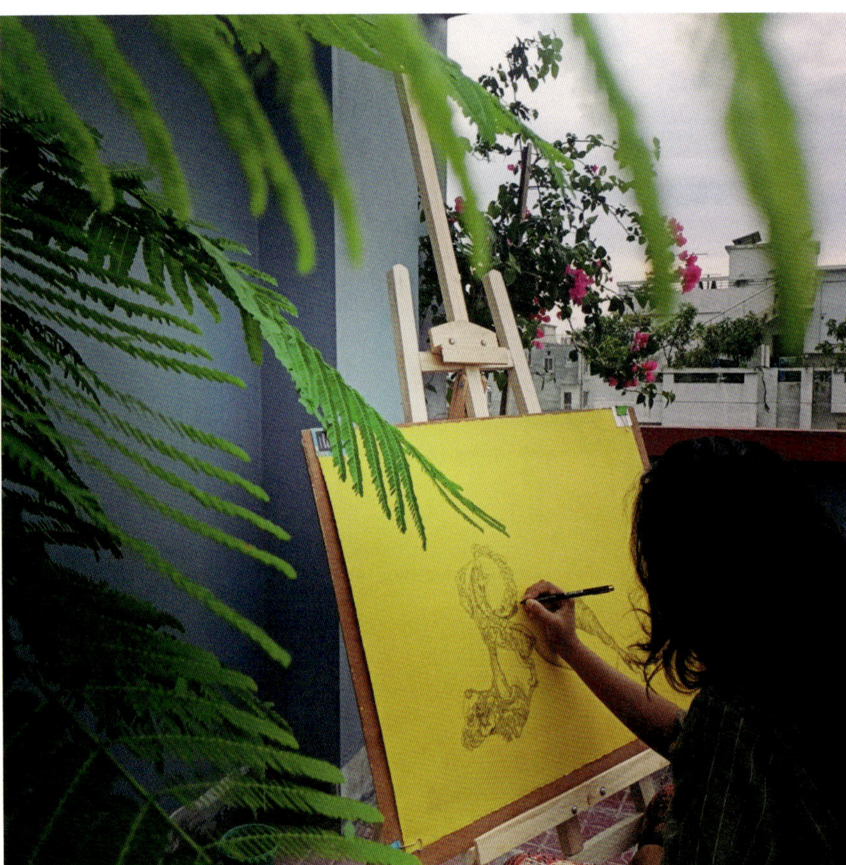

Soma Surovi Jannat in Dhaka, Bangladesh, at home on her terrace, working on the painting *Where Every Leaf Holds a Tale (Tiger Leg)*, 2024. (7.8)

understanding of art. Many classes were outdoors under trees, the library was large and accessible, and we met renowned artists like Sudhir Patwardhan (b.1949) and Atul Dodiya (b.1959). The Centre for Interdisciplinary Arts (CIAS) in Kala-Bhavan became a special space for films, discussions, and informal learning.

I also participated in art tours organised by an art historian from Mumbai, visiting Mahabalipuram, Thanjavur, Pondicherry, Chennai, and museums like CSMVS Mumbai, Indian Museum Kolkata, and the National Gallery of Modern Art Delhi. Exploring local homes and communities in Haryana and Mumbai suburbs broadened my perspective on Indian art and culture. Meeting students from across India further enriched my experience, minimising judgements based on background.

Some realities, however, were familiar: both Dhaka and Shantiniketan had only one female faculty member, and girls had to leave the studio by 10pm, while boys could stay out late. This was a reminder of broader safety issues for women on the subcontinent.

MKL: I'm interested in the ashram you brought up earlier. Could you share more about it?

SSJ: The Radha Krishna Ashram, where I lived in Shantiniketan, was a beautiful place. The student hostel for women had early curfews, closing at 8:30pm, which often felt too early, especially when I had work to finish and dinner to eat. The women's international hostel was farther away and had many restrictions. However, in the ashram, I enjoyed more freedom and had my own room, which made for a comfortable living situation. There were only a few girls from other departments in the ashram, creating a unique sense of community. The atmosphere was peaceful and affordable, allowing me to enjoy good, simple vegetarian food and the company of wonderful peers. Every morning, I woke up to the soothing sounds of the girls from Sangeet Bhavan practising their music, which added to the meditative quality of my mornings there.

I used to spend time at the ashram during festival celebrations. There, I would do makeup on the little boys and girls, dressing them up as Krishna. I loved using blue face paint, decorating the girls with flowers in their hair, and helping them wear beautiful sarees. The ashram was a sacred place with a temple and provided accommodation for girls. As a Muslim, I never felt uncomfortable there.

I would pray in my room during Ramadan, when I would wake up very early to have a meal before sunrise, and Nepal Dada, who took care of the place, would prepare food for me. He would even come to my door to wake me up before sunrise. Overall, my experience there was very positive. I felt a deep respect for the space and never felt that my religion or beliefs were disrespected. It was a comforting environment, and I felt secure there, unlike in some other places where locking my door was a constant worry. As time went on, I encountered many new ideas, experiences, and friendships.

MKL: Have you gone back to Shantiniketan since you finished your studies?

SSJ: After I graduated in 2016, I returned to Dhaka on 15 August. I spent a few months there, but felt a strong desire to return to Shantiniketan, where I had felt more at ease and free from political tensions. It was my mother who encouraged me to go back for a visit, so I obtained a tourist visa and returned. Upon my arrival, I didn't have a studio space since I was no longer a student. The ashram rooms were full, but Nepal Dada helped me find an available room near the Santal village.

Without the pressure to participate in exhibitions, I had the freedom to explore my creativity. I devoted a lot of time to drawing. Without a studio or financial stability, I took just a pen, rice paper, and canvas with me on a bicycle. I cycled to various locations in the area and spent most of my time drawing. As my tourist visa allowed for only a three-month stay in India, I focused solely on drawing, and fell in love with the process.

When I returned to Dhaka, I felt a sense of relief because I was free from the burden of working on large oil paintings that required a lot of space. I realised that I could draw anywhere in the world as long as I had simple materials. I also discovered that I truly loved Shantiniketan. At first, I thought my love was for the people around me, but after graduation, most of my friends moved to different cities. While I stayed in touch with some of my peers, ultimately, I realised it was the place – Shantiniketan –that I loved deeply.

Shantiniketan changed me, and in the process, I got to know myself better. During the monsoon season, I recall it rained every day, and I would step out into the rain, embracing the solitude both day and night. This time alone allowed me to truly connect with myself, away from family, friends, and any external pressure or judgement.

MKL: After finishing your studies, what came next?

SSJ: After graduating in 2016, the following year proved crucial for me. I abandoned the idea of a studio and began working in open spaces, travelling frequently, and developing my practice. This period of exploration culminated in my first solo exhibition in 2018, titled *Grey Contours.* That period was characterised by exploration and creativity for me. I made several trips to China, participated in Serendipity arts festival in Goa, moving back and forth between India and China, as well as visiting Bangladesh. In Bangladesh, I ventured into various locations, such as the Santal village and scenic spots like the hill tracks of Chittagong.

During my bachelor's studies, I taught art classes on weekends to children, which helped me financially during my university years. After my master's, I devoted myself fully to art, keeping my practice spontaneous and true to my vision, occasionally illustrating books or selling works, with my family's support sustaining me throughout.

I worked in a few art camps in Bangladesh. This provided some financial support for my own practice, allowing me to continue focusing on my art for several months. Much of my international travel was funded by others, while I financed most of my trips within Bangladesh myself. Limited resources sometimes sparked greater creativity, and, overall, these experiences have greatly enriched my life and practice.

MKL: It looks like you were travelling a lot starting in 2017. How did the Covid-19 pandemic and subsequent lockdown in 2020 impact your travels?

SSJ: The lockdown in 2020 certainly interrupted my travel plans, but it didn't slow down my practice. I've always tried to adapt to my surroundings, and during that time I attended two long programmes online, one based in Bangladesh and the other in London.

It was also during the pandemic that I met my husband, Siam, through a mutual friend. At first, we spoke only over the phone, and when we finally met in person we were both wearing masks. We discovered a shared love for art, culture, animals, and nature, and I was drawn to his sensitivity and openness. Today, he's not only my partner in life but also my greatest cheerleader, a thoughtful art critic, a dedicated animal lover, and someone deeply passionate about planting trees.

We married in December 2020, and shortly after that my father fell seriously ill with Covid. Through Siam's support, I realised that the focus and dedication we bring to our art can guide us through even the most uncertain moments in life.

MKL: Given that you obtained your master's degree four years prior to the pandemic, in what ways did this period affect you in your career?

SSJ: During that time, I faced both challenges and opportunities that significantly shaped my career. Initially, while I exhibited my work in Bangladesh and participated in various government exhibitions, I noticed that the

DURING THE MONSOON SEASON, I RECALL IT RAINED EVERY DAY, AND I WOULD STEP OUT INTO THE RAIN, EMBRACING THE SOLITUDE BOTH DAY AND NIGHT.

recognition I sought was limited. This period taught me a great deal about the politics of the art world and the factors that influence acknowledgement, particularly for younger, emerging artists.

A turning point came when I applied to the Dhaka Art Summit. My first attempt in 2018 was unsuccessful, but in 2020 I was selected as one of the top 11 artists. The experience included an interview with art historian, curator, and critic Philippe Pirotte, and a jury of international artists, which ensured a fair and enriching process. Winning my first award through this platform opened many doors, including a residency at Delfina in London, and helped my peers in the art community recognise and appreciate my work, especially my exploration of transitioning two-dimensional drawings into three-dimensional installations, which is a relatively uncommon approach in Bangladesh.

While the Covid-19 pandemic delayed my trip to Delfina until 2022, the overall journey has been transformative, providing me with recognition, opportunities, and a stronger sense of direction in my artistic practice.

MKL: Can you share your initial reactions when you were invited for the residency at the Ashmolean in 2023?

SSJ: It was during Ramadan, at iftar one evening, that I first noticed your email in my inbox. Seeing that it was from the University of Oxford completely surprised me. I replied right away and vividly recall the joy I felt after our initial virtual meeting. When you shared the details of the residency I felt immensely privileged and honoured. Now, as I look back, it's hard to grasp how many years have passed since that time. At that moment, I had not realised the significance it would have for me. I now reflect on how swiftly time has flown and the influence the Oxford experience has had on my life and work. Before I arrived, I experienced a range of emotions, primarily excitement. I was genuinely looking forward to being there, and I wasn't particularly anxious. The slight nervousness I felt vanished as soon as I met you, Mallica. Truly, the most beautiful part of this journey was getting to meet you. It is a memory I will always cherish.

MKL: It was a pleasure meeting you in Oxford, Surovi. And I am really thankful to Sree of Gallery Project 88 for connecting me with you. At that time, you didn't have a website or any social media presence, so I had no way of contacting you. Even though you aren't part of the Project 88 artists, Sree generously facilitated our introduction.

SSJ: I remember the moment I received an email from Sree of Project 88. She reached out to me, and I initially thought it might be related to an exhibition or something else from India. I sent her my portfolio, which I had already prepared for another potential project, so I did not need to prepare anything extra. I really appreciate her generosity and thoughtfulness in facilitating this introduction.

A TURNING POINT CAME WHEN I APPLIED TO THE DHAKA ART SUMMIT. MY FIRST ATTEMPT IN 2018 WAS UNSUCCESSFUL, BUT IN 2020 I WAS SELECTED AS ONE OF THE TOP 11 ARTISTS.

MKL: Recognition for the Frere Hall artist-in-residence initiative truly belongs to our benefactor, Taimur Hassan. He appreciates the importance of providing opportunities for artists based in South Asia, rather than limiting it to one specific country. His support has been selfless in aiding artists throughout the subcontinent.

SSJ: Absolutely, and I am immensely thankful for the chance to gain experience in Oxford. I have realised that having a residency, particularly one at the Ashmolean, is essential for many artists from the subcontinent. My time there kept me engaged and allowed me to reflect post-residency. During and after my time at the Ashmolean, I developed a greater sense of empathy toward history and museums. I discovered that these historical fragments could serve as metaphorical, and incredibly impactful, elements for my art.

I am especially grateful to Taimur Hassan, whose support made this residency possible. None of this would have been feasible without the sponsored artist-in-residence programme.

MKL: How was the Oxford experience?

SSJ: Coming from Dhaka, I found Oxford to be a friendly environment, which encouraged me to tap into my creativity and explore the collections without reservation. Several small moments stood out for me. For example, when I would arrive at the Museum early, the security guards greeted me warmly. Gestures like that truly mattered, especially when contrasted with other places where staff often appear unapproachable or overly formal. The warmth shown by the Ashmolean's team, whether from the guards or the Eastern Art team, resonated with me deeply. I took part in a few guided tours, and even in smaller groups, the staff treated us with such generosity. Those positive experiences made my time there unforgettable. I also cherish the connections I formed and the trust I developed during my residency, particularly with members of your team, like Ben Skarratt, Alessandra Cereda, Marie Sinclair, and Yuliia Spolitak. I couldn't be more appreciative of the experiences I've had.

Soma Surovi Jannat in Dhaka, Bangladesh, at home, working on the painting *Between the Sea and the Sky, Who Holds the Ground?*, 2024–25 (fig.28).

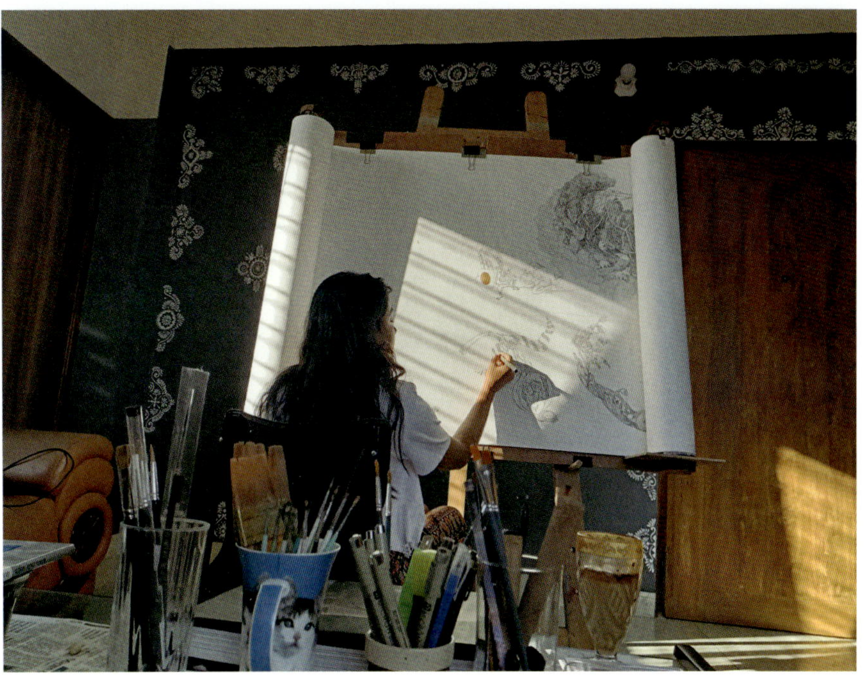

In the Eastern Art Department, creating a safe and welcoming environment seemed to be a high priority. Honestly, even though you mentioned that I would have full access to the works in the collections, I didn't anticipate the level of access I received. Initially, I believed that only those formally trained in museum studies or research could access the collections due to particular permissions and expertise. However, at the Ashmolean, it felt almost magical, like a scene from a tale where a genie grants you wishes! When I visited the Jameel Centre, they inquired if there was anything specific that I wanted to see, which made me a bit anxious. You suggested I make requests in advance. Your team was incredibly accommodating, and in the final weeks of my residency, they provided even broader access to works in the stores.

This experience granted me a delightful sense of freedom that I hadn't anticipated. I had initially assumed that the Museum would be a rigid environment where I would need to tread carefully. Instead of feeling apprehensive, I felt inspired and attentive in an affectionate way. Over the month I spent there, there were days I was alone and on others I encountered numerous individuals studying in the same research room. Researchers, scholars, professors, students, and the general public, all these visitors enriched my experience. While examining the objects I had requested, I noticed how others also interacted with the works they had chosen to see. I gained so much through these exchanges, even though I can't recall the names of every person who visited the study room.

I was captivated by the vibrant colours and textures of the objects, initially forgetting to analyse them critically. I was astonished that I was allowed to actually handle objects. My attention was mainly drawn to the beauty of the artworks, overlooking any technical aspects. My earlier experiences, with photographs and paintings, allowed me to appreciate everything I encountered, and I was interested in how others perceived the artworks as well. By the conclusion of my residency, I realised there was an abundance of works still to explore! The team was keen to ensure I had ample opportunity to discover as much as possible in the time left. They encouraged me to review works that I hadn't initially selected. The artist-in-residence following me, Anindita Bhattacharya (b.1985), shared a similar experience – the staff also urged her to view pieces she hadn't originally chosen, motivating her to examine all the paintings stored in the boxes available.

I came to understand that while I had previously seen some of these images in books, experiencing them in person was an entirely different sensation. My surprise peaked when I discovered the extensive collection of

EACH DAY, I WOULD RISE EARLY, AROUND 5AM, AND SPEND QUIET HOURS CONTEMPLATING AND CREATING IN THE MORNING LIGHT. MY FLAT ON THE TERRACE, WHICH OVERLOOKED THE OXFORD SKYLINE, WAS IDYLLIC.

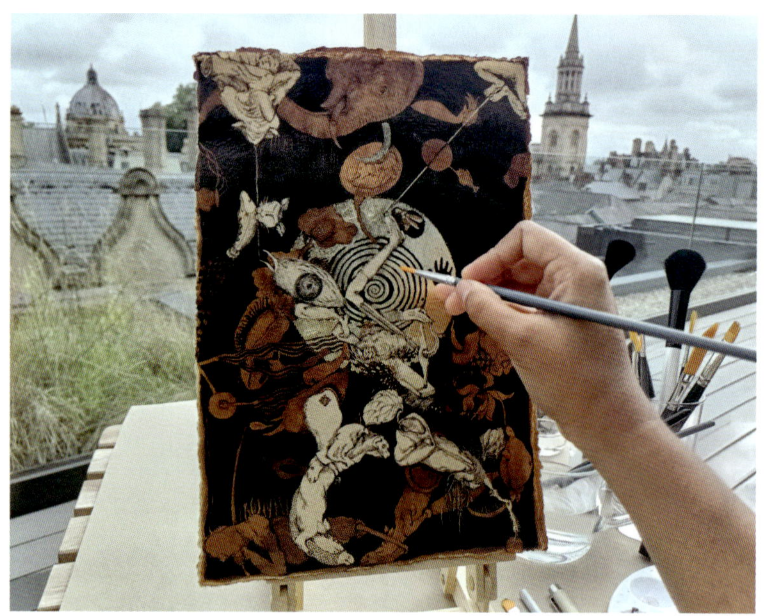

Soma Surovi Jannat in Jesus College, Oxford, during her residency at the Ashmolean, working on the painting *Resensitizing the Brown Narrative*, 2023 (fig.2)

nineteenth-century ethnographic clay figures, particularly those from Krishnanagar in West Bengal, India. I had never encountered anything quite like them before, and their size and intricacy left me in awe. I am really thankful to the entire Ashmolean team, whose warmth, guidance, and openness transformed this experience into a space of learning, inspiration, and connection.

MKL: Although I know that you enjoyed your residency, you later expressed that it took several months for you to truly comprehend its importance. Could you elaborate on how this experience has impacted you on a personal level and whether it has also sparked inspiration in your artistic practice?

SSJ: The word that comes to mind is 'transformational'. My visit altered my perception of history and has left a lasting impression on my work. It's fascinating to observe the connections that exist across cultures and eras. At the Jameel Centre, I found myself engrossed in the concept of crossing boundaries that link both culture and history. I also acquired the publication, *The Ashmolean Museum: Crossing Cultures, Crossing Time* (2017), and this resonated with me, since my work frequently investigates links between various locations and periods. I believe that this experience has also influenced my research methods, which have become both more relaxed and more focused. I began taking notes at the Museum and have kept a diary to document my thoughts and reflections, transforming the way I engage with art. This is an ongoing journey, and this more tranquil approach has allowed me to delve deeper into my work.

Since the residency in Oxford, I have become more organised. In the past, I struggled to maintain order, often feeling uncertain about my approach. My process used to be more instinctive, and reactive. Collaborating with you has provided a soothing influence as you anticipate my needs and respond efficiently. You've contributed to my sense of calm, and through this experience, I've gained so many insights.

Even my friends and colleagues have noticed a difference in my post-residency series. They pointed out that my earlier works exhibited a hurried energy in my pen lines, while the newer pieces appear much more serene and intentional. Each line seems to convey its own emotion, reflecting the time and effort I have put into them. I drew a great deal of inspiration from the exquisite details of various artefacts at the Ashmolean, especially the miniature paintings and sculptures. I was also intrigued by the small, yet meaningful artefacts showcased in the Egyptian galleries, admiring how museums cherish and preserve even the smallest pieces. These encounters motivated me to pay greater attention to every detail in my drawings. Furthermore, the complex compositions found in traditional *ragamala* and Mughal miniature paintings further stimulated my creativity. In the end, I aimed to capture a similar level of detail and emotion in my own work.

I've noticed that my work has become more complex and layered since the Ashmolean residency. Rather than progressing in a straightforward way, I now delve deeper into my ideas, uncovering what truly lies beneath the surface. This increased depth has introduced me to new concepts and images in my artwork that I hadn't previously acknowledged. I've discovered that certain aspects, such as symbols and themes, really ignite my creativity. In the past, I focused on experimenting with my art, but I wasn't as interested in trying out new materials. Now, I'm exploring how to use materials more effectively in my creations. I've come to understand that there's a significant depth to the narratives I wish to convey through my work. It's important to me that people from around the world connect and resonate with what I produce. My experiences at the Ashmolean and our discussions have greatly helped me comprehend a more global audience.

My experience at Delfina was quite different to that at the Ashmolean, as I was part of a group of eight artists. We not only formed personal connections but also exchanged artistic practices. Despite the limitations imposed by Covid, there were chances to visit artists' studios in London. I had the opportunity to meet several, including Rana Begum (b.1977), who graciously invited me into her space. Also, Oswaldo Maciá (b.1960) visited me in Delfina. It was a valuable experience where I could present my portfolio, talk about my creative approach, and consider how to advance my work. The freedom to explore museums and exhibitions made my time at Delfina both enjoyable and flexible.

However, my stay in Oxford felt much more introspective, personal, and productive. With a vast array of museums and attractions to explore in Oxford, I initially found it overwhelming. But after a few days, I achieved a sense of tranquillity and clarity regarding my weekly goals. Being in Oxford gave me the chance to spend meaningful time alone, reflecting on my practice and drawing inspiration from my environment, as well as from the staff and visitors at the Ashmolean. This focused time allowed me to connect more deeply with my own creative process.

MKL: It seems that you appreciated organising plans and enjoyed your own company in Oxford.

SSJ: During my residency at the Ashmolean Museum, while I was housed at Jesus College, my mornings were serene. Each day, I would rise early, around 5am, and spend quiet hours contemplating and creating in the morning light. My flat on the terrace, which overlooked the Oxford skyline, was idyllic. This solitude did not feel isolating; rather, it gave me space to ponder and uncover my own ideas. My time there felt structured and soothing, which greatly aided my focus.

I loved spending time in the Botanic Garden, sitting for hours in bookshops, and walking through Oxford's streets. These quiet moments gave me space to reflect and absorb the subtle rhythms of my surroundings.

Many artist residencies host several artists simultaneously, which is excellent for networking. However, the Ashmolean residency accommodates one artist at a time. This is quite uncommon, and I believe it offers numerous advantages. By focusing on a single artist, it fosters deeper involvement and personalised attention, which can be challenging to achieve when multiple artists are present. The act of creating art often necessitates solitude, and I think many artists generally favour working independently.

Reflecting on my time in Santiniketan, where I began shifting my painting style from Western influences to something more intertwined with my cultural roots, I saw how the right environment and thoughtful guidance encourage experimentation. One of my instructors noticed my use of highlights and encouraged me to release preconceived notions about art, motivating me to take creative risks.

Ultimately, my experiences both in Shantiniketan and at the Ashmolean have highlighted for me the significance of environment, solitude, and personal development in my artistic journey.

MKL: I've seen images of some of your earlier, pre-Oxford works. Would it be accurate to say that your art has significantly developed in the last decade?

SSJ: Yes, over the past decade my work has changed and grown in ways that feel both natural and deliberate. My earlier pieces were more intuitive, but over time I've learned to immerse myself fully in layers of emotion, especially those found in nature. Feedback from peers encouraged me to explore contrasts and subtle complexities, which led me to a more thoughtful, patient approach. My residency at the Ashmolean in Oxford was particularly transformative. For example, studying Mughal and Rajput miniatures up close taught me how layers of colour, texture, and detail can carry emotion and narrative in quiet, profound ways. I've realised that while some colours, like certain blues, don't resonate with me, others, such as warm browns with touches of gold, allow me to capture the depth and richness I feel in the world around me.

Even as my work engages with intricate and sensitive themes, I strive to balance them with beauty, hope, and empathy. I am drawn to fragments – objects, memories, and landscapes – that carry traces of resilience, disruption, or overlooked lives. There's a continuity between my early and recent work: a commitment to observing closely, listening deeply, and translating lived experiences into visual stories that invite reflection, wonder, and connection. For me, each piece is a conversation across time, a way to honour what has been, and to imagine what might be.

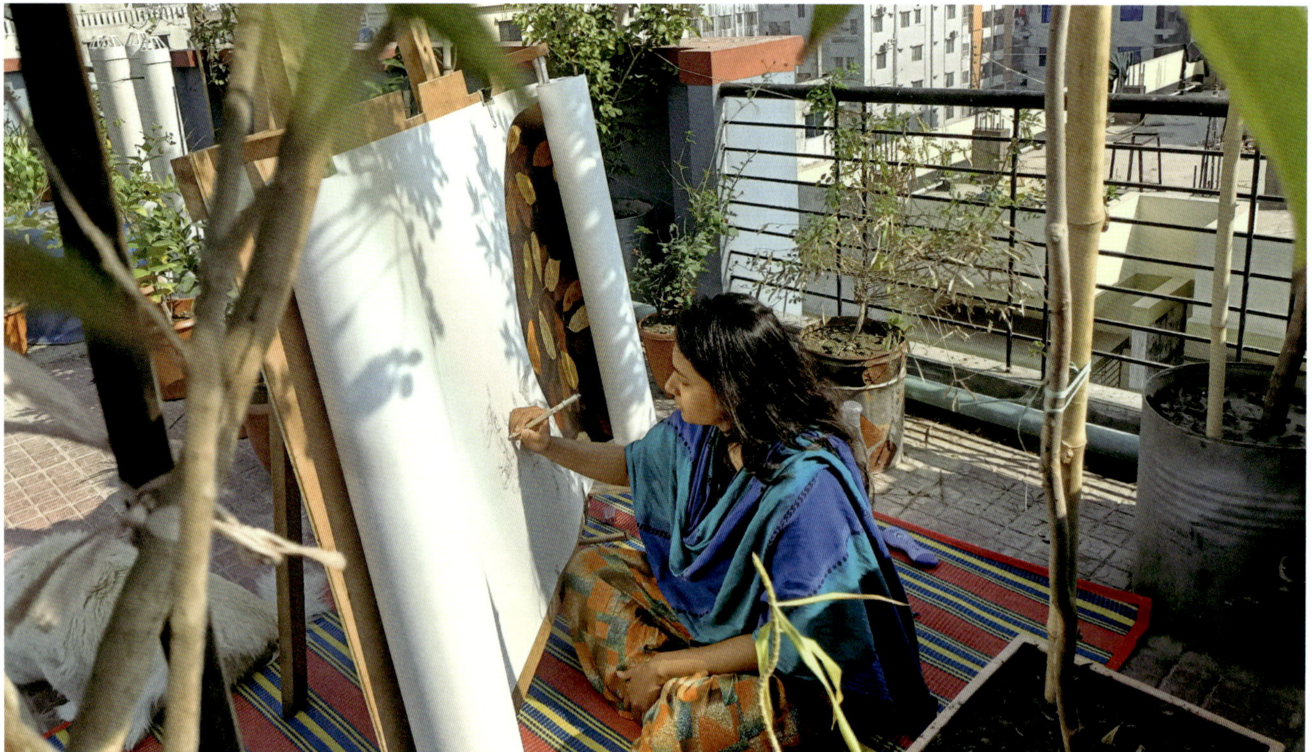

Soma Surovi Jannat in Dhaka, Bangladesh, at home on her terrace, working on the painting *Between the Sea and the Sky, Who Holds the Ground?*, 2024–25. (fig.28)

MKL: You've captured the essence, in my opinion, of one of my favourite artists, Nilima Sheikh (b.1945). Someone whose work makes me weep, because it can break my heart and make it sing at the same time. I also greatly admire Nalini Malani and her works, which strongly engage with history, literature, poetry, and politics through a feminist lens. I see her interests and the themes she explores in your works, for example, the impact of social injustice and gender inequities. Considering your time in Oxford, are there additional insights you would like to share with us?

SSJ: Thank you for saying that. To me, Nilima Sheikh's work has always felt like a quiet conversation with history. There's a gentleness in the way she attends to ordinary lives, memories, and overlooked stories; an empathy that makes you pause and reconsider what truly matters.

At the Ashmolean, I experienced a space that felt alive in a similar way. We would sit on the carpet, drink tea, and exchange ideas freely. The team, especially the many women working there, created an atmosphere of collaboration and care. It made me realise how rare such spaces can be. When I studied over a decade ago, both at Dhaka University and Santiniketan, my departments had only one female faculty member. Even today, gender representation in art education remains limited, and I see how this absence shapes what is valued and remembered.

This awareness of inclusion extends to how we preserve our history. The recent unrest in Bangladesh was devastating, with student protests, political turmoil, and the resulting damage to the museums. Valuable artefacts, photographs, and murals that chronicled our struggles and victories were destroyed.

I have also witnessed grassroots efforts to protect our heritage and the environment. Amirul Rajiv, *co-founder of Duniyadari Archive,* for instance, fought to preserve a small park in Dhaka threatened by an elevated expressway. His 'sit-in protest' in the park, which he undertook with several others, lasted for 168 days, enduring winter chills, summer heat, and relentless rain, protecting a space that offers respite to the local community. They said they would fight even if there were only one bird. This reminded me that preserving the everyday requires patience, care, and courage, whether green spaces, artefacts, or local traditions.

Art, history, and activism are deeply intertwined. My father and I once dreamed of creating a small museum in our village to celebrate local crafts. That experience taught me that objects carry memory, identity, and resilience. Nilima Sheikh's work often reflects this

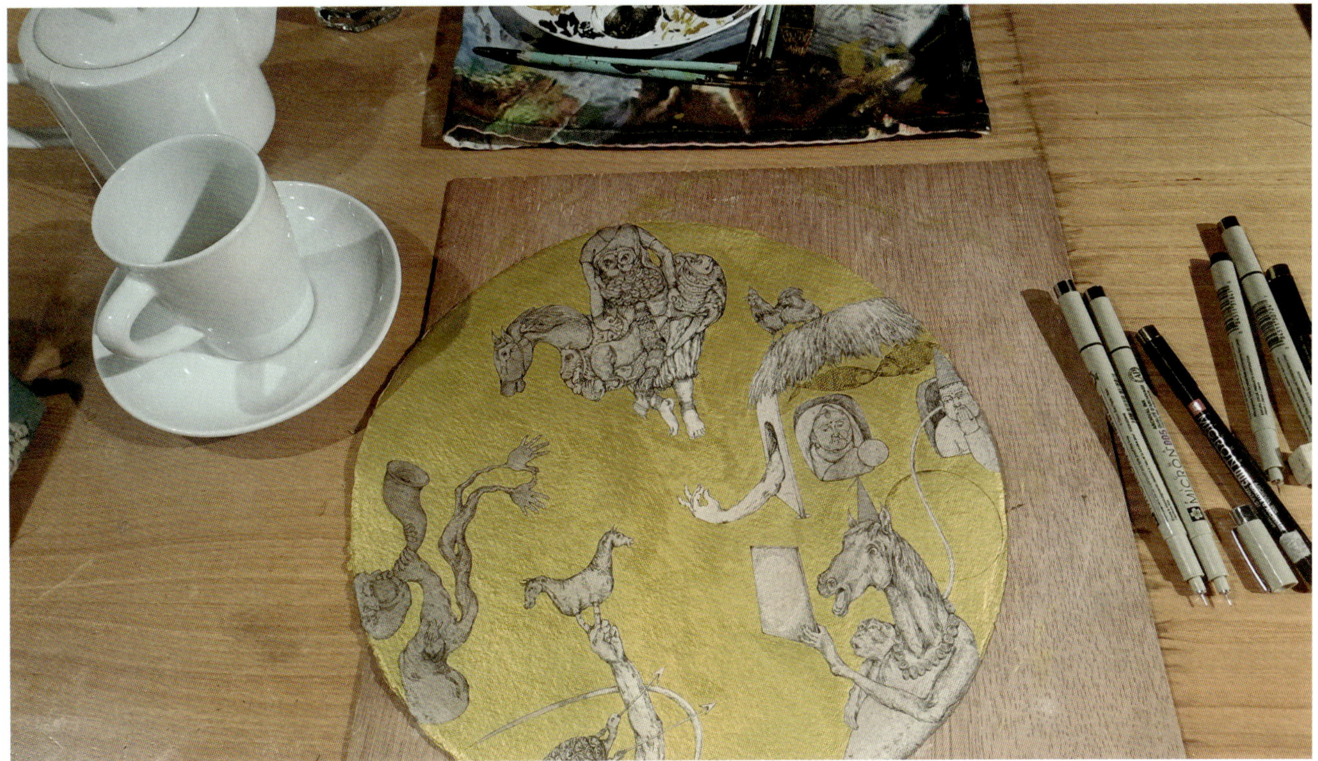

Soma Surovi Jannat in Dhaka, Bangladesh, in a local cafe, working on the series *Who Carries Whom?*, 2025. (fig.24.10)

principle: that paying attention to the seemingly small or fragile can reveal the profound.

I also greatly admire Nalini Malani, not just for the histories, literature, and politics her work engages with, but for the care, patience, and courage with which she confronts injustice. Her art feels alive to me, not as distant objects, but as conversations across time, inviting reflection, questioning, and empathy. In my own practice, I am drawn to fragments, objects, memories, and landscapes, that carry traces of disruption, resilience, or overlooked lives. In both her and Sheikh's art, I see a commitment to amplifying silenced voices and to creating spaces where difficult truths can be faced with honesty and imagination.

In Bangladesh today, this sensitivity is urgently needed, whether in defending our museums, supporting artists, or safeguarding public spaces. Living in Dhaka now, I feel the weight of these losses. Speaking out can be risky, and threats are real. Yet, witnessing how art and activism can sustain memory and community keeps me committed. Nilima Sheikh's and Nalini Malani's examples remind me that even in the face of danger or neglect, creativity can bear witness, preserve stories, and inspire hope. It is this vision that I carry with me in my work and my life.

ART, HISTORY, AND ACTIVISM ARE DEEPLY INTERTWINED. MY FATHER AND I ONCE DREAMED OF CREATING A SMALL MUSEUM IN OUR VILLAGE TO CELEBRATE LOCAL CRAFTS.

SELECTED REFERENCES

P Barua, Chowdhury SN, Sarkar S: Climate change and its risk reduction by mangrove ecosystem of Bangladesh. Bangladesh Res Pub J, 4:218–225 (2010)

Ranjan Chakrabarti, 'Local People and the Global Tiger: An Environmental History of the Sundarbans' in Global Environment, Vol. 2, No. 3, pp. 72–95 (2009)

J M Coleman, Brahmaputra river: channel processes and sedimentation. Sediment Geol, 3:129–239 (1969)

Ralph Crane and Lisa Fletcher. "Picturing the Indian Tiger: Imperial Iconography in the Nineteenth Century." *Victorian Literature and Culture* 42, no. 3, 369–86 (2014)

P J Crutzen and Stoermer EF: The 'Anthropocene'. Global Change News, 41:17–18 (2000)

S Dasgupta, Laplante B, Murray S, Wheeler D: Exposure of developing countries to sea-level rise and storm surges. Clim Change, 106:567–579 (2011)

Calynn Dowler, 'Water and human nonhuman agency in India's Sundarbans' in The Newsletter No. 85 (Spring 2020)

Femi Ferreira, Bangladesh and the sea-level rise, EBSCOhost (2024)

Amitav Ghosh, The Hungry Tide. Thomson Press (2004)

Suddhasil Halder, 'The Parable of Bon Bibi and "Being" in the Sundarbans' in Network in Canadian History & Environment (25 October 2022)

Wing Ka Ho, 'The Looming Threat of Sea Level Rise in Bangladesh' in Earth.org (14 July 2022)

Saleemul Huq, et al, Mainstreaming Adaptation to Climate Change in Least Developed Countries (LDCs). London, International Institute for Environment and Development (2003)

M S Iftekar and M R Islam, Degeneration of Bangladesh's Sundarbans Mangroves: a management issue. Int For Rev, 6:123–135 (2009)

Ayesha Imtiaz, The nation learning to embrace flooding, bbc.co.uk, (2 December 2020)

Annu Jalais, 'Bonbibi: Bridging worlds' in Indian Folklife 28:6–8 (2008)

Annu Jalais, Forest of Tigers People, Politics and Environment in the Sundarbans, Routledge, (2010)

J Jian, P J Webster, and C D Hoyos CD: Large-scale controls on Ganges and Brahmaputra river discharge on intraseasonal and seasonal time-scales, Q J R Meteorol Soc, 135:353–370 (2009)

C Loucks, S Barber-Meyer, Md A A Hossain, A Barlow, R M Chowdhury, Sea level rise and tigers: predicted impacts to Bangladesh's Sundarbans mangroves, 98:291–298, Clim Change (2010)

Dipawali Mitra, 'Here, tiger kills men, widows await justice' in Times of India (September 11 2022)

M R Mohammed, M M Rahman, and K S Islam, The causes of deterioration of Sundarban mangrove forest ecosystem of Bangladesh: conservation and sustainable management issues. AACL Bioflux 3 (2010)

Anuja B. Patel, From Reverence to Destruction: An Eco-critical approach to Amitav Ghosh's 'The Hungry Tide' in the Journal of Emerging Technologies and Innovative Research, Volume 7, Issue 12 (December 2020)

Fabrice G Renaud, James PM Syvitski, Zita Sebesvari, Saskia E Werners, Hartwig Kremer, Claudia Kuenzer, Ramachandran Ramesh, Ad Jeuken and Jana Friedrich, 'Tipping from the Holocene to the Anthropocene: How threatened are major world deltas?' in Current Opinion in Environmental Sustainability, 5:644–654 (2013)

Priya Srinivasan, 'The Sundarbans dilemma: Islands swallowed by water, and nowhere else to go' feature article in Climate Crisis, Aljazeera (27 January 2024)

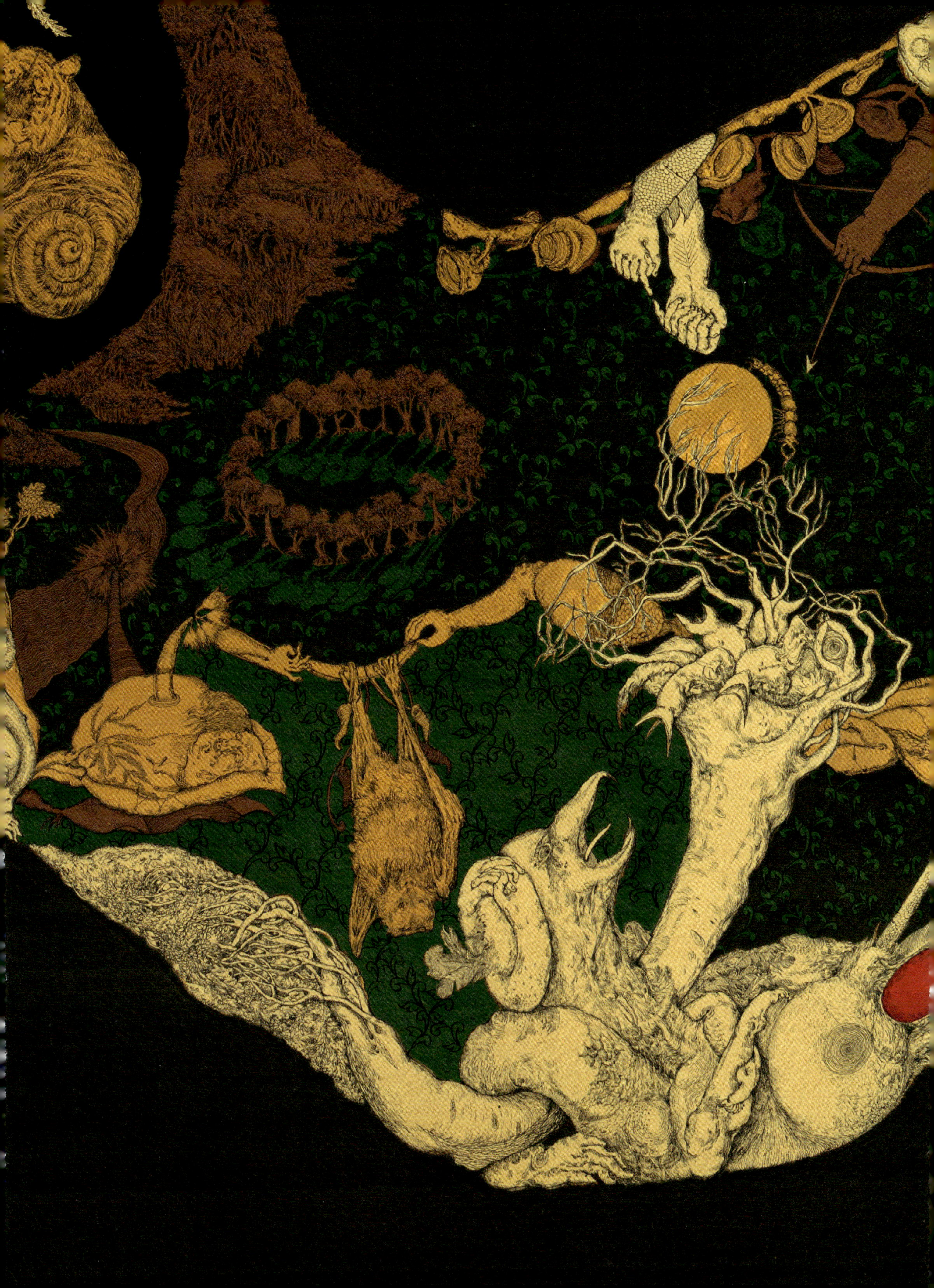

Ashmolean NOW
Soma Surovi Jannat: Climate, Culture, Care
28 March–1 November 2026

The South Asia-based Frere Hall artist-in-residence programme at the Ashmolean and this exhibition's publication is supported by Seher and Taimur Hassan.

Arts Council England using public funding through the National Lottery

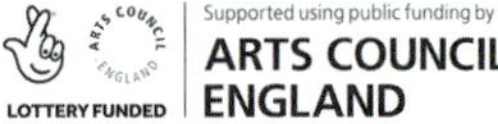

We thank the artist, the Samdani Art Foundation and Gallery Espace for helping with all the arrangements for the artworks.

Exhibition is supported by:

The Patrons of the Ashmolean Museum

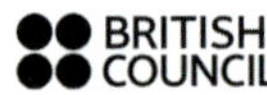

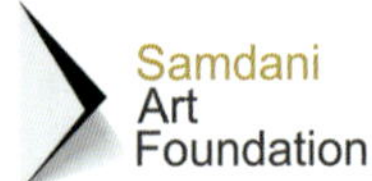

Sotheby's

Neha & Sumedh Jaiswal via Goldman Sachs Gives

Charles Wallace Bangladesh Trust

Gallery Espace, New Delhi

British Library Cataloguing in Publications Data
A catalogue record for this book is available from the British Library

ISBN: 978-1-910807-71-2

Catalogue designed by Ocky Murray
Printed and bound in Wales by Gomer Press

Detail images:
p.2: detail of fig.2
p.4: detail of fig.24.10
p.6: detail of fig.24.1
p.8: detail of fig.7.8
p.11: detail of fig.7.2
pp.12–13: detail of fig.28
p.94: detail of fig.7.5
p.111: detail of fig.7.7

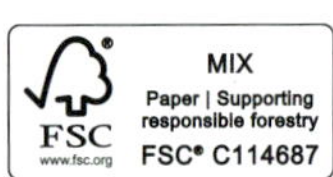

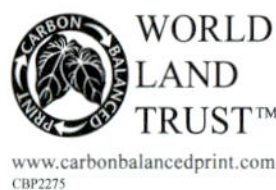

For further details of Ashmolean titles please visit:
www.ashmolean.org/shop

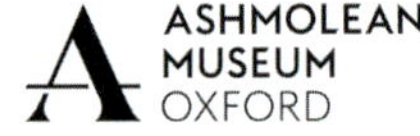

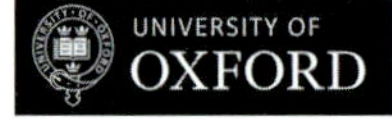